1962

The Theater of Marivaux

Pierre Carlet de Chamblain de Marivaux (1688–1763)

Painting by L. M. Van Loo,
Salle de Comité, Comédie Française.

THE

Theater

OF

Marivaux

by KENNETH N. MCKEE
with an appreciation by JEAN-LOUIS BARRAULT

WASHINGTON SQUARE, NEW YORK UNIVERSITY PRESS 1958

© 1958 BY NEW YORK UNIVERSITY PRESS, INC.
LIBRARY OF CONGRESS CATALOG CARD NUMBER: 58–6823
MANUFACTURED IN THE UNITED STATES OF AMERICA

To my wife
for her unfailing assistance
in the preparation of this book

PREFACE

THERE have been many studies on Marivaux—more perhaps on his novels and on his style than on his theater—and innumerable articles touching one facet or another of his talent, but heretofore there has been no complete study of his plays in chronological order. Gustave Larroumet's book, written in 1881, is still the best; it is the indispensable source book on Marivaux, though difficult to use because it has no index and the plays are discussed in many parts of the book without regard to chronology. Works by Jean Fleury, Gaston Deschamps, and Eugène Meyer do not treat the theater thoroughly. Editions of Marivaux are equally unsatisfactory. Since Marivaux himself was not particularly interested in the published versions of his plays, he never saw to it that they were all collected under his supervision. It has therefore been difficult to ascertain what he considered the definitive versions of his plays. The principal editions since his death—that of 1781, published by La Veuve Duchesne with an introduction by d'Alembert; of 1825–30 by Duviquet; and of 1878, by Edouard Fournier—all suffer from lamentable errors and omissions. The excellent five-volume edition of Xavier de Courville in 1929 covers only fifteen of the most important comedies. It was not until 1946 that Jean Fournier and Maurice Bastide brought out a complete definitive edition of Marivaux's theater[1] in two volumes, with an introduction by Jean Giraudoux and some critical material and notes for each play. The equally complete one-volume edition that Marcel Arland prepared in 1950 for the Editions de la

[1] *Théâtre complet de Marivaux,* "Texte établi et annoté par Jean Fournier et Maurice Bastide" (2 vols.; Paris: Les Editions nationales, 1946).

Pléiade of the Nouvelle Revue Française uses the Fournier and Bastide texts with practically no notes or explanatory material.

Strange as it may seem, what is still lacking is a systematic critical analysis of Marivaux's theater. The purpose of this book is to fill that lacuna—to study each play in chronological order with an *historique,* to point out the innovations that Marivaux introduced and that have been imitated so freely, and to highlight those qualities in his plays that have given them enduring and increasing prestige in the French theater. Each play is treated as a unit and all the necessary facts about it are brought together in a single essay with cross references to ideas that reappear in other plays. At the same time, the various characteristics of Marivaux's technique are discussed as they develop from one play to another, so that as the book progresses a cumulative exposition of his talent as a playwright comes into relief. In conclusion, a summary essay recapitulates the ideas that emerge in the course of the book.

A quandary arose during the preparation of the manuscript. So little scholarship has been devoted to Marivaux's theater that the subject is fraught with unresolved literary problems, such as the exact extent of Molière's influence on Marivaux or the prefiguration of Figaro in Marivaux's valets or Marivaux's contribution to the *drame.* Some readers might prefer it if the present text contained a detailed discussion of these and other problems. But this would require the insertion of an unwieldy mass of material that would distort the primary purpose of the book, which is to present a complete exposition of the essential facts about a play in a single essay. Therefore it has seemed unwise to burden the book with lengthy digressions that would constitute articles in themselves. So problems are stated and conclusions given without elaboration.

Spelling, punctuation, and capitalization of eighteenth-century documents have been carefully transcribed, for any alteration short of complete modernization would be purely arbitrary. One can never be sure whether the seeming mistakes are due to the carelessness of printers or to the peculiarities of the authors.

presenting in their native land, the *commedia dell'arte.* These plays were very different in structure from those in the French and English theater. They were not plays with the dialogue and directions written by the author; rather, they were merely scenarios, or *canevas,* to use the French word. The Italian author outlined the plot and the actors improvised the dialogue at each performance. This resulted in considerable variation in the staging of a comedy from one performance to the next and required skillful co-operation among the actors of the troupe. At the same time, the actors were free to inject stage business on the spur of the moment (this was in sharp contrast to the convention at the Théâtre Français, where the presentation of the classics had become formalized, even with respect to intonation and gestures), and sometimes when an actor had struck the proper mood with his audience he could prolong an interlude as much as a quarter of an hour with his bag of tricks. These tricks, or *lazzi,* covered the whole range of slapstick devices from comic grimaces to tumbling, suggestive poses, indecent gestures, and acrobatic stunts.

The plays of the *commedia dell'arte* were conventional in plot and utilized a standard collection of characters: a young lover, a sweetheart, a jealous rival, an old doctor, a nurse, some wily servants, and above all a buffoon. Language was no barrier when they were performed in Paris, for the Italian actors were excellent mimics and the spectators had little difficulty in following the antics on the stage, which were usually obscene. At the same time the Italian players, though always under police surveillance, took the liberty of parodying public figures and ridiculing religion, all of which regaled the bourgeois of Paris.

There was great variety within the scope of the *commedia dell'arte,* but the scope was limited. As time went on, the troupe added bits of French to the Italian farces, usually in the form of couplets in the final *divertissement,* and the director eventually enlisted French writers to supply comedies for his troupe. A repertory of some forty

French plays was soon built up with the works of such well-known dramatists as Dufresny, Fatouville, and Regnard. The actors of the Comédie Française objected on the ground that the Italians were infringing on their rights. Baron, spokesman for the French troupe, protested to Louis XIV, and Dominique (like Molière, a favorite of the monarch) answered for the Italians, with the result that the king granted them permission to perform in either language. Thereafter, the Théâtre Italien presented original French comedies along with their traditional *commedia dell'arte*.

But the success of the Italians was doomed to be short-lived. The troupe had always been opposed by two groups: one, the actors of the Comédie Française, by reason of professional jealousy, and the other, the *dévot* clique at the court, by reason of the licentious character of the performances. The latter group, which had gained in influence especially since the marriage of Louis XIV to Mme. de Maintenon in 1683, worked assiduously to oust the Italian players from the capital. In spite of the aura of religious rectitude that the king tried to create in order to atone for the follies of his earlier years, he was loath to impose restrictions on his friends at the Théâtre Italien, and he resisted the pressure of the *dévot* clique. However, in 1697 an episode occurred that sealed the fate of the Italians. In May the troupe announced the première of *La finta matrigna, ou La Fausse prude,* by Fatouville. Now, a few months earlier there had been published in Amsterdam a novel of the same title that satirized Mme. de Maintenon. There is no evidence that Fatouville followed the text of the novel, but at least he capitalized on the title, and the *dévot* clique was irate that the Italians should parody the wife of the king. The records do not show whether the comedy actually reached the première. In any event, on May 13, 1697, a royal decree closed the theater and banished the troupe, and there were no more Italian players in Paris as long as Louis XIV lived.

When the king died in 1715, the court reacted against the severity he had practiced in his late years, and the prince regent, the Duc d'Orléans, requested the Prince de Parme to send another company of Italian comedians to enliven the Parisian scene. The new troupe arrived the following spring. Under the protection of the regent they were installed in the Palais Royal, opening there May 18, 1716, with an Italian *canevas, L'inganno fortunato.* The première, which the regent attended with his daughter, the Duchesse de Berry, was an outstanding success. The following month the Italian players were assigned to the stage of the Hôtel de Bourgogne, where they remained during the years that Marivaux was writing for them.

Luigi Riccoboni was the man who was responsible for assembling the troupe in Italy and for guiding its activities in Paris. Riccoboni had been a famous actor at the court of Parma, excelling in the role of the young lover in the *commedia dell'arte* and also acting with distinction in classical tragedy. He adopted the name of Lélio in the Italian farces presented in Paris. The *Mercure de France* said of him: "Personne n'a jamais mieux caractérisé les passions outrées et avec plus de vraisemblance." Like Molière, he was not only the leading actor of the troupe, but he also directed the company, managed its business affairs, and wrote many of its *canevas* and parodies. He was a practicing Catholic and insisted that the rites of the church be open to his troupe. In the decadent atmosphere of the Regency, Riccoboni saw to it that the performances and manners of his actors were above reproach. The leading feminine roles in the Italian farces were taken by Riccoboni's wife, Elena Balletti, known as Flaminia. She played ingénues and soubrettes with equal ease. A woman of great personal integrity, her presence added dignity to the troupe. Flaminia's brother, Antoine-Joseph Balletti, played the second male lead, or *le jaloux,* under the name of Mario. The second feminine lead, or *l'ingénue* of the Italian farces, was played by Zanetta-Rosa-Giovanna Benozzi, better known as Silvia. She soon emerged as the leading actress of the troupe, eclipsing Flaminia, and became the most famous interpreter of Marivaux heroines. She married Antoine-Joseph Balletti in 1720; they had four sons who in their turn followed the theatrical profession. The incomparable Thomas-Antoine Vicentini, known in France as Thomassin, performed the role of Arlequin. This celebrated buffoon was one of the delights of the Théâtre Italien. His wife, Margarita Rusca, was the soubrette Violette. Later Dominique, son of the illustrious Biancolelli, joined the troupe as Trivelin, and in 1725 the brilliant comedian Jean Romagnesi added new luster to the Parisian performances. These, then, together with a few less known but equally talented minor performers, made up the troupe that captivated the Parisian public in the 1720's and 1730's by the charm of the individual actors and by the excellence of its productions.

It was not long before Riccoboni began to invite French writers to contribute plays to his company. The list of names includes some of the best-known playwrights in the early eighteenth century: Autreau, Piron, Lesage, Boissy, Fuzelier, Legrand, and, of course, Marivaux. Although the spoken French of the Italians left something to be desired, their acting was so fluid and so free from the mannerisms of French actors that they were able to give, in Marivaux's comedies in particular, delicate shades of interpretation, which were necessary to reflect the subtlety of his writing.

It is unfortunate that, because some of the registers of the Théâtre Italien have been lost, precise information regarding the date of a première or the exact number of performances is often unavailable.

The Théâtre Français

At the Théâtre Français Marivaux fared badly when his plays were first performed there. Most of them failed dismally at the première— only two had what might be called modest runs. Though the Comédie Française was eager to present his plays, the actors lacked the knack or judgment to stage them properly. However, during the French Revolution and under the guidance of Mlle. Contat, the Comédie Française began to revive some of Marivaux's comedies presented originally at the Théâtre Italien. In the course of the nineteenth and twentieth centuries, still others have been added to the repertory so that to date nineteen of Marivaux's plays have been performed at one time or another at the Théâtre Français. At present, Marivaux ranks fourth among the classical authors in the total number of performances of his plays at the Théâtre Français, and he undoubtedly ranks next to Molière as the classical author most performed currently by the Comédie Française and other professional troupes.

1 Le Père prudent et équitable

[One act in verse. Performed privately in Limoges, 1709;[1] published, 1712.]

MARIVAUX wrote two comedies before he attained maturity as a professional dramatist. The first, *Le Père prudent et équitable,* composed while he was still living in Limoges, has all the earmarks of the work of an amateur. The second, *L'Amour et la vérité,* written in collaboration with Saint-Jory in 1720 for the Théâtre Italien, failed at its première; the play is lost, but a dialogue published in the *Mercure de France* (March 1720) is purported to be a fragment of the text. These two comedies merit only the briefest discussion; they hardly give a clue to the succession of brilliant works that were to follow.

It is said that Marivaux wrote his first play as a wager. A strict imitation of Regnard and Dancourt, *Le Père prudent et équitable* shows none of the characteristics of style and content that one finds in Marivaux's writing as a mature person, after his taste has been refined by the influence of the most elegant salons in Paris.

The plot relates that Démocrite, having decided to marry off his daughter Philine, allows her to select her husband from among

1 In his book *Marivaux et le marivaudage* (Paris: Société d'édition, Les Belles lettres, 1955), pp. 81–85, Frédéric Deloffre contends that the date 1706, heretofore accepted as the year of composition, is based on a false assumption by Lesbros de Versan and that the play was written in 1709 and possibly as late as 1711.

Ariste, a middle-aged farmer, the Chevalier de la Minardinière, and the Financier; but he forbids her to marry Cléandre, the man of her own choice, chiefly because the young man is impoverished. When Philine and Cléandre have a lovers' spat, Crispin, the young man's valet, conceives the idea of intercepting the three suitors and turning them away from marriage with Philine by some sort of trickery. As Ariste approaches with his peasant servant, Maître Jacques, Crispin arranges with Philine's maid, Toinette, to pose as Démocrite's daughter and disgust Ariste with her brazen effrontery. When the Financier appears, Crispin tells him that Philine is cursed with an incurable disease. Then, before the arrival of the Chevalier, Crispin poses as a woman who tells Démocrite that she is the discarded mistress of the irresponsible Chevalier. These machinations bring about a situation in which the father has no alternative but to yield his daughter to Cléandre, and this is a satisfactory solution in view of the fact that the young man is informed in the very last scene that he has won a lawsuit that will greatly enrich him.

The idea of a wily servant working on behalf of his young master to outwit an elderly parent or guardian is, of course, one of the most commonplace themes in the French theater of this period. But in this instance it is obvious that Crispin's antics in deceiving Démocrite are borrowed almost bodily from *Le Légataire universel* by Regnard (1708), in which another Crispin poses as a country nobleman and also as a provincial widow to deceive the old Géronte. *Le Père prudent et équitable* contains much that is common to Molière, too. The lovers' quarrel in Scene 3 is reminiscent of the quarrel between Marianne and Valère in *Tartuffe* (II, 4). Scene 15 is imitated from *Monsieur de Pourceaugnac*. Even the ending savors of Molière in its abruptness and contrived unreality. It should be noted that as a youth Marivaux imitated Molière, although some fifteen years later as a professional playwright in Paris he consistently refused to follow the Molière tradition.

The versification is so faulty and so devoid of poetic imagery and polish that it is scarcely worthy of being called poetry. Why Démocrite is considered "un père prudent" is hard to see, for he is easily outwitted by Crispin. He is interesting, however, in that he does not want to force a disagreeable marriage on his daughter, and in this respect he is the forerunner of several admirable fathers who will appear in Marivaux's later plays.[2]

Le Père prudent et équitable is distinctly an "œuvre de jeunesse," understandably lacking in the literary and dramatic merits that will later distinguish Marivaux's comedies.

[2] See *Le Dénouement imprévu,* Chapter 9; *Le Jeu de l'amour et du hasard,* Chapter 16; *Les Serments indiscrets,* Chapter 19.

2   L'Amour et la vérité

[Three acts in prose. First presented at the Théâtre Italien, March 3, 1720.]

MORE than ten years elapsed before Marivaux wrote again for the theater. He had already been in Paris eight years, during which time his literary efforts had been devoted chiefly to the writing of novels[1]—rather bad ones in the seventeenth-century tradition—and articles for the *Mercure de France*. Now he turned for the first time to the professional theater. Riccoboni, the enterprising impresario of the Théâtre Italien, had been trying to interest young authors in writing plays for his troupe, and Marivaux's first venture in this direction was in collaboration with a certain Chevalier de Saint-Jory.[2]

The manuscript of *L'Amour et la vérité* is lost, and little is known about the play itself. A dialogue, purported to be a fragment of the text, was published in the *Mercure* in March 1720. Love complains that his influence is being usurped by "un petit effronté d'Amour" for whom he is partly responsible.[3] He had quarreled with Debauch-

---

[1] *Pharsamon, ou Les Folies romanesques* (1712), *Les Aventures de ***, ou Les Effets surprenants de la sympathie* (1713–14), *La Voiture embourbée* (1714), *L'Iliade travestie* (1717), *Le Télémaque travesti* (1717).

[2] The Chevalier de Saint-Jory, a relatively unknown figure in the literary circles of the day, had previously collaborated with Riccoboni on several comedies and therefore had entree to the Théâtre Italien.

[3] Love makes the same complaint in *La Réunion des amours*. See Chapter 17.

ery and Avarice, and to avenge themselves the two goddesses tempted Plutus into an affair with Venus. The offspring of the liaison is the rogue who is now inspiring men to debauchery and greed rather than to modesty and tenderness in love. Truth has likewise been driven out of the hearts of men by Falsehood and Flattery. Truth is going to enter a near-by well in the hope that all who drink from it will be imbued with the spirit of truth; Love plans to take his position in the tree above the well so that those who eat its fruit will be guided by his precepts.

This dialogue would seem to be a prologue; if so, the comedy that follows would likely be a sort of *pièce à tiroir,* with different characters undergoing the influence of Love and Truth.

Whatever the plot, there is no evidence that it was a success. Since the records of the Théâtre Italien are incomplete for this period, the number of performances is not known; nor are there any reviews in periodicals of the day to give an indication of public reaction. Gueullette,[4] quoting the Frères Parfaict, says that the first and second acts were favorably received, "mais le troisième eut un sort bien différent. L'auteur qui était dans une seconde loge, sans être connu, dit que la pièce l'avait plus ennuyé qu'un autre, attendu qu'il en était l'auteur."

In any event, *L'Amour et la vérité* contains the sort of allegorical fantasy that Marivaux is fond of and that he will use in several subsequent plays, particularly in *Le Triomphe de Plutus* (1728) and in *La Réunion des amours* (1731).

[4] J. E. Gueullette, *Notes et souvenirs sur le Théâtre-Italien au XVIIIe siècle* (Paris: E. Droz, 1938), p. 94.

3 Arlequin poli par l'amour

[One act in prose. First presented at the Théâtre Italien, October 17, 1720.]

WITH *Arlequin poli par l'amour,* Marivaux made his entrance into the French theater as a successful dramatist. After years of literary apprenticeship on the *Mercure de France* and grooming in the salons of Mme. de Lambert and Mme. de Tencin, where "l'amour demeurait la grande et principale affaire,"[1] Marivaux at last found his true vocation, and his talent began to take shape. At the same time he was working on *Arlequin poli par l'amour,* he was also fashioning a tragedy, *Annibal,*[2] which was presented a few months later at the Théâtre Français.

Arlequin poli par l'amour is hardly a comedy: it is more a *féerie,* a mixture of reality and fantasy (much like Shakespeare's *A Midsummer Night's Dream*) with the fanciful element predominating. Since the play was written for the Théâtre Italien, Marivaux was not bound by the usual conventions governing the French drama, and he therefore gave free rein to his imagination. The scene changes four times in the course of the play; on several occasions the Fairy is supposed to become invisible by turning her ring; and with the actor Thomassin in mind as Arlequin, Marivaux wrote out stage

[1] Dr. Grasset, *Le Médecin de l'amour au temps de Marivaux* (Paris, 1896), p. 162.
[2] See Chapter 4.

directions unheard of before 1720. Note the indications for Arlequin's first appearance: "Arlequin entre, la tête dans l'estomac, ou de la façon niaise dont il voudra" (Sc. 2); for his clumsiness when his dancing master teaches him to make a bow: "Arlequin égaie cette scène de tout ce que son génie peut lui fournir de propre au sujet" (shades of M. Jourdain!); or for his surprise when he sees Silvia for the first time: "Arlequin entre en jouant au volant; il vient de cette façon jusqu'aux pieds de Silvia; là, en jouant, il laisse tomber le volant, et en se baissant pour le ramasser, il voit Silvia. Il demeure étonné et courbé; petit à petit et par secousses, il se redresse le corps; quand il s'est entièrement redressé, il la regarde; elle, honteuse, feint de se retirer; dans son embarras, il l'arrête" (Sc. 5). The comedy is replete with opportunities for Arlequin to employ the *lazzi* for which he was so justly famous.

The Fairy has kidnaped Arlequin because she has fallen in love with him even though she is supposed to marry Merlin within a few days. Arlequin has been in the palace for two weeks, and the Fairy is in despair because he has slighted her attentions. In the palace park Arlequin sees and falls in love with the shepherdess Silvia, who is likewise unresponsive to her shepherd. Arlequin and Silvia naïvely discover their attraction for each other. The Fairy becomes enraged at Arlequin's continued indifference and suspects a rival. To see for herself, she follows the youth, making herself invisible, and she comes upon a delightful scene of first lovemaking between Arlequin and Silvia. Furious, she touches Silvia with her wand, rendering her motionless; she leads Arlequin back to the palace, where, "poli par l'amour," he is more determined than ever to resist her. She connives with her servant Trivelin to deceive the young couple; but when the time comes, Trivelin is so touched by the sincere love between Arlequin and Silvia that he sides with them to outwit the Fairy. Arlequin pretends to make love to her and in so doing he takes her wand. Without it the Fairy is powerless, and she watches helplessly while Arlequin and Silvia lead the sprites and fairies off the stage with the usual Théâtre Italien *divertissement* of dancing and singing.

All this is accomplished with disarming innocence and infectious hilarity along with many musical interludes. Much of the comedy comes from Arlequin's evasions of the Fairy's advances and her mania of interpreting each of his slights as a sign of love. For example, when the dancing master arrives, she says:

> LA FÉE: Voulez-vous prendre votre leçon, pour l'amour de moi?
> ARLEQUIN: Non.
> LA FÉE: Quoi! Vous me refusez si peu de chose, à moi qui vous aime? . . . [*A Trivelin*] Il ne m'entend pas; mais du moins sa méprise m'a fait plaisir. (Sc. 2)

And again, the Fairy has arranged a program of amorous songs to entice Arlequin; after the program ends she asks:

> LA FÉE: Cher Arlequin, ces tendres chansons ne vous inspirent-elles rien? Que sentez-vous?
> ARLEQUIN: Je sens un grand appétit. (Sc. 3)

Marivaux injects a note of originality in this Arlequin by endowing him with a capacity for love instead of treating him as a mere performer of burlesque tricks. La Harpe,[3] usually severe toward Marivaux, praises him in this instance for having been able to transform "ce personnage idéal qui jusque-là n'avait su que faire rire, et que pour la première fois il rendit intéressant en le rendant amoureux." Arlequin is not unlike the Chérubin of *Le Mariage de Figaro* in his guileless ignorance of love; Beaumarchais may even have borrowed some of Chérubin's traits and reactions from Arlequin's outburst of adolescent love. On the other hand, Xavier de Courville[4] claims that Marivaux's Arlequin is an imitation of the Arlequin in *Les Amans ignorans* by Autreau, performed April 14, 1720, and Frédéric Delof-

---

[3] J. F. La Harpe, *Lycée, ou cours de littérature ancienne et moderne* (Paris, 1801), XII, 548.

[4] *Luigi Riccoboni dit Lélio* (Paris, 1943), II, 201.

fre[5] suggests another source in *Pérsiles y Sigismunda* by Cervantes. In either case the similarity between Marivaux's play and the alleged sources is nebulous in the extreme. In a more general sense the sharpening influence of love is a concept that goes back to seventeenth-century French literature, with *L'Ecole des femmes* by Molière and *Tircis et Aramante* by La Fontaine as two outstanding examples.

The records of the Théâtre Italien, faulty as they are, show that *Arlequin poli par l'amour* was enormously successful in its initial run. Undoubtedly the talent of Thomassin as Arlequin had not a little to do with its popularity. The comedy was revived frequently by the troupe in the next several decades; and the *Mercure* reports that it was played before the court at Fontainebleau on September 12, 1725, April 7, 1731, and again January 30, 1734.

A few fragments of critical opinion show that *Arlequin poli par l'amour* was favorably received. Desboulmiers[6] says, "On admira la vérité des caractères & la finesse du dialogue. . . . Elle reussit beaucoup, & a toujours été revue avec le même plaisir." And Gueullette[7] calls it "une fort jolie pièce." Almost a century later La Harpe[8] paid a compliment to the play when he compared it to the other *arlequinades* given at the Théâtre Italien: "Je préfère de beaucoup le parti que Marivaux a su tirer, dans son *Arlequin poli par l'amour,* de ce personnage idéal. . . . Ici du moins tout est naturel et le naturel a de la grâce."

Arlequin poli par l'amour was not performed again until the end of the nineteenth century, in large part because after the Théâtre Italien ceased to exist the Comédie Française was slow to take over the repertory. By tradition the actors at the Théâtre Français had

[5] *Mélanges d'histoire littéraire offerts à M. Paul Dimoff* (Annales Universitatis Saraviensis, Philosophie-Lettres, 1954), III.

[6] *Histoire anecdotique et raisonnée du Théâtre Italien depuis son rétablissement en France jusqu'à l'année 1769* (Paris: Lacombe, 1769), I, 450.

[7] *Notes et souvenirs sur le Théâtre-Italien au XVIIIe siècle* (Paris: E. Droz, 1938), p. 95.

[8] *Op. cit.*, XII, 548–49.

always been loath to act Arlequin. It is true that the artists who remained at the Théâtre de la Nation during the Revolution performed *Les Fausses confidences* in 1793, but Arlequin was called Lubin; and when the reorganized Comédie Française produced *Le Jeu de l'amour et du hasard* in 1796, Arlequin's name was changed to Pasquin.[9] It was not until Marivaux had become a "classic," and the stigma of inferiority was removed from roles originally created for the Théâtre Italien, that the Comédie Française revived certain of his plays.

Another factor that may explain the reluctance of the Théâtre Français to add more of Marivaux's comedies to its repertory in the nineteenth century was the actors' loss of skill in performing Marivaux. Larroumet,[10] writing in 1881, deplored the trend toward long-run plays that deprived the actors of the chance to portray a wide range of roles and little by little reduced the special artistry necessary to interpret Marivaux. It is interesting to note that aside from the ever popular four, *Le Jeu de l'amour et du hasard, Le Legs, Les Fausses confidences,* and *L'Epreuve,* the Théâtre Français staged no new Marivaux comedies from 1810 to 1892.

However, under the leadership of Jules Claretie, the tide turned; and on October 17, 1892, the Comédie Française offered *Arlequin poli par l'amour* with Jules Truffier as Arlequin. This excellent actor, who was also a Marivaux scholar, made a few deletions in the text. Noël and Stoullig[11] called it "une fantaisie charmante, pleine de grâce et d'esprit," and report: "Ce petit ouvrage actuellement joué plut beaucoup et eut beaucoup de succès. Il était désormais réintégré au répertoire." Jules Lemaître[12] found it to be "la poésie du dernier siècle, avant Rousseau. Que voulez-vous? Chaque temps a

9 For details concerning the ruction at the Théâtre Français during the Revolution and its subsequent reorganization, see p. 120, note 1.

10 G. Larroumet, *Marivaux: sa vie et ses œuvres* (Paris: Hachette, 1882), pp. 186–87.

11 *Les Annales du théâtre et de la musique* (Paris, 1892), p. 81.

12 *Les Annales politiques et littéraires* (April 3, 1892), I, 216.

la poésie qu'il peut. Celle-là ne ressemble point à la poésie romantique ou parnassienne; mais c'est bien de la poésie tout de même." And Adolphe Brisson[13] associated the play with modern literary styles: "Enfin cette petite pièce est symbolique à un degré éminent: raison de plus pour qu'elle plaise en un temps où le symbolisme triomphe de toutes les parts."

A revival of *Arlequin poli par l'amour* at the Odéon in 1920 brought forth a profusion of favorable comment.[14] Marivaux delighted the critics. Bernard Lacache said: "C'est un joli conte, frais comme le printemps, tout ensoleillé." The spectators shared the enjoyment, according to Antoine Banès: "Le public prit le plus vif plaisir à la poétique fantaisie de Marivaux, enguirlandée des fines arabesques de M. Foudrain." Lugné-Poë concluded a complimentary article: "C'est une heure de spectacle fin et lumineux, dans une nature poudrée et enrubannée, un moment agréable et léger que nous offre l'Odéon," and Lucien Dubech exclaimed: "on jouait du Marivaux: que de délicats plaisirs à la fois."

Arlequin poli par l'amour reminded several critics, especially Guillot de Saxe, of Shakespeare: "Les trois tableaux galants à la manière de Watteau font songer . . . aux fantaisies shakespeariennes du *Songe d'une Nuit d'Eté*"; and André Dumas: "Cette féerie s'apparente étrangement à la fantaisie shakespearienne. . . . La fée inhumaine, fiancée à l'enchanteur Merlin comme, à Obéron, Titania, abuse comme elle de sa puissance secrète pour séparer les amoureux." The same elfin humor pervades both plays.[15]

Marivaux's comedy conquered American audiences when the Comédie Française performed *Arlequin poli par l'amour* in November 1955 during the famous French troupe's first tour of America.

[13] *Ibid.* (October 30, 1892), II, 281.

[14] The following citations are taken from clippings in the *Dossier sur Marivaux,* Rf 11723, Bibliothèque de l'Arsenal.

[15] These references to *A Midsummer Night's Dream* introduce the comparison of Marivaux to Shakespeare, which has been a favorite theme of critics over the years. For other instances of similarity, see pp. 37, 38, 40–41, 136, 148, 264.

The polished performances of the actors and the guileless charm of Marivaux's tale won the plaudits of the spectators, who were largely English-speaking. Walter Kerr[16] says: "A lightweight deft powder-box conceit from the featherweight pen of Marivaux has been given such animated gaiety that it spells out its own simple story with a kick of the heels and an irrepressible bounce into space. . . . everyone who has strayed into this lacquered wonderland is filled with a simple conviction that wonderlands exist." Recalling the French troupe's performance of *Le Bourgeois gentilhomme* the previous week, Mr. Kerr asserts that "the Comédie seems even happier with Marivaux than with its giant, Molière." With equal enthusiasm Herbert Matthews[17] calls *Arlequin poli par l'amour* "a poetic trifle, as light as a soufflé and as pleasant a dish to begin an evening feast. Only the French and only the Comédie Française could make us delight in anything so gossamer. . . . The acting is a tour de force of the first order."

In sum, in *Arlequin poli par l'amour* Marivaux created a captivating play that is the perfect combination of French comedy and the *commedia dell'arte*. Marivaux added a certain literary quality to the productions usually given at the Théâtre Italien, and in return Riccoboni's actors gave sympathetic interpretation to the play and to others that followed. Unknowingly, Marivaux and the Théâtre Italien complemented each other and created a vogue that is one of the outstanding features of the eighteenth-century French theater.

Highly successful in its own day and equally appreciated in modern times at home and abroad, *Arlequin poli par l'amour* is likely to be a perennial favorite because "les personnages évoqués en scène sont éternels comme ceux de Perrault, et l'on s'attend à voir le Prince Charmant."[18]

[16] *New York Herald Tribune,* November 9, 1955.
[17] *The New York Times,* November 9, 1955.
[18] *Dossier sur Marivaux,* Rf 11723, Bibliothèque de l'Arsenal.

4 Annibal

[Five acts in verse. First presented at the Théâtre Français, December 16, 1720.[1]]

WHILE he was still writing *Arlequin poli par l'amour* and in a way still testing his various abilities, Marivaux was also working on a tragedy, *Annibal,* his first—and what turned out to be his only—attempt in this field. Apparently he had some reservations about putting the play into production, for *Les Nouvelles littéraires* (Amsterdam, 1720) reports: "M. de Marivaux est incertain s'il fera représenter sa nouvelle tragédie d'*Annibal*."[2]

The subject had been treated several times prior to Marivaux, notably by Scudéry and Desmarets, and had been dramatized by Thomas Corneille. Marivaux's version was simplicity itself: Prusias has brought Hannibal to Bithynia to help him resist the Romans and has pledged his daughter, Laodice, to him, although the girl had earlier fallen in love with the former Roman ambassador, Flaminius.[3]

---

[1] The 1758 edition gave the erroneous date of October 16, 1720, for the première and established a long-accepted tradition that the success of *Arlequin poli par l'amour* at the Théâtre Italien on October 17 compensated for the failure of *Annibal* at the Théâtre Français.

[2] Marcel Arland, *Théâtre complet de Marivaux* (Paris: La Nouvelle revue française, 1949), p. 1494.

[3] Professor H. C. Lancaster points out that Marivaux may have followed his predecessors in general, but that he was the first to give Prusias a daughter and make her fall in love with Flaminius. *French Tragedy in the Time of Louis XV and Voltaire* (Baltimore: Johns Hopkins Press, 1950), I, 102.

Rome, worried about the possible military exploits of Hannibal in the East, has sent Flaminius back to Bithynia to seize the redoubtable general. Flaminius hopes at the same time to win the hand of Laodice, but she steadfastly honors her engagement to Hannibal. Prusias, intimidated by the ambassador and realizing that Hannibal is now a political liability, releases his daughter from her vow. She, however, consents to marry Flaminius only on condition that he will save Hannibal's life. Disheartened, Hannibal plans to leave Bithynia. The king's confidant, Hiéron, connives with Flaminius to capture Hannibal once he is outside the gates; but Hannibal, knowing that he cannot trust either the king or the Roman for protection, chooses to take his own life. Laodice, unwilling to profit by Hannibal's death, refuses to marry Flaminius.

Laodice is an appealing character. Strangely, her account of falling in love with Flaminius foreshadows the experiences of the heroines of comedies to follow in later years:

> J'en rougis, et jetai sur ce hardi Romain
> Des regards qui marquaient un généreux dédain.

> .   .   .   .

> Mes dédaigneux regards rencontrèrent les siens
> Et les siens, sans efforts, confondirent les miens. (I, 1)

Yet her determination to remain faithful to Hannibal recalls Pauline's fidelity to Polyeucte:

> Cependant, chère Egine, Annibal a ma foi,
> Et je suis destinée à vivre sous sa loi.
> Sans amour, il est vrai. . . .
> Et, dût mon cœur brûler d'une ardeur éternelle,
> Egine, il a ma foi; je lui serai fidèle. (I, 1)

At the end, when Hannibal dies rather than submit to Rome, Laodice upbraids Flaminius:

Enfin Rome a vaincu.
Il meurt, et vous avez consommé l'injustice,
Barbare! et vous osiez demander Laodice! (V, 10)

In spite of his love for Laodice, Flaminius is dominated by his devotion to Rome. Torn between love and duty, he reproaches himself for letting his own feelings interfere with his mission:

Elle fuit; je soupire, et mon âme abattue
A presque perdu Rome et son devoir de vue.
Vil Romain, homme né pour les soins amoureux,
Rome est donc le jouet de tes transports honteux! (IV, 4)

As depicted by Marivaux this Hannibal is not interesting as a character in tragedy. In his thinking and even in his speech he is more akin to the Dorantes of later comedies than to the famous warrior of history. However, he speaks boldly to Prusias, and pleads with the weakly monarch to uphold the honor of his kingdom:

. . . et j'ose encore vous dire
Qu'un prince à qui le ciel a commis un empire,
Pour qui cent mille bras peuvent se réunir,
Doit braver les Romains, les vaincre et les punir. (III, 4)

The play obediently follows the classical rules: the unities are observed, the subject and its treatment are properly classic, the structure is expert, the verse is adequate, though not lofty.[4] All the ingredients of a superior tragedy are here, yet the play failed. What is lacking is those flights of soaring poetry, the passionate conflicts, that are an integral part of a successful tragedy. One senses a dual force at work. While Marivaux was trying to write a tragedy according to the classical formula, his own natural ideas for the theater were struggling to find expression, also. Without his realizing it, he was already too much the Marivaux of the still unwritten *Surprise de*

---

[4] Marivaux's lack of skill in writing poetry has already been noted in *Le Père prudent et équitable.* See pp. 15–16.

l'amour to compose a tragedy of Racinian or Corneillian proportions. In spots, *Annibal* is reminiscent of *Polyeucte,* but in the field
of tragedy Marivaux suffers from comparison with Corneille and
Racine.

It may be that the simplicity of the play and the absence of
terror were partly responsible for its failure, too. By 1720 Crébillon
had come into vogue and audiences expected their tragedies to be
enlivened with *coups de théâtre* and episodes of horror. The acting
of Baron, Dufresne, and Mme. Desmares did not win *Annibal* more
than three performances in Paris and one at Versailles during its
nouveauté.

In 1747, after Marivaux had become a member of the Académie
Française, the tragedy was revived again. The *Mercure de France*[5]
said of it: "les beautés dont cette Tragédie est pleine nous feroient
regretter qu'il [Marivaux] ne se fût pas attaché à ce genre, si les ex-
cellentes productions qu'il a données en plusieurs autres pouvoient
laisser quelque chose à désirer. . . . La pièce a été reçûë avec beaucoup
d'applaudissemens, & elle les mérite." In spite of this glowing
tribute, *Annibal* had only a *succès d'estime* of five performances during its revival. It has never been played since.

Perhaps it was for the best that *Annibal* failed, for it showed
Marivaux that he did not have a flair for writing tragedy. Henceforth he will cast his lot with Arlequin. Although from time to time
his comedies will be presented at the Théâtre Français, the scene of
his major successes will be the Théâtre Italien.

[5] October 1747, p. 128.

5   La Surprise de l'amour

[Three acts in prose. First presented at the Théâtre Italien, May 3, 1722.]

AFTER having experimented successfully in comedy and unsuccessfully in tragedy, Marivaux next produced *La Surprise de l'amour*, which established the type of comedy most closely associated with his name. This play contains the essential features of his genius: elements of psychological analysis mixed with deft comedy, the traits of craftsmanship and style that distinguish most of his plays from now on. If Racine had already introduced the psychological analysis of love into tragedy, Marivaux was the first to elevate it to a prominent place in comedy, and he has since remained the master of this type of play. Many have imitated him[1]—indeed, Marivaux's theater was to become a sort of quarry for future dramatists—but none has equaled him, save perhaps Alfred de Musset.

As a play, *La Surprise de l'amour* contains little action or plot; for Marivaux, like Racine, is not so much concerned with what happens *to* his characters as he is with what happens *in* them. He is too skilled a writer to allow his play to be devoid of dramatic interest, but his attention is directed mainly to the thinking and feeling of his characters rather than to their actions.

[1] Within a few years Marivaux's contemporaries were trying to employ his technique, and the second half of the eighteenth century and the early nineteenth century abound with variations of Marivaux's themes and language. The influence is subtle, but it is there nonetheless.

Until this time most lovers on the stage were in conflict with parents or guardians, rivals, social conventions, or other external obstacles. But in *La Surprise de l'amour*—and here is another original feature in Marivaux—lovers are for the first time in conflict with themselves or struggle against their love for each other.

Lélio has withdrawn from Paris to a country house because his mistress has deceived him, and he vows to renounce all attention to women. As Margot has been unfaithful to him, Arlequin shares his master's resentment, although he complains: "quelquefois son petit nez me trotte encore dans la tête; mais quand je ne songe point à elle, je n'y gagne rien; car je pense à toutes les femmes en gros, et alors les émotions du cœur que vous dites viennent me tourmenter" (I, 2). Lélio tries to strengthen both his own and Arlequin's resolve in a long tirade against women that only reveals his devotion to them; his every criticism is filled with adoration: "Eh, mon cher enfant, la vipère n'ôte que la vie. Femmes, vous nous ravissez notre raison, notre liberté, notre repos, et vous nous laissez vivre! ... Quel aimable désordre d'idées dans la tête! L'homme a le bon sens en partage; mais, ma foi, l'esprit n'appartient qu'à la femme. ... Une femme ne veut être ni tendre, ni délicate, ni fâchée, ni bien aise; elle est tout cela sans le savoir, et cela est charmant" (I, 2).[2]

Next door to Lélio there lives a young countess, a widow; the two houses share a common garden. For her part, the Countess is disdainful of men; however, she desires to speak with Lélio in order to arrange a marriage between her gardener Pierre and Lélio's servant Jacqueline. Her *suivante,* Colombine, acts as intermediary in making the necessary arrangements with Arlequin. Colombine, smitten with Arlequin at first sight, warns him: "Je suis une espiègle, et j'ai envie de te rendre un peu misérable de ma façon" (I, 6). Arlequin is no less enamored of her, and his "émotions du cœur" seize him: "Ah! comme cela m'accrocherait si je me laissais faire!" (I, 7).

---

2 This scene reminds one of Cléonte's denunciation of Lucile to Covielle in *Le Bourgeois gentilhomme* (III, 9).

After most circumspect precautions on both sides, Lélio and the Countess finally meet, but their negotiations degenerate into mutual scorn for the opposite sex. The Countess suspects that Lélio's hostility is due to an infidelity:

> LÉLIO: Oui, Madame. Comment! cela vous étonne! Voilà pourtant les femmes, et ces actions doivent vous mettre en pays de connaissance.
>
> LA COMTESSE: J'ai cru d'abord, moi, qu'elle n'avait fait que se dégoûter de vous et de l'amour, et je lui pardonnais en faveur de cela la sottise qu'elle avait eue de vous aimer. Quand je dis vous, je parle des hommes en général.
>
> LÉLIO: On voit bien que vous êtes fâchée, Madame.
>
> LA COMTESSE: Moi, Monsieur! je n'ai pas à me plaindre des hommes; je ne les hais point non plus. Hélas! la pauvre espèce! elle est, pour qui l'examine, encore plus comique que haïssable. (I, 7)

Having deflated Lélio to her satisfaction, the Countess concludes the interview: "comme à la campagne il faut voir quelqu'un, soyons amis pendant que nous y resterons; je vous promets sûreté: nous nous divertirons, vous à médire les femmes, et moi à mépriser les hommes" (I, 7). They do not reach a conclusion about the marriage settlement for Jacqueline and Pierre.

As the Countess is leaving, the Baron comes onto the scene. He had met both Lélio and the Countess on separate occasions in the past, and he thinks their proximity now is "le coup de hasard le plus bizarre qui soit arrivé" in that the Countess, the only woman in the world who does not look favorably on men, should be thrown together with Lélio, who has condemned himself to languish in solitude. The Baron relates the story of the Roman ambassador who drew a circle around Antiochus and threatened war if he left the circle before yielding to the Roman's demand. The Baron therefore draws a circle around Lélio and dares him to jump out; Lélio promptly steps over. The Baron makes the same challenge to the Countess and she, not to be outdone by her neighbor, defiantly steps over the circle. The Baron, delighted, proclaims to the astonished and angry pair: "Bon! Voilà de l'amour qui prélude par le dépit" (I, 8), and he later comments to Colombine: "ils viennent de se faire une déclaration d'amour l'un à l'autre, et le tout en se fâchant" (I, 9).

Shortly thereafter the Countess and Colombine appear in the garden, the Countess absorbed in dreamy thoughts, Colombine shrewdly aware of what is on her mistress's mind. The Countess sighs that she has decided not to see Lélio again: she will continue their negotiations by letter. Lélio is piqued by the decision of the Countess to avoid him; left alone with Arlequin, he is completely absorbed in his own reaction toward her, seeking to justify his scorn for her. The Countess, returning to look for a miniature that Colombine has lost, engages Lélio in a battle of wits wherein each tries to puncture the vanity of the other with barbed remarks. Lélio happens to mention that Colombine had alluded to her love for him. She scoffs at the idea so vehemently that he is finally convinced of her indifference to him: "Non, Madame, vous ne m'aimez point, et j'en suis convaincu; et je vous avouerai même, dans le moment où je suis, que cette conviction m'est absolument nécessaire" (II, 8). After he has left the Countess is disturbed at her own feelings: "Juste ciel! que vient-il de me dire? et d'où vient que je suis émue de ce que je viens d'entendre? *Cette conviction m'est absolument nécessaire.* Non, cela ne signifie rien, et je n'y veux rien comprendre." And, as Colombine remarks: "Notre amour se fait bien grand."

Arlequin has found the miniature and has given it to Lélio, who keeps it,[3] asking Arlequin to return the empty box to Colombine. Colombine succeeds in breaking down the resistance of the all too willing Arlequin; and while pledging their love for each other, they realize that they cannot marry until the inclinations of their

[3] In eighteenth-century comedy the desire to possess a lady's portrait was a tacit confession of love.

master and mistress are harmonized.[4] Colombine thereupon sets out to make the Countess acknowledge her love. To this end she engages her mistress in a discussion as to what Lélio meant by: "Cette conviction m'est absolument nécessaire," and brings the conversation to the point where she can say to the Countess: "Tenez, Madame, dussiez-vous me quereller, vous aimez cet homme" (III, 2). Angry at first, the Countess finally admits this may be true; yet she has a presentiment of misfortune that may come out of it. Arlequin returns the box to the Countess with the explanation that Lélio has kept the portrait because it reminded him of his cousin; but Arlequin injects the suspicion that his master kept it to remind him of the Countess, since he berates and scolds the portrait, then utters dreamy sighs. The Countess leaves with the intention of demanding her portrait from Lélio herself.

The wily servants attack Lélio, and Colombine chides him for not confiding in her. To which the confused young man replies: "Eh, Colombine, le savais-je? . . . Je ne sais où je suis" (III, 4). With the Countess and Lélio thus prepared, Colombine brings them together with the inevitable result that Lélio falls on his knees before the Countess. Not, however, before Arlequin has lived through an embarrassing moment explaining to the unwitting Lélio how he was supposed to have worshiped the portrait. It goes without saying that Colombine and Arlequin will marry, as well as Pierre and Jacqueline. A *divertissement* ends the play with festivities.

What cannot be conveyed in the telling of the plot is the infinite variety of feeling expressed by the characters, all those subtle nuances of thought and emotion concerning which Voltaire is purported to have said of Marivaux: "il a connu tous les sentiers du cœur sans trouver la grande route." The first part of the statement is cer-

---

[4] Another eighteenth-century convention provided that the *suivante* of the heroine marry the valet of the hero. Conversely, the servants could not marry each other if some obstacle prevented the marriage of the masters.

tainly true, but the second part is an unjust appraisal of Marivaux's understanding of the human heart.

In *La Surprise de l'amour* Marivaux is completely at ease. The highly polished turn of phrase, the ultrarefined gradations of sentiment that his characters experience, are perfectly natural with him and an integral part of his style. Act II, Scene 7, is a gem of eighteenth-century sophisticated badinage. That special delicacy of expression called *marivaudage* begins to show itself at this time. However, this term, with its aura of fatuity, does not seem applicable to Marivaux himself; it should be applied to his imitators in the second half of the eighteenth century, who, lacking his taste and sensitivity, have reduced the art to clever inanity.

La Surprise de l'amour was an outstanding success in its day. The *Mercure de France*[5] states: "La Pièce a été fort bien reçûe du public par la simplicité de l'intrigue qui ne roûle que sur les mouvemens de deux principaux Personnages. La Dlle Silvia joüe le sien d'une manière qui ne laisse rien à désirer.[6] . . . le sieur Lélio, à qui la Langue Françoise ne devrait pas naturellement être si familière, a joüé son Rôle qui est tout François en perfection & Arlequin a joüé le sien à son ordinaire, c'est à dire à la satisfaction de tout le Public." Marivaux, a relatively unknown figure in the theater in spite of the success of *Arlequin poli par l'amour* two years earlier, was not mentioned in the review.

At this point, even the actors did not know who the author was, and Marivaux had not yet met Zanetta-Rosa-Giovanna Benozzi

---

[5] May 1722, pp. 146–50. Desboulmiers (*Histoire anecdotique et raisonnée du Théâtre Italien depuis son rétablissement en France jusqu'à l'année 1769* [Paris: Lacombe, 1769], II, 93) uses the same wording as the *Mercure*.

[6] J. E. Gueullette (*Notes et souvenirs sur le Théâtre-Italien au XVIIIe siècle* [Paris: E. Droz, 1938], p. 99) was even more extravagant in his praise of Silvia's acting: "Mlle Silvia (Baletti), qui dans *les Amans Ignorans*, *Arlequin poli par l'amour* et autres pièces était déjà reconnue pour une excellente actrice, fit sentir dans cette comédie qu'il n'y avait personne qui pût la surpasser, et même l'égaler, dans les caractères vrais et naïfs."

(married in 1720 to Antoine-Joseph Balletti), known in the annals of the French theater as Silvia. Lesbros de Versan[7] has related the story of their first meeting, and most critics have repeated it since. After a few performances of *La Surprise de l'amour,* Silvia deplored the fact that the author remained anonymous, adding that she would like very much to meet him. A friend took Marivaux to her home one evening without naming him. Conversation turned to the new play, and Marivaux complimented Silvia on her acting; she confessed that she could have played her role even better if the author had deigned to read the comedy to the troupe. Thereupon Marivaux casually picked up the script and began to read. In a few moments Silvia, overcome with astonishment, exclaimed, "Oh, sir, you are either the devil or the author." Marivaux answered that he was not the devil.[8]

So began one of the most famous friendships in theatrical history. From this time on, Marivaux wrote all his comedies for the Théâtre Italien with Silvia in mind, and she turned out to be the perfect interpreter of his feminine creations. Some critics have claimed that this friendship grew from a professional association to an amorous liaison. There is no evidence, except gossip and supposition, to support such a view, and Mme. Durry[9] has shown recently that the suggested affair never existed.

After its initial successful run *La Surprise de l'amour* was played before the court on November 18, 1724, on September 18, 1725, and again on March 10, 1731.[10] In addition, when the famous Italian actor Romagnesi joined the troupe in Paris in 1725, he

---

[7] *L'Esprit de Marivaux* (1769). Cited by Jean Fournier and Maurice Bastide, *Théâtre complet de Marivaux* (2 vols.; Paris: Les Editions nationales, 1946), I, 89.

[8] This episode was dramatized by Charles Clerc in a one-act play *Chez Silvia,* given at the Odéon on February 8, 1923, along with *Les Fausses confidences.* Also a narrative account of the same meeting, *La Galante,* was published in the *Figaro,* March 11, 1923.

[9] *Quelques nouveautés sur Marivaux, Cours et conférences,* 1938–39.

[10] *Le Mercure de France,* November 1724, p. 2464; September 1725, p. 2291; March 1731, p. 576.

"débuta pour la première fois dans la Comédie de la *Surprise de l'amour,* & joua le rôle de *Lélio* avec beaucoup d'intelligence."[11] Likewise, when Riccoboni and his wife returned to Paris in 1731 after a two-year visit to Italy, "la Dlle Lélio . . . joüa le rôle de Suivante, dans la Comédie de la *Surprise de l'Amour.* Le sieur Lélio son fils joüa le rôle d'Amant. Ils ont été tous les deux très bien reçus du Public."[12]

The play had recurrent performances at the Théâtre Italien as long as Silvia lived, and during the French Revolution, when the old classical plays became public domain, various theaters in Paris added it to their repertories.[13] Then it fell into oblivion for more than a century because of the reluctance of the actors at the Théâtre Français to present plays from the Italian repertory.

It was not until 1911 that the Comédie Française revived *La Surprise de l'amour*[14] under the expert direction of Jules Truffier. Truffier, "qui, par un exercice subtil et prolongé, a conduit son esprit au goût le plus raffiné," had become a polished technician in staging and interpreting Marivaux. In an interview before the première, Truffier said of the play: "Il y a une liberté d'inspiration, une fantaisie primesautière et alerte, qui n'est pas dans la seconde [*La Seconde surprise de l'amour,* 1728], grave et compassée. . . . Malheureusement, j'ai été obligé de réduire l'œuvre en un acte.[15] . . . Nous montrerons l'admirable Marivaux sous un aspect nouveau. Vous n'imaginez point combien il est proche de Shakespeare, combien les personnages de *la Surprise de l'amour* ont d'affinité avec ceux de *la Tempête* et du *Songe d'une nuit d'été.* Tout a été réuni dans l'acte de Marivaux: la musique, la poësie, la danse, la peinture."

11 *Le Mercure de France,* April 1725, pp. 828–29.
12 *Le Mercure de France,* December 1731, p. 2854.
13 *La Surprise de l'amour* was announced repeatedly for the Théâtre de la République, the Théâtre National de Molière, and the Théâtre du Marais.
14 The quotations on this revival are taken from the newspaper reviews found in the *Dossier sur Marivaux,* Rf 11726, at the Bibliothèque de l'Arsenal.
15 Truffier had also made revisions in *Arlequin poli par l'amour* some twenty years earlier. See pp. 23–24.

All of Truffier's hopes were realized, according to the critics. Gabriel Boissy proclaimed: "Voilà le spectacle le plus gracieux et le plus profond, c'est-à-dire le plus totalement français, que nous ayons eu depuis longtemps. Un grand succès a justement récompensé la Comédie Française de cette 'première' du merveilleux bibelot de Marivaux." Later, he makes this point: "*La Surprise de l'amour* semble d'abord n'être qu'une comédie de salon parée de divertissements. Cependant, le thème de la nécessité de l'amour, qui est le sujet des *Peines d'amour perdues* de Shakespeare s'y trouve et avec une concentration un peu raffinée, comme il convient, mais sans l'afféterie fatigante du barbare génie de Will."

Another critic echoes the same extravagant praise: "Nous avons eu le plaisir d'écouter jeudi, une des pièces les plus célèbres et les moins connues de Marivaux. . . . Il n'existe pas à la scène d'ouvrages sur lesquels on puisse réfléchir plus longuement et avec plus de fruit que sur ceux de Marivaux. Et il n'en existe pas de plus 'moderne.' " However, the same critic protests the shortening of the play: "L'œuvre, raccourcie, condensée, paraît trop touffue; elle renferme, dans un petit espace, trop de choses."

The actors, too, received universal approval for "une interprétation du premier ordre. . . . Il est impossible de dire la sûreté avec laquelle M. Dehelly a incarné Lélio. . . . M. Dehelly nous a donné une impression de perfection dans l'artificieux. M. Truffier a été excellent de mesure et de finesse dans Arlequin; Mlles Leconte et Provost se sont montrées malicieuses, tendres et un brin perverses dans Colombine et dans la Comtesse."

For the two hundredth anniversary of *La Surprise de l'amour* in 1922, performances were given at the Odéon and at the Vieux Colombier. André de Maricourt[16] expatiates on the attributes of the author: "Marivaux, tout d'abord, est le premier qui donna 'aux gens de commun' une personnalité et un caractère. Au contraire des laquais de Molière, il nous présente des intendants, des valets, des

[16] *Le Gaulois*, April 4, 1922.

paysans qui sont des *hommes*. . . . Il fit mieux encore. Réformateur de mœurs, malgré ce qu'on en ait dit, il réagit contre le théâtre ancien et contre Dancourt, Regnard et Destouches qui ravalaient la femme au second plan. Il donne à cette femme sa place essentielle aux côtés de l'homme."

In 1932, while lecturing on Marivaux in Bordeaux, where *La Double inconstance* was given, Jean Sarment made the following interesting remark: "Je me rappelle avoir joué, il y a une douzaine d'années, à New-York, un autre Arlequin, celui de *la Surprise de l'amour*. Nous étions tous surpris de voir à quel point toutes les finesses de la pièce portaient sur un public presque exclusivement américain."

The original version of *La Surprise de l'amour* was finally offered at the Théâtre Français on November 22, 1938. Once again the play was hailed enthusiastically by the press. In a review filled with analogies to music the critic for *Le Temps*[17] was delighted with "les variations ravissantes de *la Surprise de l'amour*. . . . Plus que jamais, j'ai été frappé du caractère musical de Marivaux. Il organise ses pièces comme une suite de variations, où le thème d'amour naît timidement, se fortifie, et prend, à la fin, une allégresse triomphante. . . . On y voit, de très loin, poindre Mozart." And he added: "M. Jacques Copeau a mis au point cette 'suite française,' à l'imitation d'Italie, avec une intelligence délicieuse."

Roger Martin du Gard[18] expressed the view that "Les trois actes de *la Surprise de l'amour* sont du meilleur Marivaux," and found the production "un des plaisirs les plus délicats que puisse nous offrir la Comédie-Française. . . . c'est un spectacle où tout concourt à nous charmer."

There has been an oft-repeated saying that all Marivaux's plays are "surprises de l'amour." Larroumet[19] traces the source of the

17 November 23, 1938.
18 *Le Figaro*, November 22, 1938.
19 G. Larroumet, *Marivaux: sa vie et ses œuvres* (Paris: Hachette, 1882), pp. 190–91.

saying to the Marquis d'Argens, who wrote in his *Réflexions historiques et critiques sur le goût* (1743): "Il y a dans ses pièces, d'ailleurs très jolies, un défaut, c'est qu'elles pourraient être presque toutes intitulées *la surprise de l'amour.*" This is manifestly a misconception. Although several of the plays turn on the "surprise" theme, they are so diversified that the saying is unjust. Marivaux himself had already foreseen the criticism and answered it: "tout se passe dans le cœur; mais ce cœur a bien des sortes de sentiments, et le portrait de l'un ne fait pas le portrait de l'autre."[20]

This is one of the comedies Marivaux himself preferred. Nor was he the only person who held it in high esteem. Théophile Gautier[21] liked it best because it was the comedy in which Marivaux "a poussé le plus loin le système qui consiste à tirer des sentiments seuls toutes les péripéties qui ordinairement sont le produit des circonstances extérieures." And Alfred de Musset must have had the first *Surprise* in mind when he wrote *Il ne faut jurer de rien,*[22] not to mention *Fantasio.*

The mention of *The Tempest* and *Love's Labor Lost* points up the affinity between Marivaux and Shakespeare already noted in *Arlequin poli par l'amour.* Larroumet[23] credits Gautier with being the first to see *rapprochements* between the two authors and cites Saint-Victor, Daudet, and Banville as developing the same theory. Brunetière, on the contrary, finds comparison with Shakespeare dangerous for Marivaux, and Sarcey feels any relationship between the two quite remote.[24] In general, French critics do not compare a particular play of Marivaux with one of Shakespeare; rather, here

[20] "Avertissement" of *Les Serments indiscrets.* See Chapter 19.
[21] *Histoire de l'art dramatique en France depuis vingt-cinq ans* (Paris: Magnin, Blanchard et Cie, 1858–59), V, 292.
[22] See also *La Seconde surprise de l'amour,* pp. 103–4, 181, 201n, 266.
[23] *Op. cit.,* pp. 292–97.
[24] Citations from still other critics are given on pp. 24, 37–38, 136, 148, 264.

and there, whimsical characters or imaginative details of action invite comparison. Above all, the spirit of fantasy and poetical expression are often common to the two authors. This similarity is all to Marivaux's credit, since it cannot be explained by influence. Although an English troupe appeared in Paris in the 1720's, Shakespeare was almost unknown in France until after 1734 when *Les Lettres philosophiques* of Voltaire appeared. There is no evidence that Marivaux knew Shakespeare's plays, much less imitated them. The best explanation is that both writers had certain gifts in common.

Xavier de Courville's theory that there is a whole "théâtre d'amour" in Molière which is the point of departure for Marivaux's theater, that *La Surprise de l'amour* derives from *La Princesse d'Elide,* seems farfetched. Almost every play, comedy or tragedy, has a love element in it, frequently "un dépit amoureux." Much of dramatic literature consists of variations on the same theme by different authors, and one could go back beyond both Marivaux and Molière to find the basic situations the two men used. The real difference is in the treatment. Certainly there is no connection between the robust farce and not very finely etched spite in *La Princesse d'Elide* and the delicate gradations of love expressed in *La Surprise de l'amour.* To interpret Molière as Marivaux's model strikes a false note. In terms of style and conception, Marivaux owes nothing to Molière.

From the beginning the sheer artistry of Marivaux has always appealed to connoisseurs. In the nineteenth and twentieth centuries, each time one of his plays was revived and a new public became acquainted with him, the circle of his admirers increased. La Rochefoucauld has said: "l'amour est un désir de posséder la personne qu'on aime, après beaucoup de mystères." These "mystères" of the human heart are unchangeable from one generation to another; Marivaux understood them and expressed them with sincerity and clarity. His ever-refreshing, spontaneous attitude toward awakening love makes him eternally young. Whereas the comedies of Destouches, La Chaussée, and Piron are stilted and dated—museum pieces brought out occasionally for inspection—*La Surprise de l'amour* is as entertaining and timely today as it was in 1722.

6   La Double inconstance

[Three acts in prose. First presented at the Théâtre Italien, April 6, 1723.]

THE first play Marivaux wrote for Silvia after he had come to know her was *La Double inconstance*. For a setting Marivaux conjured up a mythical kingdom into which he transplanted the main characters of the Théâtre Italien; and in a whimsical mood he carried them through a metamorphosis of their love. The law of the kingdom decrees that the Prince must marry one of his subjects, provided the girl loves him and is willing to become his queen. In this case the Prince has seen Silvia while he is on a hunting trip and has fallen in love with her; he has visited her five or six times at her cottage in the guise of an officer of the palace, but he has been unable to persuade her to renounce her love for Arlequin. In desperation the Prince has had Silvia brought to the Palace—and Arlequin, too—in the hope that they can be induced, by means of lavish gifts and entertainments, to abandon their love for each other. So far, all efforts have failed: Silvia flouts Trivelin when he tries to show her that it is her duty to respond to the Prince's love; and Arlequin canes the unfortunate courtier for suggesting that he be unfaithful to Silvia. It is Flaminia who conceives the idea of not separating the young lovers by force, but rather of subjecting each of them to the influence of love: the Prince is to continue to woo Silvia, disguised as a cavalry officer, and Flaminia, who has developed a real inclination for

43

Arlequin, aims to win him from Silvia. Arlequin and Silvia pledge undying love to each other, but soon Silvia finds she enjoys the luxuries of the palace, and Arlequin revels in the good food Flaminia serves him. Little by little the officer's courtship begins to touch Silvia, and Arlequin succumbs to Flaminia's culinary art, so that a "double inconstance" is developed. By the time the third act nears the end Silvia is completely in love with the officer and when he reveals his identity she is utterly happy; Arlequin by this time is so entranced with Flaminia that he willingly relinquishes his claim on Silvia.

This gay little comedy never lags. If the action is uneventful, the dialogue of the individual scenes is effervescent. Having found his true vocation in *Arlequin poli par l'amour* and *La Surprise de l'amour* and having discovered fine artists in Lélio and Silvia to interpret his thoughts, Marivaux plunged into his writing with gusto. Silvia's stubborn refusal to accept the Prince as a husband and Arlequin's rejection of the bounties bestowed on him by the Prince are treated with sly wit, while the Prince's advances to Silvia have a poetic delicacy.[1] *La Double inconstance* retains the best features of *Arlequin poli par l'amour* and *La Surprise de l'amour*.

Marivaux traces Silvia's transition to indifference toward Arlequin and the finely shaded gradations of her "surprise de l'amour" with artistic skill:

> I, 1   . . . qu'il [the Prince] me laisse mon pauvre Arlequin
> . . . qui m'aime sans façon, que j'aime même, et que je
> mourrai de chagrin de ne pas voir.

> I, 12   [To Arlequin] . . . je ne sais point ce que je veux dire,
> je vous aime trop.

---

[1] Pierre Lièvre (*Le Mercure de France*, Nouvelle Série, May 1, 1937) condemns the premise of *La Double inconstance*: "Le sujet de *la Double inconstance* est affreux. On ne s'y propose rien de moins que de rendre infidèles l'un à l'autre deux êtres sincèrement épris. Et l'on y réussit." See also pp. 138–39, 212, 217, 238.

II, 1   [To Flaminia] . . . si j'avais eu à changer Arlequin contre un autre, ç'aurait été contre un officier du palais . . . qui est d'aussi bonne façon qu'on puisse être . . . c'est dommage que je n'aie pu l'aimer.

II, 3   [To the Prince as an officer] Arlequin est venu le premier; voilà tout ce qui vous nuit. Si j'avais deviné que vous viendriez après lui, en foi je vous aurais attendu.

II, 9   Devine, Arlequin, qui j'ai encore rencontré ici? Mon amoureux qui venait me voir chez nous, ce grand monsieur si bien tourné. Je veux que vous soyez amis ensemble.

II, 11   [To Flaminia] . . . ne trouvez-vous pas qu'il [Arlequin] est un peu négligent depuis que nous sommes ici? il m'a quittée tantôt pour aller goûter; voilà une belle excuse!

FLAMINIA: L'aimez-vous? [The officer.]

SILVIA: Je ne crois pas; car je dois aimer Arlequin.

II, 12   [To the Prince as an officer] Je pourrais bien vous aimer; cela ne serait pas difficile, si je voulais. . . . Que faire d'Arlequin? Encore si c'était vous qui fût le Prince!

III, 8   SILVIA: J'aimais Arlequin, n'est-ce pas?

FLAMINIA: Il me le semblait.

SILVIA: Eh bien, je crois je ne l'aime plus.

III, 9   [To the Prince, after he has revealed his identity] Si vous avez cherché le plaisir d'être aimé de moi, vous avez bien trouvé ce que vous cherchiez.

This Silvia is naïvely aware of her beauty, and she does not hesitate to pit her natural grace against the studied charms of the ladies of the court. She boasts: "J'attends une dame aussi, moi, qui viendra devant moi se repentir de ne m'avoir pas trouvée belle" (II, 9), and she finds fault with one of her rivals: "Il me fâche assez d'être si jolie et que vous ne soyez pas assez belle" (II, 10). Her penchant for proclaiming her own beauty makes her the prototype of a more famous Marivaux figure, the heroine of *La Vie de Marianne*.

Though Arlequin is provided with many excellent comic scenes in which he can perform his *lazzi,* he nevertheless ceases to be the mere buffoon of the *commedia dell'arte.* When one of the court ladies is sent to lure him away from Silvia, he sees through her tricks and gives her a lesson in propriety by citing Silvia's example:

Si je vous contais notre amour, vous tomberiez dans l'admiration de sa modestie. Les premiers jours il fallait voir comme elle se reculait d'auprès de moi; et puis elle reculait plus doucement; puis, petit à petit, elle ne reculait plus; ensuite elle me regardait en cachette; et puis elle avait honte quand je l'avais vue faire, et puis moi j'avais un plaisir de roi à voir sa honte; ensuite j'attrapais sa main, qu'elle me laissait prendre; et puis elle était encore toute confuse; et puis je lui parlais; ensuite elle ne me répondait rien, mais n'en pensait pas moins; ensuite elle me donnait des regards pour des paroles, et puis des paroles qu'elle laissait aller sans y songer, parce que son cœur allait plus vite qu'elle; enfin, c'était un charme; aussi j'étais comme un fou. Et voilà ce qui s'appelle une fille; mais vous ne ressemblez point à Silvia. (I, 6)

Doubtless there is more of Marivaux than of Arlequin in that speech. As the play progresses, the transformation in Arlequin's heart is as finely drawn as that in Silvia's, although it must be pointed out that his love for Flaminia is awakened by her appeal to his gluttony.

On the serious side Arlequin predates Figaro by half a century. The ideas expressed by Figaro are usually accepted as being original with Beaumarchais, but one finds some of Beaumarchais' most trenchant criticism already clearly formulated in Marivaux.[2] In *La Double inconstance* the spirit of a free man who dares to challenge the authority of his superior finds expression. Arlequin protests the Prince's pursuit of Silvia: "Que voulez-vous, Monseigneur? j'ai une fille qui m'aime; vous, vous en avez plein votre maison et nonobstant vous m'ôtez la mienne. . . . Allez, vous êtes mon Prince, et je vous aime bien; mais je suis votre sujet, et cela mérite quelque chose" (III, 5). The basic situation is the same in *La*

[2] See also pp. 7, 46–47, 68, 81–82, 85, 211, 246, 265–66.

Double inconstance and in *Le Mariage de Figaro,* with Marivaux using a subject-monarch conflict and Beaumarchais a servant-master conflict. Marivaux remains dignified and respectful in his treatment of the situation, whereas some fifty years later Beaumarchais will become brash and truculent. Arlequin talks common sense, while Figaro shines with wit. The great difference between the two is pointed up by the plots: in the Marivaux play the Prince succeeds in winning Silvia from Arlequin by the gallantry of his courtship; in the Beaumarchais play Comte Almaviva loses to the clever Figaro.

Marivaux has come to be well known for his moralizing. The first glimpse of this tendency appears in *La Double inconstance.* The question of forced marriages is not raised as such in this play, but Marivaux's position is made quite clear through the words of Silvia in the first scene: "S'il [le Prince] m'avait dit: 'Me voulez-vous, Silvia?' je lui aurais répondu: 'Non; Seigneur, il faut qu'une honnête femme aime son mari, et je ne pourrais pas vous aimer" (I, 1), and later she defends her loyalty to Arlequin in the same tone: "Mais ne suis-je pas obligée d'être fidèle? N'est-ce pas mon devoir d'honnête fille? et quand on ne fait pas son devoir, est-on heureuse?" (II, 1). Marivaux also touches on the duties of a monarch. When the Prince asks Arlequin to relinquish his claim on Silvia, Arlequin appeals to the Prince "de montrer que la justice est pour tout le monde," telling him that he should think in this manner: "Faut-il que je retienne le bonheur de ce petit homme parce que j'ai le pouvoir de le garder? N'est-ce pas à moi à être son protecteur, puisque je suis son maître? S'en ira-t-il sans avoir justice? . . . Qu'est-ce qui fera mon office de prince, si je ne le fais pas!" (III, 5). Here indeed is advice for an enlightened despot.

It is curious to note that when a nobleman is tutoring Arlequin on the advantages of living at court and seeking the good will of those who govern, Arlequin replies: "J'aimerais mieux cultiver un bon champs" (II, 7). This is almost the wording and certainly the exact intent, of the last line of *Candide,* which Voltaire wrote some thirty years later: "Il faut cultiver notre jardin."

The *Mercure de France*[3] gave high praise to *La Double inconstance:* "Cette pièce n'a pas paru indigne de *la Surprise de l'amour.* . . . ce qu'on appelle Métaphysique du cœur y règne un peu trop, et peut-être n'est-il pas à la portée de tout le monde; mais les connoisseurs y trouvent de quoi nourrir l'esprit." And again the following year the *Mercure* had reason to applaud *La Double inconstance* in reviewing another play that "ne fut point goûtée du Public, qui trouva cependant à se dédommager à *la Double inconstance* qu'on présenta d'abord; c'est une des meilleures Comedies de M. de Marivaux."[4] Gueullette[5] called the comedy "très bonne," and it must have struck the public fancy, for it was played many times—the exact number is not known—in its initial run and remained in the repertory for many years. It was given at court October 3, 1724, October 1, 1725, and April 7, 1731.[6]

After *La Double inconstance* had run its course, there were no professional performances until the Odéon revived it in 1921. Then La Petite Scène troupe of Xavier de Courville staged a successful revival of *La Double inconstance* in 1925, which caused Gabriel Boissy to praise it as a "comédie qui unit aux grâces habituelles de

[3] April 1723, p. 771. It was in this review that the *Mercure* first used the term "métaphysique du cœur" that has been so often applied to other Marivaux comedies and that Voltaire paraphrased—shall we say, maliciously—in the expression "comédies métaphysiques." Most of the time Voltaire was hostile to Marivaux and tried to engage him in polemics. However, Marivaux, like Crébillon preferring a tranquil life to notorious and enervating quarrels, never rose to the bait. On the other hand, Voltaire borrowed, knowingly or not, from Marivaux on several occasions. It must have been a bitter pill for Voltaire that Marivaux was elected to the Académie Française in 1742 when both men were candidates for the seat left vacant by the death of the Abbé Houtteville. For the intrigue leading to Marivaux's election, see G. Larroumet, *Marivaux: sa vie et ses œuvres* (Paris: Hachette, 1882), pp. 127–31.

[4] January 1724, p. 121.

[5] *Notes et souvenirs sur le Théâtre-Italien au XVIIIe siècle* (Paris: E. Droz, 1938), p. 102.

[6] *Le Mercure,* October 1724; October 1725, p. 2492; April 1731, p. 770.

Marivaux l'esprit frondeur, l'audace satirique de Beaumarchais et même je ne sais quelle pensée politique et sociale plus ample. . . . Au goût incomparable des zélateurs de la Petite Scène nous avons dû des instants de pure grâce française." Jane Catulle-Mendès wrote of the same production in *La Presse:* "*La Double inconstance* nous est une sorte de révélation." Courville revived the production in 1929–30 and when he took it on tour it won plaudits in Lausanne.

  La Double inconstance was given on February 6, 1930, at the Théâtre Antoine to an overflowing crowd. Jean Sarment,[7] who played Arlequin, lectured at length on Marivaux and lamented that only four comedies—*Le Jeu de l'amour et du hasard, Les Fausses confidences, L'Epreuve,* and *Le Legs*—were actively used by the Comédie Française; he explains: "c'est pour cela que nous avons voulu présenter aujourd'hui une de ses comédies les plus oubliées—et les plus injustement méconnues—une de celles à qui Marivaux portait une tendresse particulière, qu'il était heureux, vieillard, d'avoir écrites, jeune." Pierre Brisson,[8] in a highly favorable review of the production, points out how dramatists have pillaged Marivaux: "Le théâtre de Marivaux est un Théâtre-réservoir. On y puisera toujours et les dramaturges, d'âge en âge, y reconnaîtront leur bien. Il occupe dans l'histoire dramatique une place remarquable par sa nouveauté"; he laments that "Son sort inévitable est d'être aimé de loin, en gros, et de rester mal connu." Sarment took his production of *La Double inconstance* to Bordeaux in February 1932.

  The first revival of *La Double inconstance* at the Théâtre Français on March 15, 1934, evoked mixed reactions among the critics. Although the cast contained such brilliant performers as Pierre Bertin, Madeleine Renaud, and Véra Korène, Jacques Copeau[9] felt that Marivaux had a special appeal to a special public and that this production left much to be desired: "Le tout sans invention notable

---

[7] *Notre temps,* March 1, 1930, pp. 244–50.
[8] *Le Temps,* February, 17, 1930.
[9] *Les Nouvelles littéraires, artistiques et scientifiques,* March 24, 1934.

ni particulière saveur." Opinions of a different sort were expressed by Lucien Dubech and Pierre Brisson. The former[10] extolled the comedy: "si elle n'est pas le plus parfait et le plus profond de ses ouvrages, elle est peut-être le plus frais, sinon le plus délicieux. . . . On a beau raconter tout ce qu'on veut; il n'y a que la Comédie-Française qui puisse nous donner des soirées pareilles. . . . jamais Mme. Renaud ne paraît mieux à son aise que dans les héroïnes de Marivaux. . . . Elle est naïve et spirituelle, coquette et fraîche, gracieuse et simple." Dubech gave equal praise to Pierre Bertin as Arlequin and to Véra Korène as Flaminia. Pierre Brisson[11] said of Mme. Renaud: "Elle eût ravi Marivaux," and of the play itself: "On trouve là Marivaux à sa source et dans sa fraîcheur. Souhaitons que la pièce, après deux siècles d'attente, ne quitte plus le répertoire."

Brisson's wish has been granted, for *La Double inconstance* has continued to appear regularly on the programs of the Théâtre Français. In 1950 a new cast gave "une magnifique interprétation"[12] of the play. Of the same production René Lalou[13] said: "Tout est perpétuel mouvement dans ces trois actes exquis où la fameuse 'métaphysique du cœur' est scandée par quelques bons coups de la batte d'Arlequin sur l'échine de Trivelin." And so *La Double inconstance* continues to regale modern audiences.

It is obvious that *La Double inconstance* does not reflect the *libertinage* for which the Regency is noted; rather, it celebrates the ethereal purity of young love, which exists in every age, whatever its licentiousness. If the Regency was notorious for the *soupers* of the Duc d'Orléans, it also had its Silvias and Arlequins. In 1723 there was a public for *La Double inconstance,* for even the courtesans needed a breath of fresh air.

Two modern references to *La Double inconstance* are worthy of

---

[10] *L'Action française*, March 19, 1934.
[11] *Le Temps*, March 12, 1934.
[12] François de Roux in *Le Figaro littéraire,* September 25, 1950.
[13] *Les Nouvelles littéraires, artistiques et scientifiques,* September 28, 1950.

mention. Writing in his journal in 1936, André Gide[14] exclaims: "Lu avec ravissement *la Double inconstance.* Je ne crois pas qu'aucune autre pièce de Marivaux m'ait plu davantage; ni même, à beaucoup près, autant." Then in 1950 Jean Anouilh, in his bittersweet play *La Répétition,* which had an outstanding success at the Théâtre Marigny with Madeleine Renaud and Jean-Louis Barrault, used *La Double inconstance* as the play that was being rehearsed. Incidentally, Anouilh apparently does not believe that the public is acquainted with Marivaux, for the Countess says of those who will witness the play: "Ils parlent tous de Marivaux. La plupart ne l'ont jamais lu."[15]

[14] *Journal* (Bibliothèque de la Pléiade, 1948), p. 1249.
[15] *La Répétition* (Paris, 1950), p. 12.

7 Le Prince travesti, ou L'Illustre aventurier

[Three acts in prose. First presented at the Théâtre Italien, February 5, 1724.]

". . . cet étonnant *Prince Travesti*," said Béatrix Dussane in the *Mercure de France*,[1] reviewing the first performance of the play at the Théâtre Francais on February 4, 1949—two hundred and twenty-five years after its première at the Théâtre Italien. For almost two centuries the play had remained in limbo, along with other neglected Marivaux comedies, except for passing references in literary histories and an excellent discussion by Larroumet,[2] who called it "fort originale et curieuse." Yet when it eventually came to public view in modern times through professional presentations in 1897, 1922, and finally in 1949, it was greeted with outbursts of acclaim: "une œuvre délicieuse,"[3] "une soirée savoureuse,"[4] "une pièce heureuse,"[5] "un magique ballet verbal,"[6] etc.

What is there about *Le Prince travesti* that excites such enthusiastic responses?

[1] Nouvelle Série, March 1949, p. 702.
[2] *Marivaux: sa vie et ses œuvres* (Paris: Hachette, 1882), p. 251.
[3] *Le Figaro,* February 7, 1949.
[4] *Plaisir de France,* March 1949, p. 35.
[5] *Les Nouvelles littéraires, artistiques et scientifiques,* March 10, 1949.
[6] *Le Mercure de France,* March 1949, p. 702.

Le Prince travesti almost defies the usual dramatic classifications. Marivaux himself labeled it a *comédie*—possibly for want of a better word in his day—but it actually contains elements of several dramatic forms. Royal personages, the jealousy of a princess,[7] a hero in disguise,[8] and grandeur of style link it with tragedy, while the general tone of the play is that of the *comédie historique* popularized by Népomucène Lemercier in *Pinto* at the end of the century; at the same time the role of Arlequin comes directly from the Théâtre Italien, and the character of Frédéric predates the statesmen of the *mélodrame* or the high-level political intriguers of the Scribe-Sardou school; combined with all this is the romantic situation between Hortense and Lélio. Modern writers have generally applied the term *comédie héroïque* to the play. Whatever the type, only a dramatist of Marivaux's genius could have combined these disparate ingredients into a coherent play—one that was eminently successful in the eighteenth century and again in the twentieth.

In *Le Prince travesti* Marivaux is more interested in situation and plot than in an analysis of love. Here there is no "surprise de l'amour." Lélio and Hortense are already in love when the play begins; it is the author's aim to lead their romance through such trials as the jealousy of a princess, the machinations of an evil counselor, and the rivalry of a king to a happy ending.

The Princess of Barcelona confides in her young friend, the recently widowed Hortense, that she would willingly marry the King of Castile, who asks for her hand through his ambassador, were it not for a dashing military hero, known as Lélio, who recently appeared at court. She has showered largess upon him and would share her

---

[7] There is a close parallel between *Le Prince travesti* and *Bajazet,* with the Princess, Hortense, and Lélio the dramatic counterparts of Roxane, Atalide, and Bajazet.

[8] In the early 1700's, when melodramatic features were being introduced into tragedy, it was a common device to have a prince in the guise of a commoner; for example, Sésostris in La Grange-Chancel's *Amasis* (1701) and Agénor in Crébillon's *Sémiramis* (1717).

throne with him, but she is puzzled by his reticence, and she also hesitates to lower her prestige by marrying "un simple gentilhomme." Hortense, whose short but distasteful marriage has disillusioned her about the value of a union undertaken for practical ends, urges the Princess to seek love. In the course of their conversation Hortense relates that some months previously, while her husband was still living, she had been rescued from highway bandits by a fearless cavalier who embodied all the qualities she sought in a man. Although he has since disappeared and she has no hope of ever seeing him again, he has created an ideal in her heart that makes it impossible for her to love anyone else. Convinced by such arguments, the Princess asks Hortense to intercede on her behalf so that Lélio may overcome the scruples that have restrained him so far.

Before this interview takes place Lélio reveals that he has been aware of the Princess's inclination and that he is not insensible to her, but that he has eluded her because he has already fallen in love with an unknown lady whom he cannot bring himself to forget. He also reveals that he is a prince of the blood whose father has allowed him to choose his own wife, and that he is traveling incognito in order to see the Princess before making a formal proposal. He is flattered by the Princess's attitude and has decided to declare himself, when he meets Hortense.

Lélio is overjoyed to find the lady he loves, and dismisses all thought of marrying the Princess. Hortense, though equally enraptured, refuses to heed Lélio's declaration because she feels his career will be ruined if he rejects the Princess because of her.

Frédéric, the wily *conseiller de la Princesse,* ambitious to be made *premier secrétaire de l'Etat,* asks Lélio to use his good offices in his behalf, and even offers Lélio his daughter as an added inducement— a proposition that Lélio spurns. At this point the Princess enters and names Lélio as *premier secrétaire.* Frédéric is furious and vows to oust the young upstart. He begins his machinations by bribing Lélio's valet, Arlequin, to spy on his master.

The Princess is displeased with Hortense's explanation of Lélio's coolness and suspects a rival. More fearful than ever, Hortense pleads with Lélio to flee before their love is discovered and the Princess avenges herself. To allay her fears Lélio reveals his identity to the astonished and delighted girl.

The ambassador from Castile arrives with Frédéric to conclude a marriage between his king and the Princess through the mediation of Lélio. Lélio postpones a decision and thereby angers the ambassador. Frédéric wants to conspire with the ambassador to overthrow Lélio, but the ambassador believes that the young man merits honorable treatment.

Arlequin tells Frédéric, in the presence of the Princess and Hortense, that he believes his master has a secret passion. The Princess, piqued at not winning Lélio, is indignant at Frédéric's method of spying and upbraids him. Once again the unscrupulous Frédéric appeals to Lélio, this time to regain favor with the Princess, explaining that previously he had merely been testing Lélio's loyalty.

The humiliated Princess imprisons Lélio and sends Hortense away in disgrace. Hortense pleads with Frédéric to save Lélio, but the statesman, anxious to rid the court of a favorite, refuses. It is the ambassador from Castile who magnanimously influences the Princess to pardon the young lovers and dismiss Frédéric. The Princess, moved by the noble sentiments of the ambassador, agrees to marry a king who chooses such worthy ministers. Elated, the ambassador reveals that he is King of Castile. Lélio, in turn, announces himself the Prince of León, and all ends happily for the two couples.

There is no specific source for this curious mixture. Some historians of the theater have sought to connect it with Rotrou's *Occasions perdues,* with which it has some peripheral similarities, and others have tried to associate it with an episode taken from one of Marivaux's early novels, *Les Effets surprenants de la sympathie.* The nearest influence might be *Bajazet,* already mentioned. However, the most important source, according to Xavier de Courville,[9] is really to be found in "ces pièces d'intrigue, mi-comiques, mi-tragiques, toujours romanesques, que les Italiens avaient jouées au cours de leurs années d'essai."

Frédéric is an absolutely original creation. Nothing like him had ever appeared in French comedy before. Although Trivelin[10] had the role of a statesman in *Arlequin poli par l'amour* and *La Double inconstance* and will be seen many times hereafter in other political roles, it is in *Le Prince travesti* alone that he is involved in high diplomacy. He is depicted as a shrewd but selfish courtier, hardened by years of court intrigue, now within reach of the pinnacle of a diplomatic career and bent on attaining it. Striving to defeat the noble plans of Lélio and the Castilian ambassador, Frédéric shows himself a menial and vile minister, justifying his improbity with a cynical lack of conscience (II, 13). The Princess has already called him "le plus lâche et le plus indigne de tous les hommes" (II, 11), and Hortense, having been callously rebuffed when she appealed to him to save Lélio, tells him: "vous êtes trop méchant pour être à craindre" (III, 7). To those who claim that Marivaux's range was limited to depicting one lovesick hero after another, Frédéric can be cited as an outstanding example of his ability to create new and distinct characters. If Frédéric has a fault, it is that he is generations ahead of his time.

Another proof of Marivaux's originality is that he was the first writer to give royalty a prominent part in French comedy; the mythical prince of *La Double inconstance* excepted, royal protagonists occur for the first time in *Le Prince travesti,* in which the Princess of Barcelona, the King of Castile, and the Prince of León all bear the imprint of their royal birth. Lélio and the ambassador are, in a way,

[9] *Théâtre de Marivaux* (Paris: A la Cité des livres, 1929–30), II, 7.
[10] Most of the personages bear Spanish names, but they are still the stock characters of the Théâtre Italien: Trivelin becomes Frédéric; Silvia is Hortense; Flaminia, the Princess; Mario, the King of Castile.

cast in the same mold: both are royal suitors in disguise, both are endowed with lofty attributes of honor and generosity. Their intuitive feeling for rank—like the *cri du sang* in tragedy—makes each of them recognize the sense of honor of the other, and they treat each other with a respect that exasperates Frédéric. The scene (II, 8) in which they discuss the proposed marriage has a dignity worthy of Corneille; it is an excellent piece of writing, which might surprise a reader expecting the glib badinage of *La surprise de l'amour* or *La Double inconstance.* The royal personages in this play speak a more elegant and fluid French than do Laodice and Flaminius in *Annibal.*

The role of Hortense, made to order for Silvia, covers a wide range of emotions. In the first act Hortense appears as a gay, witty young girl, the typical Silvia far removed from the serious aspects of life. But as the play progresses, and she discovers that she is the rival of her best friend, she passes through stages of fear and love, uncertainty and anguish, until toward the end, as she believes herself guilty of disgracing her suitor, she is called upon to portray emotions not unlike those of a Racinian heroine. In no other play does Marivaux get as close to the tragic as he does in *Le Prince travesti,* and it is a tribute to Silvia's ability that she could enact such a part. One might say that the whole play turns on the role of Hortense.

Arlequin alone remains the simple buffoon of the Théâtre Italien. His innocent greed and hilarious bungling, in an otherwise dignified atmosphere, are in the strict tradition of the role. And yet his *lazzi,* skillfully integrated into the rest of the play, do not strike a false note—perhaps because one expects Arlequin and his bag of tricks in any play presented by the Italian troupe.

Marivaux's penchant for moralizing is manifested once again in *Le Prince travesti,* in which Arlequin and Lélio discuss goodness in a prince. Arlequin instinctively feels that his master is no ordinary soldier and believes him to be some great nobleman; he even goes so far as to say, "personne n'a si bon cœur que vous, et il m'est avis que c'est là la marque d'un prince." To which the Prince answers: "On peut avoir le cœur bon sans être prince, et, pour l'avoir tel, un prince a plus à travailler qu'un autre" (I, 4). Marivaux points out, without censuring, the extravagance of the court when Arlequin bluntly observes to the Princess: "il y a ici un si grand tas de chambres que je voyage depuis une heure sans en trouver le bout. . . . que de fatras de meubles, de drôleries, de colifichets! Tout un village vivrait un an de ce que cela vaut" (I, 3).

Marivaux gives greater value to character than to birth by having Hortense say of the supposedly nonroyal Lélio: "Jeune, aimable, vaillant, généreux et sage, Madame, avec cela, fût-il né dans une chaumière, sa naissance est royale" (I, 1). When the Princess weighs the disadvantages of marrying Lélio, Hortense argues: "donnez à vos sujets un souverain vertueux; ils se consoleraient avec sa vertu du défaut de sa naissance" (I, 1). In *Le Jeu de l'amour et du hasard* six years later, Marivaux will repeat the same idea in words that have since become proverbial: "le mérite vaut bien la naissance."

It is interesting to note that Lélio's father, like Dorante's father in *Le Jeu,* gives the prince complete freedom in the choice of a wife. Although we never see the King of León, he is to be added to the list of liberal fathers depicted by Marivaux.

Xavier de Courville,[11] like many others, criticizes the ending of the play, stating that the brusque denouement is "une véritable pirouette d'Arlequin," whereas the situation in the middle of Act III would seem to lead to a death or a declaration of war. In tragedy, perhaps, but not in comedy. We have known from the beginning that all would end happily, and any other finale would have been false.

A curious circumstance surrounded the first performance. Marivaux, who always shunned publicity and disliked the *cabale,* permitted the play to be given without announcements, a device that his colleague Boissy used many times. The reporter for *the Mercure de*

11 *Op. cit.,* II, 5.

France[12] was incensed, declaring that it was "une nouvelle manière de frauder les droits de la critique." The première was therefore tumultuous, but the second showing passed without incident, and the play turned out to be popular enough to run for a total of sixteen performances, more than *Le Jeu de l'amour et du hasard* had in its *nouveauté*. Marivaux, apparently dissatisfied with his original version, lengthened it to five acts, but only the original is extant.

In spite of the hectic première the merits of *Le Prince travesti* were duly acknowledged. The *Mercure* said: "tout le reproche qu'on a fait à l'Auteur, c'est d'avoir mis trop d'esprit dans les Dialogues. Ce défaut a quelque chose de si brillant qu'on ne peut gueres se résoudre à s'en corriger." Desboulmiers[13] thought the play very pleasing. Gueullette[14] said tersely: "Il y a bien du bon."

After its eighteenth-century run *Le Prince travesti* fell into oblivion until it was performed at a *jeudi classique* on March 4, 1897, at the Odéon. The critic for *Le Journal des débats* (March 7, 1897) found it was "une excellente représentation" of "une pièce peu connue . . . qui occupe une place à part dans l'œuvre du célèbre auteur comique." He chides those who think that Marivaux explores only "les petits mouvements" of the heart, for "dans *le Prince travesti* il analyse avec beaucoup de force une passion profonde." The critic calls the ending "brusque—et faible comme tous les dénouements de Marivaux." That is not true. Brusque, perhaps, in this instance, but the generalization that all Marivaux plays have weak endings is false.

The 1897 performance was prefaced by a lecture given by M. Eugène Lintilhac:[15] "une conférence spirituelle et documentée, qui a été fort goûtée du public."

---

[12] February 1724, p. 346.

[13] *Histoire anecdotique et raisonnée du Théâtre Italien depuis son rétablissement en France jusqu'à l'année 1769* (Paris: Lacombe, 1769), II, 257.

[14] *Notes et souvenirs sur le Théâtre-Italien au XVIIIᵉ siècle* (Paris: E. Droz, 1938), p. 103.

[15] Lintilhac later includes a discussion of *Le Prince travesti* in his *Histoire générale du théâtre en France* (Paris, 1909), IV, 320–26.

The next performance of *Le Prince travesti* was given on February 25, 1922, at the Théâtre Fémina by Xavier de Courville's troupe, La Petite Scène. Here was a revival of unusual charm and intrinsic merit, and the most eminent critics of the day gave expression to their pleasure. Henri Bidou states his reaction in *Le Journal des débats* (March 6, 1922): "La Petite Scène a donné, avec le plus heureux succès, un charmant spectacle. . . . cette fois nous avons entendu *Le Prince Travesti* de Marivaux. C'est une pièce que, pour ma part, je mets fort au-dessus de la plupart des pièces restées au répertoire. . . . Elle a un accent, une émotion, une précision dans la langue . . . qui sont incomparables." He has high praise for the acting: "Mme. Jean Rivain l'a jouée [Hortense] d'une façon exquise," and for the production, too: "Les décors de M. Xavier de Courville étaient un enchantement." Lucien Dubech,[16] in *L'Action française,* placed the productions of La Petite Scène on a par with those of Le Vieux Colombier, saying, "Voilà ce qu'il y a de mieux à Paris. . . . J'ai bonne envie d'appeler cela, comme Lemaître appelait les vers de Racine, l'art suprême." André Beaunier was a bit more cautious in *L'Echo de Paris:* "*Le Prince travesti* est une comédie un peu lente, où il y a un délicieux fatras, où il y a de réelles beautés. . . . Un tel badinage met un sourire aux lèvres, une larme aux cils." André Bellesort in *La Revue de la semaine* is amazed at the effect of Marivaux's prose on the stage: "Je m'étonne que ce style précieux, travaillé comme une dentelle—il y a en littérature le *point* de Marivaux—ce style qui me fatigue au bout de dix pages soit un style de théâtre. Et il en est un. Nous ne perdons rien. Au contraire: ses finesses, ses subtilités prennent sur la scène une vivacité extraordinaire." And Marcel Boulanger in the *Figaro* finds a musical quality in Marivaux: "On croirait entendre la mélodie sans fin de quelque violon incroyablement pur, et dont les cordes seraient des fils de soie mêlés à des rais

---

[16] This and the other citations in this paragraph are taken from clippings in the archives of La Petite Scène.

de lumière. Et notez que cette langue de Marivaux frissonne de passion."

Such eulogies were not restricted to the critics of 1922. The 1949 revival at the Comédie Française brought equal praise from a new generation of critics. Gabriel Marcel[17] was enchanted with *Le Prince travesti,* calling it "une pièce fort heureuse, bien qu'assez hybride" and declaring: "Je ne pense pas qu'à aucune époque Marivaux ait été mieux interprété et mieux compris qu'aujourd'hui." Part of his enjoyment came from the acting of Mlle. Sabouret, who played Hortense "de la façon la plus sensible," and from the Arlequin of M. Hirsch, "qui l'a dansé plus qu'il ne l'a joué." Marcel felt, however, that perhaps Marivaux overreached himself by injecting jealousy into the role of the Princess: "Il est très curieux de noter que la jalousie éveillée dans le cœur de celle-ci . . . soit exprimée aussi faiblement, c'est comme si Marivaux lui-même ne parvenait pas à la prendre tout à fait au sérieux. Je serais tenté de dire qu'elle se place au-delà de son clavier parmi les ultrasons, et qu'il n'est pas équipé pour la traduire." Jean Herbault[18] also credits much of the success of the play "au jeu infiniment agréable de Mlle Marie Sabouret . . . dégageant avec une diction parfaite toute la pureté de la langue du XVIIIe siècle." If in a program consisting of *L'Epreuve* and *Le Prince travesti* he found that "cette comédie est loin d'avoir l'attrait constant de la précédente," he nevertheless asserts: "cette soirée de Marivaux est de bout en bout savoureuse."

Jean-Jacques Gautier[19] called *Le Prince travesti* a play "où tous les défauts ravissants de Marivaux apparaissent délicieusement"; and while it was not as satisfactory perhaps as some of his other plays, "celle-ci possède particulièrement la légèreté, la désinvolture, la

[17] *Les Nouvelles littéraires, artistiques et scientifiques,* March 10, 1949.
[18] *Plaisir de France,* March 1949, p. 35. Most of the other critics echoed praise for Mlle. Sabouret, but J.-J. Gautier of the *Figaro* (February 7, 1949) had reservations about her interpretation of the role.
[19] *Le Figaro,* February 7, 1949.

poésie, la grâce dansante, la bariolure qui manquent si fort aux ouvrages de ce temps-ci."

Jacques Lemarchand[20] complimented the Comédie Française for "exhuming" this work and for the splendid staging done by M. Debucourt. Like many others he was especially delighted to become acquainted again with the excellence of Marivaux's style. "Dans *le Prince travesti* . . . la langue est pure et charmante. . . . C'est une longue et agréable soirée."

Robert Kemp[21] said that after the curtain came down on the opening night of the performance by the Comédie Française the incredulous spectators were asking each other: "Comment ne l'a-t-elle pas fait plus tôt?" Kemp himself, thoroughly cognizant of the qualities of the play, sought to explain the enigma of previous indifference toward it. He believed that the delay in reviving *Le Prince travesti* at the Théâtre Français was due to the fact that the complexity of the play did not appeal to the French. For generations critics have read into it inspiration from Lope de Vega, Rotrou, Racine, Calderón, and even Shakespeare. In *Le Prince travesti,* Kemp stated, one does not find Marivaux "à l'état pur. . . . Nous aimons les talents bien tranchés, en France, plutôt que les ragoûts de talents." However, once the play was revived, this complexity did not prevent Parisian critics and audiences from enjoying an exhilarating experience in the theater.

Dussane[22] summarized the consensus of opinion, perhaps, when she said: "dans un exquis décor de Mme Lalique, l'ensemble que nous offre la Comédie-Française est, cette fois, bien proche de la perfection."

The popularity of *Le Prince travesti* has not been limited to Paris. It was performed with great success at Arras in July 1953 as a feature of the festival of dramatic art.[23]

[20] *Combat,* February 7, 1949.
[21] *Le Monde,* February 8, 1949.
[22] *Le Mercure de France,* March 1949, p. 702.
[23] *Les Nouvelles littéraires, artistiques et scientifiques,* July 9, 1953.

In reviewing the fortunes of *Le Prince travesti,* one is struck by the fact that after almost two centuries of oblivion, it is now understood and enjoyed. A happy combination of good acting and staging, and critical esteem, conspired to bring the play into popular favor. An increasing tendency of the Comédie Française to free Marivaux from traditional stylized acting and a growing public appreciation of Marivaux were necessary to attain this result. To quote Dussane again: "Nous sommes mieux préparés à goûter le charme complexe de ce chef-d'œuvre." Now that both actors and public have found a common ground, there is every reason to assume that *Le Prince travesti* will retain its rightful place in the repertory of the Théâtre Français.

8   La Fausse suivante, ou Le Fourbe puni

[Three acts in prose. First presented at the Théâtre Italien, July 8, 1724.]

IN his fondness for disguises and *travestissements*, a trait he held in common with most of his fellow playwrights of the eighteenth century, Marivaux ranges from the simple adoption of an assumed identity for expediency (*Le Dénouement imprévu, La Mère confidente*) to outright change of character (*Le Prince travesti, Le Jeu de l'amour et du hasard*) and change of sex (*La Fausse suivante, Le Triomphe de l'amour*). Marivaux handles all these disguises with expert variation in detail, and he avoids wearisome repetition by using them in new dimensions in each play.

The success of *Le Prince travesti* was so great that Marivaux set to work on a new comedy for the Italian actors and particularly for his star. Within five months he provided Silvia with a vehicle that contained an entirely new type of role for her. In *La Fausse suivante* she portrayed a young heiress who poses as a chevalier in order to observe her intended husband at first hand. Apparently Silvia attracted audiences in this guise, for "cette pièce a été bien reçûë du Public" and was given frequently as long as she lived, in spite of the fact that it is completely *invraisemblable;* it was played at court on October 24, 1724.[1] However, *La Fausse suivante* has never been

[1] *Le Mercure de France,* July 1724, p. 1588, and November 1724, p. 2461.

revived since it ended its career at the Théâtre Italien in the mid-eighteenth century.

The background of the play is clearly set forth in the second scene of the first act when the Chevalier dispatches a servant, Frontin, to Paris with a verbal message too important to be written down. The Chevalier is actually a young lady of quality who has just been affianced by her sister's husband to a certain Lélio, still believed to be in the provinces. At a masked ball that she attended two nights previously in the guise of a chevalier, she met Lélio by chance; they struck up a friendship and he invited the Chevalier to spend a few days at the château of a certain Countess. The disguised Chevalier, feeling that she might learn something to her advantage about her future husband, accepts the invitation and sends Frontin to tell all this to her sister in Paris to relieve her of anxiety about the girl's whereabouts.

Before he leaves, Frontin comes across his former friend Trivelin, whom he asks to replace him during the Parisian excursion. Frontin accidentally reveals that the Chevalier is "une fille habillée en homme," although he does not reveal her quality. Trivelin, like any crafty servant of eighteenth-century comedy, is more than interested in becoming involved in such a spicy situation.

In his first encounter with the Chevalier Trivelin insinuates that he knows her sex; to conceal her true identity—we never do learn her name—the Chevalier confides falsely to Trivelin that she is the *suivante* of *une dame de qualité,* a statement that gives the play its title. She bribes him to secrecy, but Trivelin makes it plain that he expects her to yield to his amorous desires: "je suis ton valet sur la scène, et ton amant dans les coulisses" (I, 5), and he does not hesitate to let Lélio's valet Arlequin in on the secret.

Lélio seeks out the Chevalier to ask a favor of him; after a preamble that displays his complete lack of integrity, Lélio finally comes to the point of explaining that he has been engaged to the Countess but now wants to terminate the engagement so that he can be free to marry a much wealthier young lady from Paris. The Chevalier advises him to break the engagement without more ado and gallantly to submit to the epithets of rascal and ingrate that the Countess will hurl at him. Lélio is willing to endure the Countess's wrath, but he points out a serious obstacle: he has borrowed 10,000 écus from her to buy an estate and has also signed a *dédit* for 10,000 more. Now that he has decided to break with the Countess, he feels he might as well do her out of the money, too. So he asks the Chevalier to make love to the Countess in the hope that she will prefer to return the *dédit* and cancel the note rather than marry him. When the Chevalier questions him about the girl from Paris who is to become his wife, Lélio remarks with the cynicism of a *chevalier d'industrie:* "crois-tu, par exemple, que j'aimerai la demoiselle de Paris, moi? Une quin-zaine de jours tout au plus; après quoi, je crois que j'en serai bien las. . . . Si elle n'est pas laide, elle le deviendra, puisqu'elle sera ma femme; cela ne peut pas lui manquer" (I, 7). Needless to say, the Chevalier falls in with Lélio's plan, not only to save herself, but the Countess, too, from a disgraceful marriage.

Lélio finds a pretext to quarrel with the Countess and conducts himself with such boorishness that she is pleased to listen to the advances of the Chevalier. The Chevalier's wooing and Lélio's jealous rages produce the desired effect, and the Countess determines to dismiss Lélio and marry the Chevalier.

At the crucial point Arlequin speaks to the Chevalier in the presence of Lélio in such a way as to reveal her sex. The Chevalier explains that she is the *suivante* of the Parisian girl he is to marry, and taking a cue from Trivelin's chicanery she convinces Lélio that it is to their mutual advantage to finish the plan they had started. To this end she says she needs his copy of the *dédit,* which he gladly sur-renders in view of the probable monetary advantages to him. The Chevalier succeeds in winning the Countess's affection, then asks her to tell Lélio that she has decided to marry him after all. The final imbroglio enables the Chevalier to show Lélio in his true light. The

Countess is humiliated, the Chevalier tears up the *dédit,* and Lélio is abashed at letting both the marriage and the money slip through his fingers. Since the Countess had already hired musicians for the festivities, the play ends with a *divertissement.*[2]

Incidentally, this is one of the few comedies by Marivaux that do not end in a marriage or at least in an amicable solution to the problem. One need hardly point out that this comedy has originality, *esprit,* and finesse in abundance, but little dramatic substance, little depth of characterization.

The most salient feature is the personality of Trivelin. As early as 1759 the Abbé de la Porte had noted the original quality of Trivelin,[3] and since that time most historians of the theater have discussed Trivelin to the exclusion of all else in the play. To be sure, Trivelin is a most extraordinary valet for 1724, another of Marivaux's "creations" and the prototype of Figaro, no less. Both servants resent the injustice of fate and social inequality, both feel themselves superior to the circumstances in which they live. One cannot escape comparing even their words:

TRIVELIN	FIGARO
Tantôt maître, tantôt valet; toujours prudent, toujours industrieux. (I, 1)	. . . maître ici, valet là, selon qu'il plaît à la fortune; ambitieux par vanité, laborieux par nécessité. (*Le Mariage,* V, 3)
C'est le triste bagage de ton serviteur; ce paquet enferme toutes mes possessions. (I, 1)	. . . j'ai quitté Madrid; et, mon bagage en sautoir, parcourant philosophiquement les deux Castilles . . . (*Le Barbier,* I, 2)

---

[2] Credited to the elder Frère Parfaict. J.-A. Desboulmiers, *Histoire anecdotique et raisonnée du Théâtre Italien depuis son rétablissement en France jusqu'à l'année 1769* (Paris: Lacombe, 1769), II, 293.

[3] G. Larroumet, *Marivaux: sa vie et ses œuvres* (Paris: Hachette, 1882), p. 228.

J'ai logé partout, sur le pavé, chez l'aubergiste, au cabaret, chez le bourgeois, chez l'homme de qualité, chez moi, chez la justice. (I, 1)

J'apprends la chimie . . . je me jette à corps perdu dans le théâtre . . . je vais rasant de ville en ville . . . j'ai tout vu, tout fait, tout usé. (*Le Mariage,* V, 3)

. . . démasqué par les uns, soupçonné par les autres; à la fin équivoque à tout le monde, j'ai tâté de tout; je dois partout. (I, 1)

. . . fatigué d'écrire, ennuyé de moi, dégoûté des autres, abîmé de dettes et léger d'argent . . . (*Le Barbier,* I, 2)

The analysis shows that Figaro, as he appears in *Le Barbier de Séville,* is no more than a clever imitation of Trivelin, and Beaumarchais' first delineation of the famous valet would not be worth more than a casual comparison with Marivaux's Trivelin, were it not for the stupendous development of Figaro in *Le Mariage de Figaro,* in which he becomes the personification of "la Révolution accomplie." It is his quality as the catalytic agent between the old regime and the new order that has raised Figaro to fame. Although glimpses of Figaro have already appeared in *La Double inconstance,*[4] Marivaux is still in the early stages of his conception of the Figaro type. As time goes on, he will add even more important components to the total picture, especially in *L'Ile des esclaves* and *Les Fausses confidences.*[5] Even so, Trivelin was a much bolder character in 1724 than Figaro was in 1784; Trivelin was an original type thrust on a society as yet uninformed, whereas Figaro was the dramatic expression of the revolutionary ideas of the seventeen fifties and sixties and seventies.

Trivelin is by no means the only predecessor of Figaro: his theatrical forebears—the Scapins, Crispins, and Frontins—are legion.

[4] See pp. 46–47.
[5] See pp. 81–82, 211.

But he is perhaps the most clearly defined ancestor of Figaro, and certainly Figaro's speeches resemble those of Trivelin so closely that one is tempted to accuse Beaumarchais of plagiarism. Strangely, Marc Monnier[6] does not mention this Trivelin as a prototype of Figaro. And Pierre Toldo[7] merely cites him in a footnote.

Aside from his importance as a forerunner of Figaro, Trivelin is an unusual servant in his own right. For the most part, Marivaux's servants are amusing reflections of their masters on a lower social level. But Trivelin is more aggressive, and guided by self-interest. He is not above making a deal with Lélio after he has accepted hush money from the Chevalier; when confronted with his duplicity, he blandly remarks: "C'est mon habit qui est un coquin; pour moi, je suis brave homme, mais avec cet équipage-là, on a de la probité en pure perte; cela ne fait ni honneur ni profit" (III, 2). Trivelin will be joined later by other servants who offer some special interest: Dubois of *Les Fausses confidences,* Lisette of *La Mère confidente,* and Lépine of *Le Legs,* all of whom will be discussed in their places.

The long first scene—which is completely irrelevant to the rest of the play—contains not only the history of Trivelin's wanderings but also a hilarious discussion of the "querelle des anciens et des modernes." Trivelin, coming from Paris, explains to Frontin just what the quarrel is about:

FRONTIN: Et qu'est-ce que c'est que les anciens et les modernes?

TRIVELIN: Des anciens . . . attends, il y en a un dont je sais le nom, et qui est le capitaine de la bande; c'est comme qui te dirait un Homère. Connais-tu cela?

FRONTIN: Non.

TRIVELIN: C'est dommage; car c'était un homme qui parlait bien grec.

FRONTIN: Il n'était donc pas Français cet homme-là?

[6] *Les Aïeux de Figaro* (Paris: Hachette, 1868), pp. 251–65.
[7] *Figaro et ses origines* (Milan: Dumolard Frères, 1893), p. 363.

TRIVELIN: Oh! que non; je pense qu'il était de Québec, quelque part dans cette Egypte, et qu'il vivait du temps du déluge. Nous avons encore de lui de fort belles satires; et mon maître l'aimait beaucoup, lui et tous les honnêtes gens de son temps, comme Virgile, Néron, Plutarque, Ulysse et Diogène.

FRONTIN: Et que veulent dire: les modernes?

TRIVELIN: Tu m'écartes de mon sujet; mais n'importe. Les modernes, c'est comme qui dirait . . . toi, par exemple.

FRONTIN: Oh! Oh! je suis un moderne, moi! . . . Et pourquoi ton maître nous haïssait-il?

TRIVELIN: Parce qu'il voulait qu'on eût quatre mille ans sur la tête pour valoir quelque chose. (I, 1)

Trivelin's ludicrous pedantry is not altogether without malice, for Marivaux liked to ridicule "les anciens." He had always been a partisan of "les modernes," as demonstrated in *Le Spectateur français* (1722) and in *L'Iliade travestie* (1717). In *La Fausse suivante* he again gives vent to the one antipathy he seems to have carried through an otherwise placid life.

So great has been the attention focused on Trivelin that critics have overlooked—or at least have failed to mention—another important aspect of *La Fausse suivante*. In this play we find an early expression of "le préjugé à la mode," that perverted convention in eighteenth-century manners that made it unseemly for a man to love his wife and admit it publicly. Usually La Chaussée is credited with treating it for the first time on the stage in his masterpiece, *Le Préjugé à la mode* (1735), although D'Allainval had already discussed the topic in *L'Ecole des bourgeois* (1728). Even before either of these men Marivaux presented the subject in *La Fausse suivante* (1724), when he had Lélio conniving with the Chevalier to escape his obligations to the Countess:

LÉLIO: Eh! qui est-ce qui te prie d'avoir de l'amour pour elle? Est-il besoin d'aimer sa femme? Si tu ne l'aimes pas, tant pis pour elle; ce sont ses affaires et non pas les tiennes.

LE CHEVALIER: Bon! mais je croyais qu'il fallait aimer sa femme, fondé sur ce qu'on vivait mal avec elle quand on ne l'aimait pas.

LÉLIO: Eh! tant mieux quand on vit mal avec elle; cela vous dispense de la voir, c'est autant de gagné. . . . crois-tu, par exemple, que j'aimerai la demoiselle de Paris, moi? Une quinzaine de jours tout au plus. (I, 7)

Marivaux was not the first to deal with "le préjugé à la mode," for Campistron had touched upon it in *Le Jaloux désabusé* (1709), but Marivaux should be counted as one of the earliest writers to project it in the theater.

The major characters in *La Fausse suivante* are among the least engaging in Marivaux's gallery. Lélio is an utter cad, one of those unscrupulous rogues who paraded their turpitudes across the stage in the early part of the eighteenth century. He is more akin to the Chevalier de Villefontaine in Dancourt's *Le Chevalier à la mode* or to the Marquis in D'Allainval's *L'Ecole des bourgeois* than he is to the Lélio of *La Surprise de l'amour* or the Dorante of *Le Jeu de l'amour et du hasard*. Even Dorimond of *Le Petit-maître corrigé* has virtues that triumph over his unworthy qualities in the end. Lélio, alone of Marivaux heroes, shows no redeeming traits.

The feminine characters—strangely, for Marivaux—are weak. The Countess, an ultrapolished *femme du monde*, is a character patterned on drawing-room standards. Her reactions are contrived rather than natural; her words have their origin in clichés in vogue at the time, delicately shaded, to be sure, by the inimitable Marivaux touch, but stylized nonetheless. Her analysis of jealousy (II, 2) and her bantering with the Chevalier (II, 8) come straight from the *bureaux d'esprit* rather than from the heart.

The impersonation of the Chevalier provided Silvia with the opportunity for a *tour de force* of acting, but the role has none of the feminine grace usually associated with a Marivaux heroine: the young lady is merely clever, she is not appealing. Although she is above reproach in her motives, there is something repellent about the part. Her lovemaking to the Countess, with its potentialities for *double entente*, borders on the risqué, so that her final triumph over Lélio does not bring much satisfaction to the spectator.

La Fausse suivante is one of those plays in which the details are better than the whole. It is spun out of diaphanous threads, but it has none of the fantasy that is usually associated with this type of play. It has enough cleverness to bring it professional success, but no depth to give it lasting value. Voltaire may have had *La Fausse suivante* in mind when he coined the expression: "Marivaux pèse des œufs de mouches sur les balances de toile d'araignée."

There is no denying that in this play Marivaux indulges in that minute analysis of sentiment, that piquant choice of word that some critics condemn in him. Perhaps it is due to the paucity of action in such a slender dramatic situation. Because of the complications of disguise, "le personnage véritable s'efface. . . . l'étude de l'amour n'est plus qu'un jeu d'esprit. . . . on a le droit de parler ici de marivaudage."[8]

[8] Xavier de Courville, *Théâtre de Marivaux* (Paris: A la Cité des livres, 1929–30), II, 8.

9 Le Dénouement imprévu

[One act in prose. First presented at the Théâtre Français, December 2, 1724.]

IN the early 1720's Marivaux's life was fraught with difficulty, both personal and professional. He lost his money in the Law bank in 1722 and was reduced to earning a living by his writing, a vocation that brought only meager monetary rewards early in the eighteenth century, even to the most industrious. His wife, whom he cherished, died in 1723. An internal upheaval at the Théâtre Italien was disrupting the harmony of its existence. The rivalry between Flaminia and Silvia, resulting from the growth of Silvia's popularity, had been a source of friction for some time. Now, in 1724, a serious episode occurred. Lucien Dubech[1] relates that Silvia had taken a lover. A crisis was brought on by Flaminia's gossiping, for when word of the affair reached Silvia's husband (Antoine-Joseph Balletti), he beat her, causing a miscarriage that left her in a weakened condition for many months. Xavier de Courville[2] claims that the audiences punished Flaminia for her jealousy. At any rate, in 1729, she and her husband (Luigi Riccoboni) left Paris and spent two years in Italy. This whole episode must have been disturbing to a man of Marivaux's gentle character.

[1] *Histoire générale illustrée du théâtre* (Paris, 1933), IV, 88.
[2] *Théâtre de Marivaux* (Paris: A la Cité des livres, 1929–30), II, 204.

Marivaux was troubled, too, by a gnawing ambition. He had now had five successful plays at the Théâtre Italien; he was recognized as a leading playwright, and already his colleagues were beginning to imitate his style, thus giving rise to what is called "marivaudage." But one thing was lacking: he had not had a successful play at the Théâtre Français.[3] In spite of the renown he had attained at the Théâtre Italien, at this time only the Comédie Française could "consacrer un auteur," and Marivaux aspired to have that particular stamp of approval on a play of his. The yearning to be appreciated at the Théâtre Français haunted Marivaux all his life, but he was thwarted at every turn. Although the actors of the troupe presented ten of his plays between 1720 and 1746 none achieved much success in Marivaux's lifetime. *La Seconde surprise de l'amour* and *Le Legs* later became stand-bys of the troupe, and, currently, the comedies of Marivaux rank second to those of Molière in frequency of performance, but Marivaux himself never had the satisfaction of being acclaimed after a première at the Théâtre Français.

Fournier and Bastide[4] state that because of his success at the Théâtre Italien "les Comédiens Français avaient demandé une pièce à Marivaux qui, pour aller plus vite, leur promit seulement un acte: ce fut *le Dénouement imprévu,* qu'il écrivit, suivant la tradition, avec l'aîné des frères Parfaict." The play was presented on December 2, 1724, as a curtain raiser to *Le Jaloux désabusé* by Campistron. "Cette comédie n'a pas eu beaucoup de succès; on convient pourtant qu'elle est pleine d'esprit, & fort bien écrite."[5] An examination of the play will reveal the reason for its failure.

M. Argante has picked out Eraste, a country nobleman, as a husband for his daughter. She, however, would prefer to marry Dorante, a mediocre attorney, not because she is in love with him but simply

[3] His *Annibal* had failed there in 1720.
[4] *Théâtre complet de Marivaux* (2 vols.; Paris: Les Editions nationales, 1946), I, 208.
[5] *Le Mercure de France,* December 1724, pp. 2862–67.

because she prefers him to someone she has never seen. To thwart her father's plans Mlle. Argante plots with Dorante, Lisette, and Maître Pierre, her father's farmer, to "faire la folle" and thereby discourage the unknown suitor. She encounters her father and, feigning insanity, pretends to be her father planning a marriage. Her arguments are not only valid but highly amusing in the way she imitates the pompous attitude of the old man. Needless to say, M. Argante is exasperated, but he insists on the marriage just the same: "Oh! je n'y saurais tenir. Vous êtes une impertinente; il vous épousera, je le veux, et vous obéirez. . . . je vous montrerai que je suis votre père" (Sc. 7).

Eraste's valet, Crispin, comes to warn M. Argante that his master will arrive in the guise of a friend so that he can observe Mlle. Argante before asking for her hand. M. Argante grants this privilege with some misgiving; and while he goes to fetch his belligerent daughter, Maître Pierre has the opportunity to talk with Eraste, whom he believes to be the friend. The garrulous farmer discloses Mlle. Argante's aversion to the marriage and the ill temper she plans to show the young suitor if he is fool enough to marry her. Thus disenchanted, Eraste awaits the entrance of Mlle. Argante.

Up to this point Marivaux has written an excellent, if conventional, comedy in compliance with the traditional standard expected by the audiences at the Théâtre Français. The characters bear the names common in the early part of the eighteenth century, and, of course, Arlequin is missing. The basic situation is taken right out of the cupboard of acceptable plots: the device of a girl feigning insanity to outwit her elders had been used frequently. The most recent and undoubtedly the best-known play of this type was *Les Folies amoureuses* by Regnard (1704), but before that Théâtre Français audiences had seen and liked *Les Vendanges de Surennes* by Dancourt (1695), in which the same formula was used. Both these comedies were in the repertory throughout the eighteenth century.

But Marivaux would not have been Marivaux if he had not in-

jected something unexpected into the situation. Just at the moment
when the spectators thought they could foresee the ending, Marivaux
had the originality to direct his play along other lines and bring
about a "dénouement imprévu." When Mlle. Argante and Eraste
meet, "la surprise de l'amour" operates at first sight:

> ÉRASTE [à part]: Ah! l'aimable personne! pourquoi l'ai-je vue,
> puisque je dois la perdre!

> MADEMOISELLE ARGANTE [à part, en entrant]: Voilà un joli
> homme! Si Eraste lui ressemblait, je ne ferais pas la folle. (Sc. 11)

Enlightened by awakened love, Mlle. Argante sees through Eraste's
kindly deception; and within a few minutes their hearts find each
other, Eraste falling on his knees before the now enraptured Mlle.
Argante. A brief closing scene shows parental joy and brings on the
musicians for the festivities.[6]

This ending was not only "imprévu"; it was precipitous! And
herein lies the weakness of the play. The awakening is too abrupt,
the elixir of love works too fast. Marivaux does not allow himself
enough time, and in one short scene he tries to accomplish what he
takes three acts to do in his best plays. The first ten scenes are skillfully written in the best Marivaux manner and prepare the background for a fully developed comedy. Then suddenly in Scene 11 the
whole theme is unfolded and resolved before the audience has caught
its breath.

In such a short trifle characterization amounts to little. Mlle.
Argante is all too willing to yield to her first impulse; contrary to
one of Marivaux's own precepts, her love does not grow by resistance.
Eraste has mere outline without depth. However, his concern for a
happy marriage for Mlle. Argante, his fear that she might marry
him out of obedience rather than love, prepares the way for a more
elaborate development of the same character in the person of Dorante

---

[6] The *divertissement* was by the elder Frère Parfaict.

in *Le Jeu de l'amour et du hasard.* M. Argante is unusually stern for a Marivaux father.

Six performances in 1724, three more in 1789, and one on February 1, 1894, at the Odéon constitute the entire run of the play. Apparently the *jeudi classique* in 1894 did not attract the attention of the critics, for there seem to be no reviews of it in leading papers.

Unimportant as it is, *Le Dénouement imprévu* is not without its influence. Alfred de Musset found in this comedy much of the material that went into *La Nuit vénitienne;* and, curiously, Lessing reports that *Le Dénouement imprévu* had much more success in Germany than in France.

10 L'Ile des esclaves

[One act in prose. First presented at the Théâtre Italien, March 5, 1725.]

MARIVAUX'S penchant for moralizing, already noticeable in his plays and journals, and later to show itself so mettlesome in his novels, led him to write several comedies in which the element of social satire or philosophy predominated over the dramatic—philosophy here being used in the eighteenth-century French meaning. These comedies embody in a fragmentary way many of the ideas current in Parisian intellectual circles in the 1720's and later incorporated in the works of Montesquieu, Voltaire, Diderot, and Rousseau. It is not to be assumed that Marivaux originated these ideas; it is more likely that he participated in discussing them in the drawing rooms he frequented, and was sympathetic enough to them to inject them piecemeal into his comedies before they were voiced as part of the philosophical crescendo of the 1740's and 1750's.

In any event, *L'Ile des esclaves* (1725), *L'Ile de la raison* (1727), and *La Colonie* (1729) are based essentially on philosophical ideas, with *Le Triomphe de Plutus* (1728), *La Réunion des amours* (1731), and *La Dispute* (1744) combining metaphysical concepts with allegory. As they were all planned for professional use and attained varying degrees of success on the stage, they should not be looked upon merely as philosophical dialogues. Marivaux's artistic instinct has invested each of them with a measure of dramatic entity and with a generous quantity of comic detail.

78

Marivaux's first play of this type, *L'Ile des esclaves,* was actually the most successful of his comedies in its *nouveauté,* reaching twenty-one performances in its initial run. Audiences had already become accustomed to comedies with social overtones in *Arlequin sauvage* (1721) and *Timon le misanthrope* (1722), both by La Drevetière de L'Isle and both enormously popular in their day. But Marivaux was the first author to give intellectual stature and literary polish to such a comedy.

L'Ile des esclaves has no plot—just a situation, but a situation of audacious conception: the overthrow of social classes. Iphicrate, a Grecian nobleman, has been shipwrecked on a strange island with his servant, Arlequin; likewise, the haughty Euphrosine and her *suivante,* Cléanthis. The place turns out to be L'Ile des Esclaves, founded a century earlier by escaped slaves who have evolved a utopian government, in which servitude is abolished and masters are corrected of their arrogance. Trivelin, a sort of head of state, comes across the four Greeks and, following the laws of the island, forces the two aristocrats to change places with their servants. In this transposition Iphicrate and Euphrosine learn humility and kindliness, while Arlequin and Cléanthis learn patience and respect for their superiors. Having been thus corrected, the two couples are permitted to return to Athens.

Into this simple situation Marivaux has poured an abundance of philosophical reflection and hilarious comedy. The interchange of master and servant is an old comic device, but the novelty of *L'Ile des esclaves* lies in the ideas that emerge as an integral part of the play and the ingenious way they are expressed.

The central theme of the play is the principle of equality. Marivaux maintains that equality springs from natural goodness, and that social injustice is a malady that can be cured. Through the words of Trivelin, Marivaux says of the Athenian aristocrats: "vous voilà en mauvais état, nous entreprenons de vous guérir; vous êtes moins nos esclaves que nos malades, et nous ne prenons que trois ans pour vous rendre sains, c'est-à-dire humains, raisonnables et généreux pour toute votre vie" (Sc. 2). The treatment is unfolded in rollicking scenes in which Arlequin and Cléanthis paint portraits of their masters in the La Bruyère manner and parody their foibles with such cutting merriment that Iphicrate and Euphrosine wince. The process of correction culminates in a scene of mutual understanding between Iphicrate and Arlequin. Arlequin regrets his incivilities to his master, but he frankly points out his master's faults: "tu me remontres bien mon devoir ici pour toi; mais tu n'as jamais su le tien pour moi, quand nous étions dans Athènes. Tu veux que je partage ton affliction, et jamais tu n'a partagé la mienne. Eh bien! va, je dois avoir le cœur meilleur que toi" (Sc. 9.) It is Arlequin who exclaims: "qu'il y a de plaisir à bien faire!" and who offers to return his master's insignia: "Rendez-moi mon habit, et reprenez le vôtre; je ne suis pas digne de le porter."

Arlequin's critical attitude toward Iphicrate foreshadows Figaro's captious comment to Almaviva: "Aux vertus qu'on exige d'un domestique, Votre Excellence connaît-elle beaucoup de maîtres qui fussent dignes d'être valets?" (*Le Barbier de Séville*, I, 2). But Almaviva would never have answered in Iphicrate's words: "Va, mon cher enfant, oublie que tu fus mon esclave, et je me ressouviendrai toujours que je ne méritais pas d'être ton maître" (*L'Île des esclaves*, Sc. 9).

The feminine characters are less willing to yield to correction. Euphrosine accepts her role as *suivante* with haughty stoicism, and Cléanthis vents her spite wrathfully in a word portrait of her mistress:

CLÉANTHIS: Vaine, minaudière et coquette . . . voilà ma chère maîtresse. Cela lui ressemble comme son visage.

TRIVELIN: . . . En quoi donc, par exemple, lui trouvez-vous les défauts dont nous parlons?

CLÉANTHIS: En quoi? partout, à toute heure, en tous lieux; . . . Il y a tant de choses, j'en ai tant vu, tant remarqué de toutes les espèces, que cela me brouille. Madame se tait, Madame parle; elle regarde, elle est triste, elle est gaie; silence, discours, regards, tristesse et joie, c'est tout vu, il n'y a que la couleur de différente; c'est vanité muette, contente ou fâchée. . . . Madame se lève; a-t-elle bien dormi, le sommeil l'a-t-il rendue belle, se sent-elle du vif, du sémillant dans les yeux? vite sur les armes; la journée sera glorieuse. . . . Madame, au contraire, a-t-elle mal reposé? "Ah! qu'on m'apporte un miroir; comme me voilà faite! que je suis mal bâtie!". . . (Sc. 3)

and so on until Cléanthis has completed a scathing description of a coquette of 1725.

In a final scene of reconciliation Arlequin leads the way to repentance: "Mais enfin, je veux être un homme de bien. . . . Je me repens de mes sottises" (Sc. 10), and Iphicrate and Euphrosine follow suit. But before Cléanthis repents she delivers a virulent tirade (which Figaro was to imitate some sixty years later):

Ah! vraiment, nous y voilà, nous y voilà avec vos beaux exemples. Voilà de nos gens qui nous méprisent dans le monde, qui font les fiers, qui nous maltraitent, et qui nous regardent comme des vers de terre; et puis, qui sont trop heureux dans l'occasion de nous trouver cent fois plus hon- nêtes gens qu'eux. . . . Il s'agit de vous pardonner, et pour avoir cette bonté-là, que faut-il être, s'il vous plaît? Riche? non; noble? non; grand seigneur? point du tout. Vous étiez tout cela; en valiez-vous mieux? Et que faut-il donc? Ah! nous y voici. Il faut avoir le cœur bon,[1] de la vertu et de la raison; voilà ce qu'il faut, voilà ce qui est estimable, ce qui distingue, ce qui fait qu'un homme est plus qu'un autre. Entendez vous, Messieurs les honnêtes gens du monde. . . . Allez, vous devriez rougir de honte. (Sc. 10)

[1] For other expressions of the same thought, see *Le Prince travesti* (I, 4); *La Double inconstance* (III, 5); *L'Ile de la raison* (I, 4, III, 9); and *Le Jeu de l'amour et du hasard* (I, 2).

In the same tirade Cléanthis utters the lines Beaumarchais paraphrased into another Figaro[2] quip, the most famous of them all:

CLÉANTHIS	FIGARO
Fi! que cela est vilain de n'avoir	Noblesse, fortune, un rang, des
eu pour tout mérite que de l'or,	places: tout cela rend si fier!
de l'argent et des dignités!	Qu'avez-vous fait pour tant de
C'était bien la peine de faire	biens? Vous vous êtes donné la
tant les glorieux! (Sc. 10)	peine de naître, et rien de plus.
	(*Le Mariage de Figaro,* V, 3)

Then her heart softens and she breaks down: "Il est vrai que je
pleure; ce n'est pas le bon cœur qui me manque" (Sc. 10).

Trivelin rejoices in the transformation that has been wrought in
the Athenians and adds a word of admonition: "Et vous, Iphicrate,
vous Euphrosine, je vous attendris; je n'ai rien à ajouter aux leçons
que vous donne cette aventure. Vous avez été leurs maîtres, et vous
avez mal agi; ils sont devenus les vôtres, et ils vous pardonnent; faites
vos réflexions là-dessus. La différence des conditions n'est qu'une
épreuve que les dieux font sur nous" (Sc. 11).

What may seem like heavy moralizing is so leavened with infectious good will that one can understand why *L'Ile des esclaves*
had the longest initial run of any Marivaux play. Perhaps its
popularity can be explained to some degree by the vogue of *Les
Lettres persanes,* in which the exotic and philosophic stand out
prominently. Twenty-five years before Rousseau Marivaux propa-
gated the principle of natural goodness in man. With his gift for
portraying the age in which he lived, Marivaux reflected its early
gropings toward the theory of equality.

One might wonder, though, whether Marivaux was fully con-

---

[2] For other instances where Marivaux foreshadows Figaro, see pp. 46–47, 67–
68, 211, 246. Although Marc Monnier (*Les Aïeux de Figaro* [Paris: Hachette,
1868], pp. 251–66) mentions *L'Ile des esclaves,* he erroneously calls it "un
pendant à *l'Ile de la raison*"; he does not discuss the play or cite from it. Pierre
Toldo (*Figaro et ses origines* [Milan: Dumolard Frères, 1893], p. 289) dismisses Marivaux without discussing a single play.

vinced that social equality could be achieved; for in the end the original master-servant relationships are restored. His two male characters accept their fate with good grace, but the feminine characters resist correction. When Cléanthis as mistress proposes to Arlequin as master that he marry Euphrosine, the latter haughtily rejects the idea; and when Arlequin approaches the former Athenian aristocrat to make love to her, she successfully appeals to his instincts as a faithful servant not to embarrass her. Arlequin's ambition is no match for her innate hauteur. One aspect of Marivaux's modernness can be observed in *L'Ile des esclaves,* for in this work his ideas on equality are much more akin to those of the twentieth century than of the eighteenth.

The *Mercure de France* acknowledged the première of *L'Ile des esclaves* in the issue for March 1725 and promised a longer review in the near future. It appeared the following month: "Le Public l'a reçûë avec beaucoup d'applaudissemens. M. de Marivaux, qui en est l'Auteur, est accoutumé à de pareils succès, & tout ce qui part de sa plume lui acquiert une nouvelle gloire."[3] There was a special accolade for Silvia in the role of Cléanthis: "Sylvia s'en acquitte avec des graces qui la mettent au rang des meilleures actrices qui ayent encore paru sur nos Théâtres."

L'Ile des esclaves may have regaled the Parisian populace, but Gueullette[4] reports that the play "ne plut pas à la Cour" when it was performed there April 21, 1731. It is understandable that the court would not relish a play that set about, albeit in a jovial manner, to overthrow the traditional social system. The *divertissement* only accentuated the theme: "La pièce finit par une petite Fête dont on auroit pû se passer; elle est composée d'Esclaves qui se réjouissent de ce qu'on a brisé leurs chaînes."[5]

---

[3] *Le Mercure de France,* April 1725, pp. 784–87.
[4] *Notes et souvenirs sur le Théâtre-Italien au XVIIIᵉ siècle* (Paris: E. Droz, 1938), p. 105.
[5] *Le Mercure de France,* April 1725, pp. 784–87.

Incidentally Mlle. Clairon, who later became one of the leading actresses at the Théâtre Français, made her debut as Cléanthis on January 7, 1736, at the Théâtre Italien. Her performance at that time did not qualify her to be accepted as a permanent member of the troupe. She then went to the Opéra and in 1744 joined the Comédie Française.

Philosophical plays of this type occur with increasing frequency in the eighteenth century and reach their climax—a brutal and lusterless climax—in the French Revolution. Though Marivaux gave impetus to such plays on a professional literary scale, he would hardly have recognized—and would certainly never have approved of—the fourth generation of his offspring in *Les Emigrés aux terres australes* by Gamas (1792) and *Le Jugement dernier des rois* by Maréchal (1793). Plays of "philosophical" purport abounded during the Revolution, but for the most part they are literary trash—unworthy of comparison with Marivaux, except as they show how degenerated and coarse the writers of the Revolution were and how low dramatic art had sunk.

Sainte-Beuve[6] gave a certain notoriety to *L'Ile des esclaves* by terming it "une bergerie révolutionnaire de 1792." The label is somewhat misleading. In 1792—on the stage, at least—the masters might have forsworn their aristocratic prerogatives and would have rejoiced to stay on L'Ile des esclaves where all men were equal. But most assuredly no servant in 1792 would have bemeaned himself to such a degree as to say to his master, as Arlequin did in 1725: "C'est à moi à vous demander pardon du mauvais service que je vous ai toujours rendu," nor would he have returned his master's suit on the ground that "je ne suis pas digne de le porter" (Sc. 9).

Other nineteenth-century critics scarcely did justice to *L'Ile des esclaves.* Petit de Julleville,[7] who was apparently unfamiliar with the play itself and unaware of its eighteenth-century success, classifies

6 *Causeries du lundi* (Paris, Garnier, s.a.), IX, 374.
7 *Le Théâtre en France* (Paris: Nouvelle édition, 1923), p. 276.

it among "les féeries, les pièces mythologiques," which are "la moins bonne partie de l'œuvre théâtrale de Marivaux." Lenient[8] seems to have given the play no more than a hasty reading, for his account emphasizes the conditions on L'Ile des esclaves in the early scenes and barely mentions the important doctrines formulated in Scenes 9 and 10. Lintilhac does not mention *L'Ile des esclaves* at all. Since it was not acted during the nineteenth century, there are no reviews of it.

Twentieth-century revivals of *L'Ile des esclaves* have taken place in 1931, when Jean Sarment presented a series of matinees at the Théâtre Antoine; in 1934, when students at the Sorbonne included it on a program of three plays that Professor Gaiffe produced to show the spirit of Figaro before Beaumarchais; and finally in 1934 and 1939 at the Théâtre Français. About the performances at the Sorbonne, Gérard d'Houville[9] said: "Ainsi que nous l'a dit M. Félix Gaiffe, dans une allocution aussi agréable que savante, les revendications égalitaires de Figaro se trouvent annoncées, dès 1725, dans *l'Ile des esclaves*."

[8] *La Comédie en France au XVIIIe siècle* (Paris, 1888), I, 383.
[9] *Le Figaro*, May 7, 1934.

11 L'Héritier du village

[One act in prose. First presented at the Théâtre Italien, August 19, 1725.]

L'Héritier du village is undoubtedly the least characteristic of Marivaux's comedies; it savors of nothing so much as a *dancourade,* and contains none of those special touches one has come to expect in a play by Marivaux. His sole excursion into peasant society reveals, too, that he was not as adept at portraying its people and problems as he was at depicting the powdered and bewigged aristocrats of Parisian drawing rooms. Six performances between August 19 and September 2, 1725, and three more in October of the same year label *L'Héritier du village* as a failure.

Farmer Blaise has just inherited 100,000 francs from his brother in Paris. He places the money in the hands of a usurer for investment and immediately takes on the airs of *gens de qualité* and coaches his wife Claudine to act like a *grande dame.* He has also hired Arlequin, a roguish adventurer in this play, to tutor his children, Colin and Colette, in fine manners. A wealthy neighbor, Mme. Damis and her cousin, the Chevalier, call on Blaise and his wife; when they learn of Blaise's inheritance, the Chevalier proposes that he marry Colette and that Mme. Damis marry Colin. Of course Blaise and Claudine are delighted to have their children marry into the local aristocracy. There follow hilarious scenes in which Colin

86

runs the gamut of gaucheries in making love to Mme. Damis, and Colette is too eager to accept the advances of the Chevalier. Musicians are brought on for the wedding festivities only a moment before word comes from Paris that Blaise's agent has gone bankrupt. Mme. Damis and the Chevalier withdraw their pledges, and Blaise and his family remain the crude peasants they have always been.

Since Marivaux is less original here than in his other plays, it is not surprising that he borrows—unwittingly, in all probability—from his predecessors. As Larroumet[1] says, "*L'Héritier du village* rappelle à chaque instant *Georges Dandin* et *le Bourgeois gentilhomme*." Blaise is M. Jourdain reduced from bourgeois to peasant level, and the general tone of Marivaux's play drifts from comedy to farce.

Desboulmiers[2] called it "une mauvaise copie de *l'Usurier Gentilhomme*." This comedy by Legrand had a notable success at the Théâtre Français at its première in 1713, and since it was played throughout the eighteenth century Marivaux must have been familiar with it. Desboulmiers further expressed his unfavorable opinion of the play by adding that *L'Héritier du village* "n'était pas digne de la Plume de M. de Marivaux." The *Mercure de France*[3] noted the first performance but did not deign to give it an analysis or name the author.

L'Héritier du village is not lacking in boisterous comedy. Blaise drills Claudine in using fine manners as he has observed them in Paris and then tries to impose "le préjugé à la mode"[4] on her:

> BLAISE: Je te varrions un régiment de galants à l'entour de toi, que je sis obligé de passer mon chemin; c'est mon savoir-vivre que ça, li aura trop de froidure entre nous.

[1] G. Larroumet, *Marivaux: sa vie et ses œuvres* (Paris: Hachette, 1882), p. 159.
[2] *Histoire anecdotique et raisonnée du Théâtre Italien depuis son rétablissement en France jusqu'à l'année 1769* (Paris: Lacombe, 1769), II, 413.
[3] August 1725, p. 1869.
[4] See also *La Fausse suivante* (1,7).

CLAUDINE: Blaise, cette froidure me chiffonne; ça ne vaut rian en ménage; je sis d'avis que je nous aimions bian au contraire.

BLAISE: Nous aimer, femme! morgué! il faut bian s'en garder; vraiment, ça jetterait un biau coton dans le monde!

CLAUDINE: Hélas! Blaise, comme tu fais! et qui est-ce qui m'aimera donc moi?

BLAISE: Pargué! ce ne sera pas moi, je ne sis pas si sot ni si ridicule. (Sc. 2)

Blaise attempts to dignify his new social status and imitate *les gens de qualité* by not paying his debts:

LE FISCAL: . . . je vous prie en même temps de me donner les cinquante francs que vous me devez depuis un mois.

BLAISE: Ça est vrai, je reconnais la dette; mais je ne saurais la payer; ça me serait reproché.

LE FISCAL: Comment! vous ne sauriez payer! Pourquoi?

BLAISE: Parce que ça n'est pas daigne d'une parsonne de ma compétence; ça me tournerait à confusion. . . . morgué! boutez-vous à ma place. Voulez-vous que je me parde de réputation pour cinquante chétifs francs? ça vaut-il la peine de passer pour un je ne sais qui en payant? . . . Il m'est bian parmis d'en bailler en emprunt, ça se pratique; mais en paiement ça ne se peut pas. (Sc. 7)

Yet Blaise gladly lends the Fiscal 50 francs, and he is furious when the latter accepts them in payment of the note:

BLAISE: Tenez, fiscal, je sis ravi de vous sarvir; prenez.

LE FISCAL: Je suis honnête homme; voici votre billet que je déchire, me voilà payé.

BLAISE: Vous v'là payé, fiscal? jarnigué! ça est bian malhonnête à vous. Morgué! ce n'est pas comme ça qu'on triche l'honneur des gens de ma sorte; c'est un affront. (Sc. 7)

It is worth noting that Blaise and Claudine are the first husband and wife Marivaux puts on the stage, and they are the only married couple to appear in any of his plays, except M. and Mme. Sorbin in *La Colonie* (1729) and the Marquis and his wife in the unperformed *La Femme fidèle*. Marivaux is never interested in the dramatic possibilities of marital conflict nor in the humorous episodes that might arise between husband and wife. Usually his plays contain only a widowed mother or father, perhaps in order to prevent the love story from being distorted by parental discord.

Larroumet[5] asserts—and Arland[6] repeats—that Picard derived the idea for *Les Marionnettes* (1806) from *L'Héritier du village*. However, Picard himself, who is quite frank in admitting his sources, does not say so; in his preface to *Les Marionnettes*[7] he claims Horace as his inspiration: "Horace est peut- être le meilleur poëte que puisse méditer l'auteur comique. Pour ma part, voilà trois fois qu'un seul vers de lui me fournit une comédie en cinq actes." Moreover, he states that "Gaspard et Marcelin ont quelque raison de se comparer à Fabrice et à Gil Blas," and he points out that the action resembles that of Dufresny's comedy, *La Coquette du village, ou Le Lot supposé* (1715). Picard does not mention Marivaux or his play in connection with *Les Marionnettes*. Since *L'Héritier du village* failed in 1725 and was never revived, it can be assumed that Picard did not know Marivaux's comedy and that it is purely by accident that there is some similarity in the aspirations of the newly enriched peasants in both plays.

On the other hand, it is most likely that D'Allainval, one of Marivaux's colleagues at the Théâtre Italien, used portions of *L'Héritier du village* when he wrote *L'Ecole des bourgeois* for the Comédie Française in 1728.

Once again one of Marivaux's poorer comedies, one that failed in Paris, was a great success in Germany. Lessing[8] says: "the sprightliest humor, the drollest wit, the cleverest satire: one is left breathless with laughter."

[5] *Op. cit.,* p. 273.
[6] Marcel Arland, *Théâtre complet de Marivaux* (Paris: La Nouvelle revue française), p. 502.
[7] *Œuvres de L. B. Picard* (Paris, 1821), V, 223.
[8] *Hamburgische Dramaturgie.*

12 L'Ile de la raison, ou Les Petits hommes

[Three acts in prose. First presented at the Théâtre Français, September 11, 1727.]

DURING the spring and summer of 1727 the drawing rooms of Paris were chuckling over a new philosophical comedy by Marivaux. The play contained the most sophisticated dialogue and the most ingenious ideas (the main novelty deriving from the currently popular translation of *Gulliver's Travels*), and it was the fashion in elite circles to read the play aloud to one's guests. For *L'Ile de la raison* Marivaux imagined a mythical island where a person's physical stature is determined by his reason. The natives, of course, are all rational beings and of normal size. But eight Europeans have been brought to the island—Marivaux does not explain how—and they have shrunk to Lilliputian proportions. It is the aim of the islanders to correct the Europeans of their prejudices and eccentricities and restore them to human size. In the course of the play six of the Europeans become *raisonnables,* but the other two are hilariously obtuse. All this is treated with a sparkling wit that enchants the reader.

The actors of the Comédie Française were eager to take advantage of the enormous vogue of the play. Earlier in the same year the troupe had accepted another piece by Marivaux, *La Surprise de l'amour* (his second comedy by the same title, and generally called *La Seconde surprise* to distinguish it from the first *Surprise* given in 1722 at the Théâtre Italien). However, the actors had wasted many months wrangling over the casting and production details of *La Surprise;* they now decided to stage *L'Ile de la raison* forthwith. So in the midst of considerable excitement, *L'Ile de la raison* was performed for an expectant public on September 11, 1727.

The play failed miserably! And little wonder, for the chief comic effect—the growth or shrinking of the Europeans as they showed more or less reason—could not be attained on the stage. Marivaux even wrote a special prologue[1] for the acted version to prepare the spectators for the bizarre events they were about to witness. The transformation, which can easily be imagined as one reads the play, does not materialize in the theater; therefore the illusion is lost and the pungency of the lines weakened. A successful movie version of the comedy might be produced by means of trick photography, but presumably *L'Ile de la raison* is precluded from stage production, except by *avant-garde* troupes.[2] In 1727, at least, the play was a fiasco. As the *Mercure*[3] commented, the comedy, "quoique pleine d'esprit, ne parût pas être goûtée du Public." For the third time Marivaux met failure at the Théâtre Français.

Marivaux had further reason to regret this venture. The failure at the Théâtre Français cast a stigma over the play, and *L'Ile de la raison* soon lost its popularity in the drawing rooms. Marivaux comments in a preface he wrote sometime later: "J'ai eu tort de donner cette comédie au théâtre. Elle n'était pas bonne à être représentée, et le public lui a fait justice en la condamnant."

Even though the play failed in 1727, it is extremely interesting to

[1] The idea for the prologue was borrowed from *Le Double veuvage* by Dufresny (1702).
[2] The play was given by the Compagnie de l'Equipe in 1950. See pp. 96–97.
[3] September 1727, p. 2087.

a twentieth-century reader who follows the currents of eighteenth-century thought. The play has no single theme or philosophical message but it abounds with novel ideas.

From the point of view of dramatic construction, *L'Ile de la raison* is a *pièce à tiroir.* The eight Europeans, caged like tiny animals, are brought onto the stage and inspected by the Governor and his retinue. The Governor is touched by their plight and with paternal benevolence tries to help them overcome their failings: "c'est toujours faire une bonne action que de tenter d'en faire une. Blectrue, c'est vous à qui je les confie. Je vous charge du soin de les éclairer. . . . En les voyant faits comme nous, nous en sentirons encore mieux le prix de la raison, puisqu'elle seule fait la différence de la bête à l'homme." (I, 4). They are then subjected one by one to the reasoning of Blectrue, who is the *conseiller du gouverneur,* and of other islanders including Floris, the Governor's daughter and Parmenès, his son.

The Poet agrees to be the first to submit to questioning. He does not concede that he has any faults, and he asks by what magic he has been reduced in size. Blectrue replies: "Je n'y connais point d'autre magie que vos faiblesses. . . . la petitesse de votre corps n'est qu'une figure de la petitesse de votre âme" (I, 10). Since the word "poet" does not exist in the vocabulary of the islanders, the European poet takes egotistical delight in describing his honorable profession and the glory that goes with it, and he bewilders Blectrue as he explains the kinds of plays he writes:

LE POÈTE: On appelle cela des tragédies, que l'on récite en dialogues, où il y a des héros si tendres, qui ont tour à tour des transports de vertu et de passion si merveilleux; de nobles coupables qui ont une fierté si étonnante, dont les crimes ont quelque chose de si grand, et les reproches qu'ils s'en font sont si magnanimes; des hommes enfin qui ont de si respectables faiblesses, qui se tuent quelquefois d'une manière si admirable et si auguste, qu'on ne saurait les voir sans en avoir l'âme émue et pleurer de plaisir. Vous ne me répondez rien.

BLECTRUE, *surpris, l'examine sérieusement:* Voilà qui est fini, je n'espère plus rien; votre espèce me devient plus problématique que jamais. Quel pot-pourri de crimes admirables, de vertus coupables et de faiblesses augustes! il faut que leur raison ne soit qu'un coq-à-l'âne. Continuez.

LE POÈTE: Et puis, il y a des comédies où je représentais les vices et les ridicules des hommes.

BLECTRUE: Ah! je leur pardonne de pleurer là.

LE POÈTE: Point du tout; cela les faisait rire.

BLECTRUE: Hem?

LE POÈTE: Je vous dis qu'ils riaient.

BLECTRUE: Pleurer où l'on doit rire, et rire où l'on doit pleurer! les monstrueuses créatures!

Still impenitent in his arrogance, the Poet is dismissed to reflect on his foolishness.[4] One can see that Marivaux is already propagating one of the basic ideas Rousseau was to elaborate in *La Lettre à d'Alembert* some thirty years later.

The next case, the peasant Blaise, freely admits, among other vices, his inordinate drunkenness and his lust for Farmer Maturin's wife. His repentance is so sincere and his return to normal size so complete that Blectrue asks him to work on Fontignac, the braggart Gascon. Under the tutelage of the reformed peasant, Fontignac lists lying, gossiping, and servile flattery as his chief sins, and he grows in stature in proportion to his confession of wrongdoing. He in turn cures Spinette, the *suivante* of the Countess. All three of them tackle the Doctor, now so tiny they can hardly see him in his cage. Although he is "un docteur de la Faculté," his three children died of smallpox and his wife succumbed at twenty-five to a lung ailment. Blaise

---

[4] Gossipmongers of the day liked to think that the Poet was a caricature of Voltaire. His description of tragedy and comedy recalls Montesquieu's parody of dramatic authors (*Les Lettres persanes*, No. 28).

reproaches him for earning a living "en tuant le monde." Thus insulted, the Doctor rebuffs the attempts to reform him, but Blaise predicts he will be converted in time. Next comes the Countess—"jeune, belle et fille de condition"—a worldly young woman with all the faults of her generation. At first she scoffs at those who criticize her, until Spinette draws her portrait, as Cléanthis did for Euphrosine in *L'Ile des esclaves*. Confronted with humiliating examples of her coquetry and selfishness, the Countess comes to her senses, and promises never to be unreasonable again. Her brother, the Courtier, is not so easily convinced of his faults. He berates Fontignac and Blaise for pointing out his extravagance and duplicity, but in the end he admits his errors; and when he finds himself as tall as Blaise and Fontignac, he thanks both of them.

A commotion offstage heralds the entrance of the Poet and the Philosopher, who are fighting with each other so violently that it is necessary for Blaise and the Courtier to separate them by force. The Poet has written some verses in which he satirizes the Philosopher. Both men become increasingly belligerent and incorrigible, and it is finally decided to place them "aux Petites-Maisons ou bien aux Incurables."

The play ends with a scene of rejoicing for the good things that have been accomplished for the Europeans. The Governor summarizes the philosophy of the play: "L'usage le plus digne qu'on puisse faire de son bonheur, c'est de s'en servir à l'avantage des autres" (III, 9), and announces a *divertissement*.

The romantic element is not lacking. Marivaux makes Floris fall in love with the Courtier and Parmenès with the Countess. However, he adds a novel twist to the love interest: it is the custom on this island for women to pay court to men. Blectrue explains the logic of this to the Europeans and in turn criticizes the European custom:

Que deviendra la faiblesse si la force l'attaque? . . . Que deviendra l'amour, si c'est le sexe le moins fort que vous chargez du soin d'en surmonter les fougues? Quoi! vous mettrez la séduction du côté des hommes, et la nécessité de la vaincre du côté des femmes! . . . Quelles étranges lois que les vôtres en fait d'amour! Allez, mes enfants, ce n'est pas la raison, c'est le vice qui les a faites. (II, 3)

Eighteenth-century audiences must have delighted in those scenes in which the Countess proposes to Parmenès and the Courtier waits impatiently for the timid Floris to make amorous advances to him. When Blaise calls for a notary to draw up the marriage contracts, the Governor explains still another custom of the island: "Nous n'en avons point d'autre ici que la présence de ceux devant qui on se marie. Quand on a de la raison, toutes les conventions sont faites" (III, 9). Such thinking goes beyond eighteenth-century philosophy and borders on the theory of anarchism as outlined by Bukanin in the nineteenth century.

Of particular importance are the Governor's speeches in which he charges his subjects with the responsibility of trying to correct the erring Europeans. In a way he is the forerunner of the "enlightened despot," at a time when the "absolute monarch" concept was still in vogue. His speeches (I, 3, 4) savor of the later eighteenth-century philosophy typified by Frederick II's assertion that he was "the first servant of the state." The Governor's son rejects the idea of superiority of birth and refuses to allow the Countess to call him "prince":

Nous ne connaissons point ce titre-là ici; mon nom est Parmenès, et l'on ne m'en donne point d'autre. On a bien de la peine à détruire l'orgueil en le combattant. Que deviendrait-il, si on le flattait? Il serait la source de tous les maux. Surtout que le ciel en préserve ceux qui sont établis pour commander, eux qui doivent avoir plus de vertus que les autres, parce qu'il n'y a point de justice contre leurs défauts! (II, 8)

In spite of original ideas, *L'Ile de la raison* failed on the stage, as the periodicals of the day attest. When the play was published in the sixth volume of *Le Nouveau théâtre français*, the critic for *Le*

Journal littéraire[5] enjoyed "la folie orgueilleuse et incurable du Philosophe," but he protested "qu'on ait . . . mis les Médecins au nombre des fous"; he regretted, too, that "cette Pièce manque d'intrigue et d'action, que les yeux démentent à chaque instant ce que les Acteurs disent de leur prétendue petitesse & de leur croissance prétendue."

However unsuccessful *L'Ile de la raison* may have been at the Théâtre Français, a parody of it called *L'Ile de la folie* had "dix-sept représentations très suivies"[6] at the Théâtre Italien. The *Mercure de France*[7] found "le sujet fort réjouissant et les Scènes bien écrites." Marivaux's play is not mentioned by name, but undoubtedly the Italian actors took roguish delight in punishing their companion for his temporary infidelity.

Like *Le Prince travesti*, *L'Ile de la raison* remained in obscurity for over two hundred years and then created a veritable furor when an exceptionally fine revival was staged in Paris by an *avant-garde* troupe in June 1950. Gabriel Marcel[8] paid homage to this production in extravagant terms: "Voici un spectacle qui, sur tous les plans, mérite les plus grands éloges. La compagnie L'Equipe . . . a eu le double et rare mérite d'exhumer et de monter avec une intelligence remarquable une pièce importante de Marivaux qui n'avait pas été reprise depuis sa création en 1727. . . . Or, chose étonnante, voici qu'en 1950 cette pièce a triomphé!" None of the subtlety of the dialogue was lost on the capacity audience, which was made up almost entirely of laboring-class spectators. Marcel does not hesitate to give proper credit to Marivaux: "Certes, sans le génie de Marivaux, qu'est-ce qu'un pareil sujet aurait pu bien devenir? . . . ce qui sauve tout, c'est ce don unique d'allier la malice et la bonté."

[5] 1735, p. 453.
[6] J.-A. Desboulmiers, *Histoire anecdotique et raisonnée du Théâtre Italien depuis son rétablissement en France jusqu'à l'année 1769* (Paris: Lacombe, 1769), III, 93.
[7] October 1727, p. 2313.
[8] *Les Nouvelles littéraires, artistiques et scientifiques,* June 29, 1950.

Marcel cautions against regarding the play as a revolutionary docu-
ment and points out that the ideas expressed are more akin to the
spirit of humanism: "La raison, ici, n'est aucunement séparable de la
sensibilité. Mais cette sensibilité-là n'est ni sensiblerie ni sentimen-
talité préromantique." The actors visibly experienced keen pleasure in
interpreting the play, and "c'est merveille de voir comme ce plaisir
se communique aux spectateurs." Jean-Jacques Gautier[9] lauds "une
compagnie d'amateurs qui pourrait donner des leçons d'invention, de
gentillesse, d'esprit, de goût même, à bien des troupes profession-
nelles, et des plus renommées. . . . Je suis . . . surpris . . . que la
Comédie-Française n'ait point songé à remonter . . . cette délicieuse
pièce—Cendrillon. Oui, mais voilà, la Comédie-Française, l'aurait-
elle fait aussi bien?" Jacques Lemarchand[10] is no less exuberant, calling the evening "un hommage important pour Marivaux," and prais-
ing this group of amateurs for maintaining "ce qu'il y a de meilleur
dans notre histoire littéraire. . . . il règne tout au long du spectacle
une unité, une simplicité, une ardeur qui plaisent et parfois ravis-
sent."

M. Demay, the skillful director of the Compagnie de l'Equipe, attained a measure of the desired imagery by placing the islanders on
a platform and the Europeans in a sort of concealed trough in front.
From this position the Europeans could be raised or lowered to give
the illusion of growing or shrinking with their reason.

The program for the 1950 revival carried the following statement:

L'Ile de la raison ayant été sifflée le jour de sa création, nous avons voulu
prouver que le jeu dramatique évolue et que ce qui était considéré comme
injouable au temps de Marivaux peut aujourd'hui être joué. A vous de
dire si nous avons réussi.

The glowing tributes just cited would proclaim the affirmative

9 *Le Figaro,* June 9, 1950.
10 *Combat,* June 10, 1950.

and belie Xavier de Courville's[11] assertion: "c'est une œuvre littéraire froide et morte." In fact, *L'Ile de la raison* illustrates the modernness of Marivaux. If the play is not timeless, at least it transcends the limitations of its early-eighteenth-century origin and has real piquancy for mid-twentieth-century audiences. In spite of the technical difficulties it presents, which will always limit the frequency of revivals, *L'Ile de la raison* can be acceptably staged for modern spectators.

[11] *Théâtre de Marivaux* (Paris: A la Cité des livres, 1929–30), II, 205.

13   La [Seconde] Surprise de l'amour

[Three acts in prose. First presented at the Théâtre Français, December 31, 1727.]

THE Comédie Française had been holding a new comedy by Marivaux for many months—new, that is, in the sense that he had written it especially for the troupe, although he had used exactly the same title five years earlier for a play at the Théâtre Italien.[1] After the première critics inserted the word "seconde" in the title, and since then the comedy has been called *La Seconde surprise de l'amour.*

The casting must have caused considerable disagreement among the actors, for the final distribution of roles resulted in several unusual and inappropriate assignments: Quinault l'Aîné played the Chevalier; la Thorillière, the Count; and Adrienne Lecouvreur, the Marquise. Although these actors customarily gave brilliant performances in tragedy, their special talents were misplaced in *La Seconde surprise de l'amour.* At the first performance Mlle. Lecouvreur acted with restrained lightness, but thereafter she put on airs *à la princesse,* with the result that the comedy had only a mediocre success (which seemed to be Marivaux's inevitable fate at the Théâtre Français) and was soon dropped from the active repertory.

However, a few years later *La Seconde surprise* was given in some

---

[1] For a discussion of *La Première surprise de l'amour,* see Chapter 5.

théâtres de société, where amid more intimate surroundings the inherent charm of the play became evident. A new cast was assembled by the Comédie Française, and the play was revived with considerable success. In the course of the eighteenth century it became the most frequently performed of Marivaux's comedies at the Théâtre Français, reaching a total of two hundred thirty-four showings by the end of the century.

As its title indicates, this charming comedy relates another "surprise de l'amour." The young Marquise has just lost her husband, and her love for him is so deep that she plans to spend the rest of her life in seclusion, mourning him. She has employed Hortensius, a pedant, to surround her with books from antiquity and to read to her. The Chevalier, who has lived next door for some time, is equally afflicted because Angélique, whom he loves, has taken final vows in a convent rather than marry another man her despotic father would force upon her.[2] The Marquise and the Chevalier are drawn together by grief and console each other "en amitié." The Chevalier is about to leave Paris to pine in a remote province, but he postpones his departure in order to bring a bit of comfort to the young widow. Her maid Lisette, however, who believes that neither the Marquise nor the Chevalier can inhibit their natural instincts forever, foresees love growing out of their friendship. Conniving with the Chevalier's valet, Lubin, she presumes to offer the Marquise's hand to the Chevalier. The sudden injection of love into the situation shocks both the Marquise and the Chevalier, who believe they are keeping their relationship "en amitié." Hortensius, knowing he will

[2] This is one of the early examples in the theater of the use of convents for disciplinary purposes. In *L'Ecole des mères* (see Chapter 20), Mme. Argante threatens to put Angélique into a convent for refusing to marry the elderly M. Damis. As the century progressed, there was more and more evidence that tyrannical parents punished recalcitrant young daughters by putting them in religious orders. "Forced vows" became one of the social evils toward the end of the *ancien régime*. Cf. *Mélanie* (1770) by Laharpe, *Le Comte de Comminges* (1764) by Baculard d'Arnaud, and *Les Victimes cloîtrées* (1791) by Boutet de Monvel.

lose his job if the Marquise marries, selfishly interferes by insinuating to the lady that the Chevalier has actually spurned her. This only stirs pride and self-analysis in the Marquise: she is piqued to think that anyone would reject her, and her *amour-propre* seeks revenge; and even though she insists that she would not accept a proposal, she is determined that the Chevalier should *want* to marry her. The Count, a suitor of the Marquise and friend of the Chevalier, asks the latter to speak to her on his behalf. The Chevalier, too, passes through a turmoil of confusing emotions: his wish to be faithful to Angélique conflicts with his sympathy for the Marquise; his sense of duty to his friend cannot stifle his jealousy. Misunderstanding and *dépit amoureux* bring the plot to the point where the distraught Chevalier, keeping his word to his friend, persuades the Marquise to marry the Count; he himself will obligingly accept the Count's sister. Through all this, "la surprise de l'amour" works its alchemy and, when the Chevalier comes to bid farewell to the Marquise, it dominates them both and forces them to declare themselves to each other in spite of their pledged word. The Count enters as this tender scene is taking place; he accepts defeat graciously and withdraws. Lisette announces the arrival of the notary the Count has sent for; he is retained to draw up a contract for the Marquise and the Chevalier. Lisette and Lubin will follow the pattern of their masters.

Comparison between the two *Surprises* is inevitable. Marivaux had made much progress in his ability to delineate awakening love during the five-year period between the two plays. One senses a more polished mastery of thought and style in *La Seconde surprise,* so that "beaucoup de gens de lettres la préfèrent maintenant à la première *Surprise.*"[3] While both plays turn on a common theme (two hearts that resist love are caught in *le jeu* of their seeming indifference), each is distinct in detail. Whereas the Countess and Lélio of *La Première surprise* build their acquaintance on a basis of mutual scorn for the opposite sex, the Marquise and the Chevalier

3 *Biographie universelle ancienne et moderne,* XXVI, p. 690.

are drawn together by an understanding of each other's sorrow. The first play abounds with sententious theories about love and infidelity, by which the Countess and Lélio justify their hostility; the second play is entirely free of moralizing, as the Marquise and the Chevalier wander blindly through the unchartered pathways of their hearts to the exquisite realization of love.

The exigencies of the Théâtre Français made it necessary for Marivaux to observe conventions that further differentiate the plays. Arlequin, of course, is missing; but he is replaced by Lubin—in name only, one might add, for the words and antics are truly those of Arlequin; Marivaux could easily insert Lubin's role in a comedy for the Théâtre Italien without changing a line. Hortensius, whose ancestry might be traced back to Sorel's *Francion* or to comic types in the old Italian repertory, is a unique creation in Marivaux's theater. He was undoubtedly conceived with a view to pleasing audiences at the Théâtre Français in the early eighteenth century—although one is tempted to wonder whether these particular spectators were not irritated rather than pleased by a burlesque of "les anciens." This pretentious boor seeks to make love to the spirited Lisette with a vocabulary top-heavy with pedantry, and his clumsy interference in the affairs of the Marquise is entirely lacking in *savoir-faire*. But most of all it is his besotted attack on "les modernes" that creates much of the comedy. This outburst is filled with such bombast, and the whole character of Hortensius is so ridiculous, that the net result is a parody of "les anciens."[4]

Ordinarily it is difficult to find sources for Marivaux's comedies other than contemporary trifles at the Théâtre Italien, but two can be indicated for *La Seconde surprise de l'amour*. The most obvious is

---

[4] For some inexplicable reason, Fournier and Bastide (*Théâtre complet de Marivaux* [2 vols.; Paris: Les Editions nationales, 1946], I, 279) contend that Marivaux uses Hortensius to "décocher habilement quelques flèches contre les Modernes, comme il l'avait fait au début de *la Fausse suivante*." This assumption is untenable, since all through his life Marivaux was a partisan of "les modernes." See *La Fausse suivante*, pp. 69–70.

La Matrone d'Ephèse (1702) by Marivaux's close friend, Houdar de la Motte. Prior to La Motte, in the seventeenth century, the widow theme had also been dramatized for the *ancien* Théâtre Italien by Fatouville in *La Matrone d'Ephèse* (1681); and still earlier Mainfray had published *L'Ephésienne* (1614). All these authors had derived material from Petronius. But Marivaux's borrowing does not go beyond the basic idea of a young widow grieving for her husband; his treatment of the theme is original, and omits the macabre element so prominent in the other versions. In addition, Larroumet[5] points out that the reading of philosophy by Hortensius (II, 8) may have been imitated from *Le Joueur* (1696) of Regnard, in which Hector tries to console the gambler Valère for his losses by citing Seneca (IV, 13).

More to the point, however, is the influence Marivaux's play had in the nineteenth century. The Italian playwright Alberto Nota copied much of *La Seconde surprise* in *La vedova in solitudine* (1821). It deals with a young widow living in seclusion with the bust of her late husband; there is a plot to prevent her from remarrying, but the ending is the same as in Marivaux's comedy. Meilhac and Halévy appropriated sections of *La Seconde surprise* for *La Veuve* (1874), in which a young widow wishes to remain faithful to the memory of her husband until she finds receipts for gifts he had lavished on an unsuspected mistress. Both *La vedova in solitudine* and *La Veuve* are so rich in amorous intrigue and gay comedy that it can be assumed they are modeled after Marivaux rather than his more ghoulish predecessors.

One cannot avoid mentioning Alfred de Musset at this point, for *La Seconde surprise* is one of the plays most similar in style and spirit to Musset's comedies. He must have had Hortensius in mind when he created some of his caricatures; knowingly or not, he found the title for one of his most famous plays, *Il ne faut jurer de rien,*

---

[5] *Marivaux: sa vie et ses œuvres* (Paris: Hachette, 1882), p. 160.

in a speech by Lubin: "Eh bien, tout coup vaille, il ne faut jurer de rien dans la vie, cela dépend des fantaisies" (I, 11).[6]

Reviewing the première, the *Mercure de France*[7] referred to the outstanding success of the first *Surprise* at the Théâtre Italien and regretted that "On ne peut pas dire que celle qu'on joue actuellement sur le Théâtre François, ait été aussi généralement approuvée; mais on convient que si quelque chose a contribué à en rendre le succès moins éclatant, c'est la nouveauté du genre." The critic blames the apathy of the audience for the poor reception accorded the second *Surprise* at the Théâtre Français. Although the same spectators witnessed both plays, "on ne porte pas le même esprit à l'un & à l'autre Théâtre. Le genre que Molière a consacré au Théâtre François, est le seul qu'on y cherche." While blaming the audience, the critic made it plain that the play itself was of excellent quality: "Toutes les voix se réunissent à dire que la dernière *Surprise de l'Amour,* est une pièce parfaitement bien écrite, pleine d'esprit & de sentimens; que c'est une métaphysique du cœur très-délicate. . . . Le sujet est trop simple, dit on, soit; mais c'est de cette même simplicité que l'Auteur doit tirer une nouvelle gloire."

As has already been pointed out, *La Seconde surprise de l'amour* had a creditable run in the eighteenth century, but the history of the play at the Théâtre Français during the nineteenth century was rather bleak: revivals with Mlle. Mars in the first decade, with Mlle. Brohan in the 1850's, and with Mme. Bartet in the 1890's seemed to evoke no response from the public. Although *La Seconde surprise* was revived at the Odéon on March 17, 1929, it was not given again at the Théâtre Français until Jean-Louis Vaudoyer restaged it in 1944. At that time there were no reviews of it, undoubtedly because of the interruption of usual newspaper procedures in wartime.

The twentieth century, however, saw two brilliant revivals in

6 See also p. 181.
7 December 1727, pp. 2957–58.

other theaters. Xavier de Courville, who had become a master at interpreting and staging Marivaux, offered a limited number of performances of *La Seconde surprise de l'amour* March 18–23, 1929.[8] Gérard d'Houville[9] was captivated: "La Petite Scène nous a offert un de ces spectacles d'un goût parfait dont elle a le charmant secret. Certes, la *Seconde surprise de l'amour* n'est pas un des chefs-d'œuvre de Marivaux,[10] mais le dialogue est délicieux," and he found the production blessed with: "Ravissant décor; excellente mise en scène et très jolis effets d'éclairage." Unfortunately, because other critics did not review the play, this splendid revival did not have as much influence as it merited; but it did demonstrate what could be done with the play.

An acme of perfection was achieved when the Compagnie Madeleine Renaud–Jean-Louis Barrault presented *La Seconde surprise de l'amour* at the Théâtre Marigny on February 18, 1949.[11] Witnessing this production a few days after the brilliant revival of *Le Prince travesti*[12] at the Théâtre Français, critics were at a loss to find new superlatives for *La Seconde surprise*.

Once again Mme. Renaud, already so well known for her interpretation of Marivaux's heroines, illumined the theatrical season with her portrayal of the Marquise. Jean-Jacques Gautier,[13] like his colleagues, praised her because "elle avait répudié les traditions, elle s'était affranchie des conventions, elle jouait librement, elle interprétait son personnage d'une façon si moderne. . . . renouvelait le miracle de ce texte enchanteur." In the second act, "Elle a commencé à brûler les planches, à nous ravir. . . . Successivement pointue,

[8] M. de Courville toured Belgium, Holland, Switzerland, and Yugoslavia with his production.

[9] *Le Figaro*, March 28, 1929.

[10] Most critics would not agree with d'Houville on this point.

[11] M. Barrault took his production of *La Seconde surprise de l'amour* on the company's tour of South America in 1950.

[12] For reviews, see pp. 61–62.

[13] *Le Figaro*, February 21, 1949.

aigre, hargneuse, coquette, souriante, entreprenante, audacieuse . . .
passant d'un registre à l'autre et conservant tout de même à son jeu
une merveilleuse unité." Jean Herbault[14] says succinctly: "Madame
Renaud, parfaitement assistée par ses camarades, joue avec sa voix,
avec son visage, avec ses mains, avec des doigts même: marquise infiniment femme." Bernard Simiot[15] found her "riche de sortilèges."

The staging won the plaudits of the critics. Gabriel Marcel[16]
called Barrault's spectacle "un des plus parfaits qu'il nous a donnés.
Il a d'ailleurs été aux nues." Jean Herbault credited it with "la
réussite incontestable," and Bernard Simiot labeled it "un très intelligent régal . . . dans un décor rose, gris et crème qui eût fait
sourire de reconnaissance Marivaux lui-même."

This was not, however, one of those instances where superior acting and staging gave undue luster to the play itself. Rather, the
production highlighted the inherent value of *La Seconde surprise
de l'amour* and revealed the merits that now make it one of the
favorites of the twentieth century. The critics recognized the enduring quality of the play itself and paid homage to its author. Simiot,
who was reviewing several openings in the April issue of *La Revue
hommes et mondes,* began by sorting out the very good plays from
the mediocre or poor productions: "Venons tout de suite au meilleur,
et décernons sans tarder la palme à trois auteurs dont on n'a pas fini
de chanter les louanges: Marivaux, Molière, Racine." The awareness
of Marivaux's worth as a dramatist has been steadily increasing, and
it is now commonplace for critics to classify him with the great
classical masters of the French theater. Simiot calls their plays
"quelques louis d'or bien frappés" in comparison with the counterfeit
or valueless paper money of the usual theatrical currency. Gabriel
Marcel states that "*La Seconde surprise de l'amour* est du Marivaux
essentiel," and he stresses the musical qualities of Marivaux's writ-

---

14 *Plaisir de France,* March 1, 1949.
15 *La Revue hommes et mondes,* April 1949, p. 667.
16 *Les Nouvelles littéraires, artistiques et scientifiques,* March 10, 1949.

ings:[17] "Je ne crois pas qu'il existe rien au théâtre de plus mozartien que ce deuxième acte de *la Seconde surprise de l'amour*."

To return once again to Bernard Simiot: he gives a clue as to why Marivaux is so popular in the twentieth century. He describes the delicate sentiments of Marivaux's characters as they thread their way "à travers les multiples sentiers de la carte du tendre." Then he adds: "Il paraît qu'aujourd'hui nous allons plus vite en besogne et que nous précipitons nos affaires de cœur, mais c'est aussi que le théâtre d'amour du XXᵉ siècle place le cœur à un niveau nettement plus bas. . . . Chez Marivaux, le tourment de la chair n'apparaît pas en gros plan, et, cependant, toutes les coquetteries de son théâtre sont chargées de désir. . . . Le public d'aujourd'hui s'y trompe si peu, qu'habitué cependant à recevoir en plein visage les ondes de choc prodiguées par nos spécialistes de l'obsession sexuelle, il délaisse volontiers ces brefs délires pour aller prendre un plaisir plus secret aux cheminements amoureux que nous propose Mme Madeleine Renaud."

The observation is well taken. In Marivaux's theater one never finds the exploitation of coarseness, the exposition of tawdry passions. Strangely, his novels, reflecting as they do the society of the day with realistic accuracy, contain a fair share of lewd characters indulging in amorous intrigues; yet his plays are singularly free of these elements. The idealized love of Marivaux's theater comes as a breath of fresh air in the midst of a theatrical atmosphere too often polluted since *La Dame aux camélias* by unsavory exhibitions of love.

Like *Le Prince travesti*, *La Seconde surprise de l'amour* has joined the ranks of other Marivaux comedies that in modern times have captured the fancy of the public. Its success gives Marivaux added stature in the French theater.

[17] For other instances where modern critics have discussed the musical qualities of Marivaux's style, see pp. 39, 60, 217.

14   Le Triomphe de Plutus

[One act in prose. First presented at the Théâtre Italien, April 22, 1728.]

AFTER a two-year absence from the Théâtre Italien, during which he had undergone two failures at the Théâtre Français, Marivaux returned to his favorite actors with a racy one-act comedy that is a curious mixture of mythological personalities and stock characters of Italian farce, but a typical example of the genre for which the Italian troupe had become famous. In spite of its levity, *Le Triomphe de Plutus* deals realistically with the money question—one that was of immediate interest to Marivaux himself, for he was in financial straits at this moment. The question was very real to the public at large, too, since this was the era of financial upheaval following the collapse of the Law bank, which in turn had led to the rise of a powerful class of parvenus. Although the general tone of the play is one of flip comedy, the remarks about money matters and the influence of wealth carry a serious meaning.

Apollo has assumed an earthly role as a *bel esprit,* Ergaste, in order to win the heart of Aminte, and has vaunted his conquest to Plutus. The latter, piqued by Apollo's boasting, comes to earth as a *financier,* Richard, for the express purpose of captivating the girl by pitting his money against Apollo's virtuous qualities.

When the two meet in front of the home of Armidas, who is Aminte's uncle, Apollo counsels Plutus against using coarse language as he pursues earthly ladies; to which Plutus replies: "Bon! bon! vous voilà toujours avec votre esprit pindarisé; je parle net et clair, et outre cela mes ducats ont un style qui vaut bien celui de l'Académie. . . . avec de l'argent j'ai tout ce qu'il me faut." Apollo realizes that they are rivals for the love of Aminte, but he is sure that "sans vanité, elle est dans d'assez bonnes dispositions pour nous." Plutus is unconcerned: "Qu'est-ce que cela me fait à moi? J'ai un écrin plein de bijoux qui se moque de toutes ces dispositions-là; laissez-moi faire" (Sc. 2).

Spinette, the *suivante* of Aminte, greets the two visitors on behalf of her mistress and the girl's uncle. Apollo, eager to see his beloved, leaves Spinette to talk with Plutus. The latter wastes no time as he sets about buying Spinette's good will: "je ne m'appelle pas Ergaste, moi; j'ai nom Richard, et je suis bien nommé; en voici la preuve. (*Il lui donne une bourse*)" (Sc. 4). The promise of other gifts wins over the girl; she warns Plutus that he will have to overcome Apollo's attractiveness: "il parle de mariage, aussi, il est d'une figure assez aimable; beaucoup d'esprit; il faudra lutter contre tout cela." Plutus is sure of himself: "Et moi je suis riche; cela vaut mieux que tout ce qu'il a. . . . dis-lui encore que mon or et mon argent sont toujours beaux; cela ne prend point de rides; un louis d'or de quatre-vingt ans est tout aussi beau qu'un louis d'or du jour" (Sc. 4).

Plutus has no difficulty in bribing Apollo's valet, Arlequin, who is unpaid and thirsty:

PLUTUS: Tu me touches, tu as la physionomie d'un bon enfant. Tiens, voilà de quoi boire à ma santé.

ARLEQUIN: Mais, Monsieur, cela me confond; suis-je bien éveillé? Dix louis d'or pour boire à votre santé! Spinette, fait-il jour? N'est-ce pas un rêve?

SPINETTE: Non; Monsieur m'a déjà fait rêver de même.

ARLEQUIN: Voilà un rêve qui me mènera réellement au cabaret. (Sc. 5)

Aminte's uncle, Armidas, falls an easy victim. The wily Plutus
buys a piece of property from Armidas at an extravagant price, then
offers to make a deal with him: "Eh bien, troquons; reprenez la terre
gratis, et je prends la fille sur le même pied" (Sc. 6). Not only does
Plutus propose to take the girl without a dowry, but he promises to
set a lavish table to which Armidas will always be invited: "Vraiment! si j'épouse Mademoiselle Aminte, je prétends bien que dans
six mois vous soyez plus en chair que vous n'êtes. Voilà un menton
qui triplera, sur ma parole" (Sc. 6). The old man cannot resist such
temptations and assures Plutus that Aminte will conform to his
wishes.

While Apollo remains indoors to compose a *divertissement* for
his fiancée, Aminte comes out to talk to her friends. Plutus flatters
her with gallantries that she finds ridiculous at first, but during his
momentary absence Armidas, Spinette, and Arlequin vie with one
another to show her that Plutus' generosity far outweighs Apollo's
manly graces. When Plutus returns he says to Aminte: "Ergaste vous
fait là-haut des vers; chacun a sa poésie et voilà la mienne" (Sc. 10),
and he presents her with a magnificent bracelet. Spinette comments:
"Une rime à ces vers-là serait bien riche." Overcome by other lavish
gifts, Aminte finally admits: "Je veux mourir si je suis la maîtresse
de dire non. Il y a dans ses manières je ne sais quoi d'engageant qui
vous entraîne" (Sc. 10).

When Apollo enters with his musicians to rehearse the *divertissement,* the others are bored; one by one they abandon him, and Apollo
can justly reproach Aminte for her infidelity and Arlequin for his
desertion. Plutus has hired elegantly dressed musicians and dancers
to give an entertainment for his newly won love; this is the *coup de
grâce* for Apollo: "Il ne manquait plus que ce trait pour achever ma
défaite; et me voilà pleinement convaincu que l'or est l'unique divi-
nité à qui les hommes sacrifient" (Sc. 17), and he admits as much to
his rival: "Plutus, vous l'emportez sur Apollon; mais je ne suis point
jaloux de votre triomphe. Il n'est point honteux pour le dieu du

mérite d'être au-dessous du dieu des vices dans le cœur des hommes" (Sc. 18).

Having won his bet, Plutus announces his identity and that of Apollo to the guests and says that they must return to Olympus; he is confident that his bounty will compensate them for his absence. He bids the musicians to start the festivities.

Such was the comedy Marivaux presented in 1728. Evidently he was not proud of it, for "L'Auteur de ce petit ouvrage ne se nomme point."[1] However, the *divertissement* written by Panard with music by Mouret "a fait grand plaisir" and no doubt accounts for much of the success of the play, which had twelve performances in its *nouveauté* and six more the following season.

One might wonder what moral Marivaux had in mind. The plot suggests the rather cynical proposition that money triumphs over virtue. Yet the situation is handled with such an air of buffoonery that one is not inclined to accept this proposition seriously; in fact, one might even conclude that the author was suggesting the opposite. The real moral of the play is not to be found in the triumph of Plutus but rather in the repellent character of Plutus that negates his triumphs.

In fact, this play, like some of Marivaux's minor comedies, sheds light on the author. Marivaux respected virtue, condemned vice, scorned wealth. Yet he was too much a man of his day not to realize that vice was often practiced to the detriment of virtue and that money influenced people to an alarming degree.

In many respects *Le Triomphe de Plutus* echoes the sentiments expressed so trenchantly by Lesage in *Turcaret* (1709). The prodigalities of Plutus recall the infamous *traitant*. When Plutus insolently scoffs at Apollo: "Homme de mérite, lui! il n'a pas le sou," and in turn vaunts himself: "Un homme comme moi! c'est un trésor" (Sc. 6), he reflects the spirit of Turcaret. When he tempts Spinette with largess: "je te ferai ta fortune, mais une fortune qui sera bien

_____
[1] *Le Mercure de France*, April 1728, pp. 811–12.

nourrie," and asks her to influence Aminte: "Vante-moi seulement auprès d'elle, je lui donnerai tout ce qu'elle voudra; elle n'aura qu'à souhaiter," he exudes Turcaret's sensuality. Plutus' brash assertion "avec de l'argent, j'ai tout ce qu'il me faut" (Sc. 2) brings to mind the scoundrel Frontin in Lesage's play. Whereas Lesage exposed the *traitant* with such mordant realism that he incurred the wrath of powerful money interests, Marivaux treated the same subject with a levity that did not offend. Or perhaps sophisticated Parisians had become inured to the offensiveness of the crude newly rich.

If Marivaux owed something to Lesage for the conception of Plutus, his play in turn became source material for two other dramatists. Destouches modeled his ribald parvenu, Lisimon, in *Le Glorieux* (1732) after Plutus,[2] and in 1756 Mlle. Hus (better known for her *galanteries* than for her acting or writing) offered a mediocre comedy at the Théâtre Italien entitled *Plutus rival de l'amour,* which, as Fournier and Bastide[3] point out, "doit à Marivaux plus que son titre."

One of the least consequential of Marivaux's comedies, *Le Triomphe de Plutus* nevertheless enjoyed a successful run. It has some value as a commentary on the money problems of the day, and the not inconsiderable honor of contributing to one of the masterpieces of the eighteenth-century French theater.

[2] Larroumet, Fournier and Bastide, and Arland concur on this point.
[3] *Théâtre complet de Marivaux* (2 vols.; Les Editions nationales, 1946), I, 306.

Les Acteurs de la Comédie Italienne.
Nicolas Lancret's realistic portrayal of the troupe
that performed most of Marivaux's comedies.

Silvia. Portrait by L. M. Van Loo of the actress
who created Marivaux's heroines at the Théâtre Italien
in the 1720's and 1730's.

Les Comédiens français. Watteau's
graceful rendering of a group of French actors
at the time Marivaux began to write for the theater.

Préville. Portrait by C. A. Van Loo of an actor of the
Comédie Française who had great success in *Le Legs*.

15   La Colonie

[Three-act version first presented at the Théâtre Italien, June 18, 1729.
One-act version published in the *Mercure de France*, June 1750.]

La Colonie finds Marivaux in a philosophical mood again. This time he deals with the obliteration of class distinction and carries the ·discussion of women's rights into hitherto unexplored areas, broaching the as yet unformulated question of their participation in government.

In general, what theorizing was done about women in the sixteenth and seventeenth centuries placed them in a position distinctly inferior to men, relegating them to the duties of raising families or beautifying themselves to serve the pleasures of men. Montaigne summarized his ideas on the subject in *De trois commerces* (Book III, Chapter 3): "C'est le vrai avantage des dames que la beauté. Les discours, la prudence et les offices de l'amitié se trouvant mieux chez les hommes: pourtant gouvernent-ils les affaires du monde."

In the seventeenth century *Les Femmes savantes* by Molière (1672) created a veritable furor and stirred new debates on the position of women in society. In 1687 Fénelon, who attached more importance to the education of girls than did most of his contemporaries, published his *Traité de l'éducation des filles.* He proposed a system of instruction that would inure a girl against boredom and frivolity and that would combine useful studies with training to prepare her to take her place in society. La Bruyère,[1] touching on education for women, blames their ignorance on themselves, for they do not seek to improve their condition: "Pourquoi s'en prendre aux hommes de ce que les femmes ne sont pas savantes? Par quelles lois, par quels édits, par quels rescrits leur a-t-on défendu d'ouvrir les yeux et de lire, de retenir ce qu'elles ont lu et d'en rendre compte ou dans leur conversation ou par leurs ouvrages?" According to La Bruyère, women choose to devote their efforts to the wiles of coquetry; they already have so many advantages that men "sont heureux que les femmes qui les dominent d'ailleurs par tant d'endroits aient sur eux cet avantage de moins." Montesquieu[2] enlivened the question without coming to definite conclusions: "C'est une grande question, parmi les hommes, de sçavoir s'il est plus avantageux d'ôter aux femmes la liberté, que de la leur laisser. Il me semble qu'il y a bien des raisons pour et contre." Europeans—so Montesquieu asserts—argue that there is nothing admirable in bringing unhappiness to those one loves, while Asiatics believe that it is weakness on the part of men to renounce their natural control over women. If it is true that men exercise tyrannical power over women, it is likewise true that women have a universal authority over men: that of beauty. Montesquieu ends the debate with a citation from Mohammed: "Le prophète a décidé la question, & a réglé les droits de l'un & de l'autre sexe. Les femmes, dit-il, doivent honorer leurs maris: leurs maris les doivent honorer; mais ils ont l'avantage d'un degré sur elles."

Against this background Marivaux presented his play. First performed in a three-act version under the title of *La Nouvelle colonie, ou La Ligue des femmes,* it did not succeed. The *Mercure de France*[3] commented: "Cette Pièce n'a pas été aussi heureuse que la plupart de celles qui sont sorties de sa plume." Marivaux withdrew the play after the first performance; he never published his original version

[1] *Des femmes,* p. 49.
[2] *Lettres persanes,* No. 38.
[3] June 1729, p. 1403.

and the manuscript has never been found. However, the review in the *Mercure* gives the substance of the play. On an unidentified island the election of two governors (one representing the nobility and the other the third estate) is to take place. The women, led by Silvia, believe they have lived long enough under the domination of men, and they demand a voice in the new government. Silvia charges her noble suitor, the newly elected Timagène, to carry their demands to the council. M. Sorbin, the governor representing the third estate, opposes this plan, although his wife shares Silvia's ideas. Rather than lose their loves, both men plan to resign—not, however, until they have passed a law stating that women are to be prosecuted only by entreaties and remonstrances. A *philosophe* named Hermocrate, acting as an adviser to the two governors, reproaches them for their weakness. In a new meeting of the council called to accept the resignation of Timagène and Sorbin, Hermocrate is elected the sole governor. His first act is to banish Silvia's father, Timagène, M. and Mme. Sorbin, and their future son-in-law Arlequin. This severity makes the women renounce their demands. The play ends with a *divertissement* in which the singers point out that love gives women an advantage over men that should compensate them for not participating in government.

Some twenty years later Marivaux rewrote his comedy in a one-act version and published it in the *Mercure de France,* June 1750, under the title of *La Colonie.* Obviously he made radical changes. Since the new version was not intended for the Théâtre Italien, Silvia was designated as a noblewoman named Arthenice, and the Sorbin daughter's suitor was called Persinet instead of Arlequin.

The characters are apparently Europeans who have fled their native land in order to avoid death or slavery at the hands of a conquering enemy. Since they are no longer bound by the laws of the homeland, they are free to set up a government to their own liking. As the play begins, the men are about to assemble to make the laws. But the women, guided by lofty revolutionary theories of social and political equality, want a share in the government. The aristocratic Arthenice and the bourgeoise Mme. Sorbin harass Timagène and M. Sorbin with their demands. During the council meeting Arthenice harangues the women and pledges them to withhold their favors from the men if the latter do not recognize them as equals. Some of the women would demur, but Arthenice's will prevails. The men are nonplussed by the women's audacity. The philosopher Hermocrate thinks of a plan to disunite the women: he starts negotiating with them on the basis of their social status, and they fall to quarreling among themselves, Arthenice refusing to concede the privileges of her birth. As the women are disputing, some men enter with weapons, saying that the colony is attacked by natives and that if the women are to have equal rights they must fight alongside the men. The women decide to withdraw their demands and return to their subservient positions if the men will protect them. So the play ends just where it started. An innocuous romance between Persinet and Lina Sorbin is interwoven in these doings.

It is not, however, the dramatic content of *La Colonie* that attracts the reader, but the ideas. Here Marivaux projects theories on women's suffrage and social equality so far in advance of his time that they scarcely touched his contemporaries, although they have become commonplace in the twentieth century. True, Marivaux peppered his ideas with joyous comedy and witty dialogue (a frequent complaint of eighteenth-century critics is that Marivaux has "trop d'esprit"), for he realized that the reforms he conceived were unworkable in his day; yet the seriousness of intent in the play is obvious.

A plea for equal rights for women pervades the play. Arthenice expresses the resentment of the women: "nous sommes dans une occurrence où l'amour n'est plus qu'un sot. . . . le mariage, tel qu'il a été jusqu'ici, n'est plus aussi qu'une pure servitude" (Sc. 5). In her tirade to the women she proclaims: "Je fais vœu de vivre pour soutenir les droits de mon sexe opprimé; je consacre ma vie à sa gloire" (Sc. 6). As chief spokeswoman for her irate confederates, Arthenice decries the traditional political subjugation of her sex: "L'oppression dans laquelle nous vivons sous nos tyrans . . . n'en est pas devenue plus raisonnable; n'attendons pas que les hommes se corrigent d'eux-mêmes" (Sc. 9), and she bewails the fact that the use of women's intelligence has been limited to the supervision of household chores: "Venons à l'esprit, et voyez combien le nôtre a paru redoutable à nos tyrans; jugez-en par les précautions qu'ils ont prises pour l'étouffer, pour nous empêcher d'en faire usage; c'est à filer, . . . c'est à l'économie de leur maison, c'est au misérable tracas d'un ménage . . . que ces messieurs nous condamnent" (Sc. 9). Then Arthenice berates the women for being so stupid as to be flattered by the pretty compliments of their suitors: "Il est vrai qu'on nous traite de charmantes, que nous sommes des astres, qu'on nous distribue des teints de lis et de roses . . . et qu'en arrive-t-il? que par simplicité, nous nous entêtons du vil honneur de leur plaire, et que nous nous amusons bonnement à être coquettes, car nous le sommes, il en faut convenir" (Sc. 9). Therefore she decrees that the women make themselves ugly, clothe themselves in sacks, and scorn the company of men.[4]

Arthenice presents her ultimatum to the men: "je n'ai plus qu'un mot à dire, profitez-en; il n'y a point de nation qui ne se plaigne des défauts de son gouvernement; d'où viennent-ils, ces défauts? C'est que notre esprit manque à la terre dans l'institution de ses lois, c'est que vous ne faites rien de la moitié de l'esprit humain que nous avons, et que vous n'employez jamais que la vôtre, qui est la plus faible. . . . C'est que le mariage qui se fait entre les hommes et nous, devait

---

[4] This scene is obviously reminiscent of the *Lysistrata* of Aristophanes. Marivaux did not know Greek, and the play was not translated into French until 1730, the year after the première of *La Colonie*. However, it is most likely that Marivaux had heard Aristophanes' plays discussed in the drawing rooms. Furthermore, there is no evidence in the 1729 review of the play in the *Mercure de France* that this particular scene was in the original version; Marivaux may have written it as late as 1750.

aussi se faire entre leurs pensées et les nôtres; c'était l'intention des dieux, elle n'est pas remplie, et voilà la source de l'imperfection des lois" (Sc. 13). In the end the women have to abandon their claims, but the idea of equal rights for women, a major political issue in the nineteenth and twentieth centuries, was projected in dramatic form in 1729 (and in 1750) with amusing, yet serious, forcefulness. It is impossible to determine how much of the succinct wording appeared in the 1729 version, but certainly the spirit and intention were embodied in the original draft.

The theory of social equality is also set forth. At the beginning of the play Arthenice generously sweeps away the social barriers between herself and Mme. Sorbin: "Madame Sorbin, ou plutôt ma compagne, car vous l'êtes, puisque les femmes de votre état viennent de vous revêtir du même pouvoir dont les femmes nobles m'ont revêtue moi-même, donnons-nous la main, unissons-nous et n'ayons qu'un même esprit toutes les deux" (Sc. 1), and she states bluntly to the men that since they have all cast their lot together in this venture: "la fortune y est égale entre tous . . . personne n'a droit d'y commander" (Sc. 2). However, when Hermocrate proposes the suppression of rank and places her on the same level as Mme. Sorbin, Arthenice rebels: "Je n'y consentirai jamais; je suis née avec un avantage que je garderai, s'il vous plaît" (Sc. 17). Finding Mme. Sorbin's company intolerable, Arthenice explodes: "La brutalité de cette femme-là me dégoûte de tout, et je renonce à un projet impraticable avec elle" (Sc. 18).

Arthenice's ideas would no more succeed on the mythical island than they would in the France of Marivaux's day; almost at the beginning Arthenice and Mme. Sorbin admit as much, although they have hopes for the future:

ARTHENICE: Je vous garantis un nom immortel.

MADAME SORBIN: Nous, dans vingt mille ans, nous serons encore la nouvelle du jour.

ARTHENICE: Et quand même nous ne réussirons pas, nos petites-filles réussiront. (Sc. 1)

It is not to be assumed that Marivaux originated these ideas; theorizing about the status of women was "in the air" at the time, especially in the elite circle Marivaux frequented. Mme. de Lambert incorporated some of the current thinking in her *Réflexions sur les femmes* (1732), although Marivaux borrowed little from her.

The originality of Marivaux is to have taken up the question of freedom for women when it was still little discussed, and to have presented arguments in favor of such freedom when it was generally frowned on. So far as *La Colonie* is concerned, the most striking ideas in the play seem to be Marivaux's own. He removed the discussion of women's suffrage and social equality from a nebulous realm, and set forth bold and coherent theories. Marivaux could make proposals for reform because in 1729 and even in 1750 they were so far beyond the possibility of implementation that one could discuss them glibly on a purely theoretical basis. Nevertheless, Marivaux gave new dimensions to social thinking on women's rights and political equality.

La Colonie was given at the Odéon on February 5, 1925, together with *La Surprise de l'amour* under the aegis of Professor Gaiffe.

16   Le Jeu de l'amour et du hasard

[Three acts in prose. First performed at the Théâtre Italien, January 23, 1730.]

THE best-known and most frequently performed of Marivaux's comedies—and, by critical acclaim, his masterpiece—is *Le Jeu de l'amour et du hasard*. The play had a successful run in its *nouveauté* at the Théâtre Italien, was played before the court on February 10, 1731, and was frequently revived by the Italian actors over the next several decades. During the French Revolution, when the plays of the classical theater were consigned to the public domain, *Le Jeu de l'amour et du hasard* was a popular piece at the *petits théâtres* several years before it entered the repertory of the Théâtre Français in 1796.[1] Since then it has continued in the active repertory, often as a showpiece for a gifted actress. In addition, *Le Jeu de l'amour et du hasard* has been a perennial favorite at the Odéon and also at uncounted *petits théâtres* and with *avant-garde* troupes in the nine-

[1] During the French Revolution political differences among the actors caused the Comédie Française to split into two factions: the loyalist group headed by Fleury, Dazincourt, and Mlle. Contat remaining at the traditional theater (called at that time the Théâtre de la Nation) and a dissident group led by Talma, Dugazon, and Mme. Vestris establishing its own house (called the Théâtre Français de la Rue de Richelieu and later the Théâtre de la République). The Théâtre de la Nation was considered the official theater until September 1793, when the loyalist troupe was arrested for treason and their theater closed. After the Reign of Terror the actors of the Comédie Française tried their luck individually or in groups on various stages in Paris, but the Théâtre de la République was considered the official theater. It was not until May 1799 that old grievances were forgotten and the Comédie Française was re-established as a united troupe in their old theater.

teenth and twentieth centuries. Such popularity is not undeserved, for time has proved *Le Jeu de l'amour et du hasard* to be a gem of dramatic literature.

The action of the play is based on an ingenious and highly diverting situation. M. Orgon has arranged to marry his daughter Silvia to the young nobleman Dorante, who is the son of an old friend living in Burgundy. Since the two young people have never seen each other, their parents, with leniency uncommon in the eighteenth century, have granted them complete liberty to accept or reject the marriage. Although Silvia has been assured that Dorante is "un des plus honnêtes hommes du monde . . . bien fait, aimable, de bonne mine" (I, 1), she feels that when she meets him she may not like him, and she does not want to be trapped into a loveless marriage, as some of her friends have been.[2] It is not that she is afraid of marriage; rather, she wants to be sure that superficial attributes of appearance and manners do not conceal a knave whose true character will come to light only after they are married. In order to examine the young man for herself, Silvia has asked her father to be allowed to exchange places with Lisette and act as a maid during Dorante's visit. M. Orgon agrees with kindly indulgence. When Silvia goes to change clothes with Lisette, M. Orgon explains to his son Mario that he has just received a letter from Dorante's father in which it is revealed that Dorante, who is taking his marriage seriously and is as much concerned about the happiness of the girl as about his own, has persuaded his father to permit him to visit the Orgon household in the guise of his valet Arlequin so that he may observe Silvia incognito. M. Orgon is aware of a possible indelicacy in the situation and asks Mario whether he should warn Silvia of Dorante's plan. Amused at the novelty of the situation, Mario suggests that they let the intrigue take its course: "Voyons si le cœur ne les avertirait de ce qu'ils valent. Peut-être que Dorante prendra du goût pour ma sœur,

---

[2] Boissy got his idea for *Les Dehors trompeurs* (1740) from Silvia's description of the unhappy households she observed (I, 1).

toute soubrette qu'elle sera, et cela serait charmant pour elle" (I, 4). So the stage is set for a double *travestissement*.

Dorante arrives. He assumes the name Bourguignon. The gracious charm of the supposed maid augurs well for the mistress he expects to see; likewise, his own good breeding, ill concealed in the garb of a valet, arouses in Silvia's heart high hopes for the master. Left alone, Dorante and Silvia go through an enchanting scene (I, 7) in which the quality of the maid attracts Dorante ("cette fille m'étonne! Il n'y a point de femme au monde à qui sa physionomie ne fît honneur"), and the innate superiority of the valet touches Silvia ("ce garçon-là n'est pas sot, et je ne plains pas la soubrette qui l'aura"). Although each believes he is dealing with a person beneath his station, "la surprise de l'amour" begins to operate, and they are instinctively drawn to each other. Imagine, then, Silvia's dismay when Arlequin appears, oafish and arrogant, as the young suitor, and offends her by referring to M. Orgon as "mon beau-père" and to the daughter as "ma femme." Comparing him to the valet, Silvia sighs: "Que le sort est bizarre! aucun de ces deux hommes n'est à sa place" (I, 8). Dorante scolds Arlequin for his clumsy beginning and ill-mannered remarks to the maid; he himself is a bit bewildered by the curious turn of affairs: "Je ne sais plus où j'en suis; cette aventure-ci m'étourdit: que faut-il que je fasse?" (I, 9).

In the lapse of time between acts, Lisette has met Arlequin, and they have discovered such an affinity for each other that Lisette is disturbed. She informs M. Orgon that she had offered to play the role of mistress without attaching any consequence to it, but now she fears she has won the heart of Silvia's suitor: "malgré toutes les règles de la modestie, il faut pourtant que je vous dise que, si vous ne mettez ordre à ce qui arrive, votre prétendu gendre n'aura plus de cœur à donner à Mademoiselle votre fille" (II, 1). To Lisette's astonishment, M. Orgon compliments her and encourages her to continue; Lisette warns: "Monsieur, prenez-y garde; jusqu'ici je n'ai pas aidé à mes appas, je les ai laissés faire tout seuls, j'ai ménagé sa tête; si je m'en mêle, je la renverse; il n'y aura plus de remède" (II, 1). Lisette pursues her course, and Arlequin matches her advances with lusty appetite; a ribald "surprise de l'amour" takes hold of them and, like water seeking its own level, Lisette and Arlequin regale themselves in each other's company. Their misuse of elegant language and fine manners is a constant delight to the spectator: witness Arlequin's attempt to make love to the supposed daughter of the house: "Hélas! quand vous ne seriez que Perrette ou Margot; quand je vous aurais vue, le martinet à la main, descendre à la cave, vous auriez toujours été ma Princesse" (II, 5). Both are fearful that their new sentiments will not be able to stand the shock of the revelation that must come sooner or later; Arlequin proposes: "Pour les fortifier de part et d'autre, jurons-nous de nous aimer toujours, en dépit de toutes les fautes d'orthographe que vous aurez faites sur mon compte" (II, 5). To which Lisette replies: "J'ai plus d'intérêt à ce serment-là que vous, et je le fais de tout mon cœur" (II, 5).

Silvia is so irritated by Arlequin that she asks Lisette to dismiss the bumpkin on her behalf. She unwittingly finds herself defending the supposed valet and her outburst becomes so vehement that Lisette is astounded: "je ne reviendrai de longtemps de la surprise où vous me jetez" (II, 7). Silvia herself is no less annoyed at her bewilderment, though she does not blame the young man: "ce n'est pas sa faute, le pauvre garçon; et je ne dois pas m'en prendre à lui" (II, 8). At this taut moment Dorante approaches. Silvia tries to maintain a cool indifference in their conversation, but Dorante cannot prevent himself from talking of love. Both are aware of a potential misalliance in their situation. Silvia chides herself for listening to the chivalrous declaration of a valet: her pride as a *jeune fille bien élevée* does not permit her to be on friendly terms with a servant; yet when he turns to leave she detains him. Dorante is torn between the respect he owes the daughter of M. Orgon and the love he feels for the maid. As if to cure himself of his passion, he begs her: "Eh bien! chère Lisette, dis-le-moi cent fois que tu ne m'aimeras point.

. . . Il faut que je le croie. . . . accable mon cœur de cette certi-
tude-là. . . . donne-moi du secours contre moi-même; il m'est nécessaire; je te le demande à genoux" (II, 9), and he falls on his knees
before her. She is panic-stricken at the extremity to which her
escapade has brought her: "Ah! nous y voilà! il ne manquait plus
que cette façon-là à mon aventure. Que je suis malheureuse!" (II,
10); yet she succumbs to his sincerity: "Je dirai ce qu'il te plaira; que
me veux-tu? je ne te hais point. Lève-toi; je t'aimerais, si je pouvais;
tu ne me déplais point; cela doit te suffire." Unnoticed by either
of them, M. Orgon and Mario enter the room as Dorante continues:

> DORANTE: Quoi! Lisette, si je n'étais pas ce que je suis, si j'étais
> riche, d'une condition honnête, et que je t'aimasse autant que je
> t'aime, ton cœur n'aurait point de répugnance pour moi?
>
> SILVIA: Assurément.
>
> DORANTE: Tu ne me haïrais pas? Tu me souffrirais?
>
> SILVIA: Volontiers. Mais lève-toi.
>
> DORANTE: Tu parais le dire sérieusement, et, si cela est, ma raison
> est perdue.
>
> SILVIA: Je dis ce que tu veux, et tu ne te lèves point. (II, 10)

Dorante is about to reveal his secret when M. Orgon interrupts
jovially: "cela va à merveille, mes enfants; courage!" Silvia is humiliated at being caught thus by her father and her brother with a
servant at her feet. After Dorante leaves, M. Orgon and Mario
take loving joy in teasing her about her predicament. Once again
she finds herself defending the young man: "On accuse ce valet, et on
a tort; vous vous trompez tous, Lisette est une folle, il est innocent,
et voilà qui est fini; pourquoi donc m'en reparler encore? car je suis
outrée" (II, 11), and they leave the girl in a state of despair: "Ah!
que j'ai le cœur serré! Je ne sais ce qui se mêle à l'embarras où je me
trouve: toute cette aventure-ci m'afflige" (II, 12).

Dorante returns, this time to make his confession in spite of
Silvia's desire to escape him:

DORANTE: Arrête donc, Lisette; j'ai à te parler pour la dernière fois: il s'agit d'une chose de conséquence qui regarde tes maîtres. . . . tu vas voir les choses bien changer de face par ce que je te vais dire.

SILVIA: Eh bien, parle donc; je t'écoute, puisqu'il est arrêté que ma complaisance pour toi sera éternelle.

DORANTE: Me promets-tu le secret?

SILVIA: Je n'ai jamais trahi personne.

DORANTE: . . . tu m'as promis le secret; achevons. Tu m'as vu dans de grands mouvements; je n'ai pu me défendre de t'aimer.

SILVIA: Nous y voilà; je me défendrai de t'entendre, moi; adieu.

DORANTE: Reste; ce n'est plus Bourguignon qui te parle.

SILVIA: Eh! qui es-tu donc?

DORANTE: Sache que celui qui est avec ta maîtresse n'est pas ce qu'on pense.

SILVIA [*vivement*]: Qui est-il donc?

DORANTE: Un valet.

SILVIA: Après?

DORANTE: C'est moi qui suis Dorante. (II, 12)

In a flash all becomes clear to Silvia, and she says to herself with infinite relief: "Ah! je vois clair dans mon cœur." Dorante hastens to explain that he is willing to break with tradition to marry her: "Mon père, en partant, me permit ce que j'ai fait, et l'évènement m'en paraît un songe: je hais la maîtresse dont je devais être l'époux, et j'aime la suivante." But Silvia keeps her secret; she asks: "Votre penchant pour moi est-il sérieux? m'aimez-vous jusque-là?" To which Dorante answers without hesitation: "Au point de renoncer à tout engagement." Overwhelmed by such magnanimity of heart, Silvia cannot help reflecting: "Allons, j'avais grand besoin que ce fût là Dorante."

At this point Marivaux might well have ended the play by having Silvia admit her identity and bringing to a suitable conclusion the romance of Arlequin and Lisette. But he has not finished exploring all the complexities of feeling in these young people, and he contrives means to continue his comedy.

Dorante, feeling that the disguise has gone beyond the bounds of propriety, demands that Arlequin reveal his identity to the supposed Silvia; if she still persists in her infatuation for a valet, at least his own conscience will be free. Mario, coached by Silvia, torments Dorante by insinuating that he is seriously attached to the comely maid. Dorante has difficulty in retaining his disguise and in not answering Mario like an *homme de condition*. When Silvia arrives Dorante is further embarrassed by being ordered out of the room by Mario. He refuses to go until Silvia, seeming to play up to Mario as if there were an understanding between them, repeats the order. Dorante is disenchanted and reproaches Silvia as he leaves: "Vous ne m'aviez pas dit cet amour-là, Lisette" (III, 3). Overjoyed, Silvia confesses to Mario: "Si je n'aimais pas cet homme-là, avouons que je serais bien ingrate" (III, 4). She is utterly happy in her love for Dorante, which is now free of all taint of misalliance: "Dorante et moi, nous sommes destinés l'un à l'autre; il doit m'épouser" (III, 4). But a remnant of feminine vanity makes her want to ascertain that Dorante will marry her in spite of what he believes to be her humble position: "Il pense qu'il chagrinera son père en m'épousant; il croit trahir sa fortune et sa naissance; voilà de grands sujets de réflexion: je serai charmée de triompher. Mais il faut que j'arrache ma victoire, et non pas qu'il me la donne: je veux un combat entre l'amour et la raison" (III, 4).

Lisette, giddy with the success of her conquest, comes to give final warning to the family that Dorante is "une tête bien conditionnée" and asks if Silvia will yield him to her. Not only Silvia, but M. Orgon and Mario approve. Although she is unable to understand their consent, she is nonetheless willing to take them at their word; she clears the deck for action: "ayez donc la bonté de me laisser le champ libre: il s'agit ici de mon chef-d'œuvre" (III, 5). There follows one of the fine comic scenes on the French stage when Arlequin, obeying Dorante, tries to tell the truth to Lisette.

> ARLEQUIN: Je suis . . . N'avez-vous jamais vu de fausse monnaie? Savez-vous ce que c'est qu'un louis d'or faux? Eh bien, je ressemble assez à cela.
>
> LISETTE: Achevez donc: quel est votre nom?
>
> ARLEQUIN: Mon nom? [*A part.*] Lui dirai-je que je m'appelle Arlequin? Non; cela rime trop avec coquin.
>
> LISETTE: Eh bien?
>
> ARLEQUIN: Ah dame! il y a un peu à tirer ici. Haïssez-vous la qualité de soldat?
>
> LISETTE: Qu'appelez-vous un soldat?
>
> ARLEQUIN: Oui, par exemple, un soldat d'antichambre.
>
> LISETTE: Un soldat d'antichambre! Ce n'est donc point Dorante à qui je parle enfin?
>
> ARLEQUIN: C'est lui qui est mon capitaine.
>
> LISETTE: Faquin!
>
> ARLEQUIN [*à part*]: Je n'ai pu éviter la rime. (III, 6)

Far from being incensed, Lisette can scarcely restrain her laughter long enough to scold him a moment for deceiving her; then she declares: "Touche là, Arlequin; je suis prise pour dupe. Le soldat d'antichambre de Monsieur vaut bien la coiffeuse de Madame." They both accept the reality of the situation with hearty good humor, and Arlequin settles the issue: "Pardi! oui: en changeant de nom tu n'as pas changé de visage, et tu sais bien que nous nous sommes promis fidélité en dépit de toutes les fautes d'orthographe" (III, 6).

Now all the characters are apprised of the secret except Dorante. As he enters in search of the girl he believes to be Lisette, Arlequin cannot resist the temptation to heckle his master; he boasts of his conquest of M. Orgon's daughter; and when Silvia approaches, Arlequin says with affectionate insolence: "Bonjour, Lisette: je vous recommande Bourguignon; c'est un garçon qui a quelque mérite" (III, 7).

But Dorante is too heavy-hearted to continue the deception any longer. Not only has the daughter of the house proved to be common enough to consort with a valet, but, even worse, the charming *suivante* is involved with Mario. He therefore announces ruefully to the girl that he thinks it best for him to leave incognito as he has arrived. Silvia is dismayed, but she cannot bring herself to detain him. She watches him leave, and for a breathless moment she fears he does not love her enough to stay. But Dorante hesitates on the threshold, then turns back in anguish to make sure that it is right for him to leave; he pleads with her to tell him whether she is really in love with Mario. With a simple honesty she explains that the distance in social position between a *suivante* like herself and a young man of quality like him would soon spoil their love, that her diffidence is only a wish to protect him:

SILVIA: . . . Moi qui vous parle, je me ferais un scrupule de vous dire que je vous aime, dans les dispositions où vous êtes; l'aveu de mes sentiments pourrait exposer votre raison, et vous voyez bien aussi que je vous les cache.

DORANTE: Ah! ma chère Lisette, que viens-je d'entendre? tes paroles ont un feu qui me pénètre; je t'adore, je te respecte. Il n'est ni rang, ni naissance, ni fortune qui ne disparaisse devant une âme comme la tienne; . . . Ne consentez-vous pas d'être à moi?

SILVIA: Quoi! vous m'épouserez malgré ce que vous êtes, malgré la colère d'un père, malgré votre fortune?

DORANTE: Mon père me pardonnera dès qu'il vous aura vue; ma fortune nous suffit à tous deux; et le mérite vaut bien la naissance: ne disputons point, car je ne changerai jamais.

SILVIA: Enfin, j'en suis venue à bout; vous . . . vous ne changerez jamais?

DORANTE: Non, ma chère Lisette.

SILVIA: Que d'amour! (III, 8)

Her victory complete, Silvia joyously calls her father and reveals to Dorante that it is she who was all along destined to be his wife. Their double disguise has only brought them closer together, and Dorante is happy to say: "ce qui m'enchante le plus, ce sont les preuves que je vous ai données de ma tendresse" (III, 9).

The special merit of *Le Jeu de l'amour et du hasard* is its perfection. By 1730 Marivaux was a thoroughly experienced playwright; knowingly or not, he lavished all the resources of his talent on the play and made it one of the finest comedies to be written in the eighteenth century.

The style is an impeccable blending of elegant prose and its raucous imitation by Arlequin and Lisette. The delicate shades of sentiment expressed and the sensitive choice of words bring the language perilously close to *marivaudage,* but the speeches are so much a part of the characters that, given the situation, they do not savor of overaffectation. As Fleury[3] puts it, Marivaux "voit les choses d'une certaine façon, sous un certain jour, avec certains rapprochements et certains contrastes; il faut bien qu'il trouve des mots et des tournures pour exprimer ce qu'il voit. . . . A un état social raffiné, il faut également un style raffiné." Comedies written in verse often contain phraseology that could well demonstrate the worst affectations of *marivaudage;* yet because they are in verse one accepts them. In reviewing *Arlequin poli par l'amour,* Lemaître[4] called Marivaux's prose "la poésie du dernier siècle, avant Rousseau," and the same observation is applicable here. *Le Jeu* is a splendid illustration of Marivaux's ability to fuse character and style into an indissoluble unit.

Oddly, this play does not contain strikingly original elements such as have heretofore characterized most of Marivaux's comedies; rather, *Le Jeu* is a synthesis of the best that is in Marivaux. The "surprise de l'amour" has long since become an identifying stamp of Mari-

[3] *Marivaux et le marivaudage* (Paris: Plon, 1881), pp. 671–72.
[4] *Annales politiques et littéraires* (1892) I, 216. See also p. 23.

vaux's art, and he uses it again in *Le Jeu* with superb skill. Silvia is a composite of several heroines that Marivaux had created in the persons of the Silvia of *La Double inconstance,* the Hortense of *Le Prince travesti,* and the Marquise of *La Seconde surprise de l'amour;* she is the embodiment of the ideal *jeune fille bien élevée* and the prototype of a dozen lovely heroines to follow. Zanetta-Rosa-Giovanna Benozzi, who was Marivaux's favorite actress and who interpreted the role at the première in 1730, became so identified with the part that today she is usually called Silvia instead of by her own name. Dorante, the young lover who is so solicitous of the feelings of his betrothed, was tentatively sketched in Eraste of *Le Dénouement imprévu* and is here developed into a well-rounded character. In the course of several comedies Marivaux had humanized Arlequin, and in *Le Jeu* he is still farther removed from the domain of mere buffoonery and appears as a genuine person; his tricks and *lazzi* are not superimposed farcical gestures but rather an integral part of the play. When *Le Jeu* was performed at the Théâtre Français in 1796, Arlequin's name was changed to Pasquin as a concession to actors who refused to play a role traditionally looked upon as a clown's.

M. Orgon, Silvia's father, is an exceptionally liberal parent for 1730. The freedom he gives Silvia and the kindliness that pervades his entire being (and that he sheds over the whole play) differentiate him from the usual stern fathers who have appeared heretofore. Nor is he a unique figure in Marivaux's theater. His kindliness is almost equaled by another M. Orgon in *Les Serments indiscrets,* by the father of Hortense in *Le Petit-maître corrigé,* by still another M. Orgon in *La Joie imprévue,* and by M. Damis in *L'Ecole des mères.* Even off-stage fathers, such as the King of León in *Le Prince travesti* and Dorante's father in *Le Jeu,* seem endowed with the same liberalism. One wonders what factors in Marivaux's background account for this idealized conception of a father. Did his own father inspire it? Or was his experience with his own father so unhappy that he compensated himself by inventing an ideal type? So little is known about Marivaux's parents that it is impossible to answer these questions. The fact remains, however, that Marivaux never failed to present the fathers in his plays in an admirable light.

The idea that a father should refrain from abusing his *autorité de père,* new on the stage in Marivaux's time, is traceable to *L'Astrée.* Ménandre, the father of Silvanire, wants to force his daughter to marry Théante, even though he knows she loves Aglante. The Druid priest, Cloridamante, is asked to judge the case. After hearing the arguments of each one, the priest decides:

Nous disons, déclarons, et ordonnons, que le mariage, sur toutes les actions qui sont libres, doit obtenir le premier lieu, et ne peut jamais estre contracté sans le consentement des deux parties, qui se lient d'un si sainct et sacré bien, et que toutes les fois que la rigueur des pères en use autrement, il est tyrannique, et doit estre tenu pour nul.[5]

Marivaux added nothing new to the moralizing he had done in earlier plays, but in *Le Jeu* he polished some of his previous *mots* to the point where they became maxims worthy of La Rochefoucauld. His tendency to phrase precepts relative to goodness in man in *Le Prince travesti* and in *L'Ile des esclaves* comes to a climax here. Silvia is grateful to her father for permitting her to change places with Lisette; M. Orgon replies: "dans ce monde, il faut être un peu trop bon pour l'être assez" (I, 2); he himself is the living example of it. Another famous Marivaux sentiment—"le mérite vaut la naissance"—had been expressed less simply as early as *Le Prince travesti* and even *Arlequin poli par l'amour.* It is a precept that permeates Marivaux's social thinking and that will recur, differently worded, in *La Mère confidente, Les Fausses confidences,* and *Le Préjugé vaincu.* The one new idea is Dorante's willingness to cut across social lines and marry a *suivante.* The spectators know that when the time comes he will not be reduced to that extremity; but in his own mind he is willing to do so, and the mere proposal of such a

[5] *L'Astrée,* ed. by Hugues Vaganay (Lyon, 1925), IV, 155.

radical innovation was bold for 1730.[6] A few years later Marivaux was to develop the idea and create a situation wherein an aristocratic young widow marries her *intendant*.[7]

In addition to borrowing from himself, Marivaux took a leaf here and there from his predecessors. *L'Epreuve réciproque* (1711) and *Le Galant coureur* (1722), both by Legrand, and *Le Portrait* (1727) by Beauchamp all present a young suitor or heroine trying to examine his intended without the other's knowledge. (A suggestion that Marivaux imitated a Danish play, *Henrik and Pernille* (1722), seems farfetched in spite of certain points of similarity.) And, of course, the use of disguise was a common dramatic device. But no one before this time had conceived and executed a four-way *travestissement*. As Alphonse Daudet[8] remarked: "on chercherait vainement dans tout le dix-huitième siècle un écrivain autre que Marivaux capable de tirer de cet impertinent imbroglio une œuvre aussi chaste et aussi distinguée."

Critical reception of *Le Jeu de l'amour et du hasard* at its première was of the highest order, with the *Mercure de France*[9] reiterating expressions oft used for Marivaux by this time: "reçûë très-favorablement du Public . . . très-grand succès . . . très-goûtée. . . ."; and Gueullette[10] called it "très bonne."

The play must have caused considerable public discussion, for a few months later the *Mercure*[11] again drew attention to it with a compilation of *remarques* that it had received from its readers since the première. Briefly summarized, these remarks fall into three categories: "(1) On dit qu'il n'est pas vrai-semblable que Silvia puisse

[6] In 1732 Valère in *Le Glorieux* by Destouches imitates Dorante in that he wants to marry his sister's *suivante*. But Valère is cold and unconvincing; furthermore, he is the son of a crude *parvenu*, so that the question of his violating prestige of birth does not enter into the case.

[7] See *Les Fausses confidences,* p. 209.

[8] *Le Journal officiel,* July 6, 1877.

[9] January 1730, pp. 145–46.

[10] *Notes et souvenirs sur le Théâtre-Italien au XVIIIe siècle* (Paris: E. Droz, 1938), p. 115.

[11] April 1730, pp. 770–79.

se persuader qu'un Butor tel qu'Arlequin soit ce même Dorante dont on lui a fait une peinture si avantageuse. La seule vûë du faux Dorante ne doit-elle pas faire soupçonner du mystère? . . . (2) Arlequin ne soûtient pas son caractère par tout; des choses très-jolies succedent à des grossieretés. . . . (3) On auroit voulu que le second Acte eût été le troisième, & l'on croît que cela n'auroit pas été difficile; la raison qui empêche Silvia de se découvrir après avoir appris que Bourguignon est Dorante, n'étant qu'une petite vanité, ne sçauroit excuser son silence." These criticisms, which have been voiced from time to time by other critics during the intervening generations, have their justification perhaps from a theoretical point of view; but if acted on they would spoil the flawless character of the play as it stands. If Silvia had recognized Dorante under his disguise, there would have been no play at all, or at best nothing more than a repetition of *Le Dénouement imprévu;* if Arlequin had retained his traditional character, much of the comedy would have been lost; and if Silvia had revealed her identity at the end of Act II, Marivaux would have had to sacrifice the charm of the unexpected in love. Once the spectator has accepted the original premise of the double *travestissement,* the play moves forward through the *sentiers du cœur* with a subtle combination of logic and ingratiating sentiment that few writers achieve.

Le Jeu de l'amour et du hasard was a notable success at the Théâtre Italien for many years. Then, when Favart combined the Italian actors with his own troupe to form the Opéra Comique in 1762, plays of the Italian repertory were given with less and less frequency, and some of them, including *Le Jeu,* disappeared altogether. It was not performed again until the French Revolution, when complete liberty was granted to all theaters. It was first revived as *Les Jeux de l'amour et du hasard*[12] on April 29, 1791, at

12 This name originated with Desboulmiers (*Histoire anecdotique et raisonnée du Théâtre Italien depuis son rétablissement en France jusqu'à l'année 1769* [Paris: Lacombe, 1769]) and persisted until the middle of the nineteenth century.

the Théâtre de la République, which Talma and his group founded after having broken with the Comédie Française, and soon thereafter at a variety of *petits théâtres* including the Théâtre de la Citoyenne Montansier, Théâtre National de Molière, and Théâtre des Jeunes Elèves. Other Marivaux comedies from the Italian repertory performed in this period were *Les Fausses confidences, La Mère confidente, Le Legs, La Surprise de l'amour, L'Epreuve,* and *L'Ecole des mères.*

Some historians have claimed that *Le Jeu de l'amour et du hasard* did not enter the repertory of the Comédie Française until 1802 when Mlle. Mars began to play Silvia. Actually, the first official inscription of *Le Jeu de l'amour et du hasard* on the records of the Théâtre Français occurred in 1796, with Louise Contat as the guiding light of the project.[13] A decade later the personal magnetism of Mlle. Mars in the role of Silvia gave great impetus during Napoleonic days to the popularity of *Le Jeu* and other plays from Marivaux's Italian repertory; she played Silvia as late as 1841 on the eve of her retirement. Throughout the nineteenth century the rosters of the Théâtre Français were filled with the names of brilliant comediennes from Mlle. Mars to Julia Bartet in the part of Silvia or Lisette, with the greatest number of performances occurring in the 1850's when Mmes. Arnould-Plessy and Brohan were the luminaries of the troupe. *Le Jeu* was also a favorite vehicle for young actresses making their debuts at the Théâtre Français or at the Odéon. However, it must be pointed out that more often than not, according to critical opinion, an actress chose Silvia primarily to display her own personality, and all too frequently Silvia was sacrificed to the actress

[13] Mlle. Contat had previously been responsible for reviving *Les Fausses confidences* and *L'Epreuve* at the Théâtre de la Nation in 1793; these were the first of Marivaux's plays from the Italian repertory to be staged at the Théâtre Français. Fournier and Bastide (*Théâtre complet de Marivaux* [2 vols.; Paris: Les Editions nationales, 1946], I, 30) state erroneously that "les comédies italiennes de Marivaux furent de 1794 à 1796 inscrites au répertoire du Théâtre de la République," whereas the revivals actually started several years earlier.

herself. Théophile Gautier,[14] comparing the performance of Mlle. Judith in 1848 with the earlier performances of Mlle. Mars, declared that Mlle. Mars had always been "plus occupée de déployer ses manières de grande dame et d'établir sur toute la pièce son écrasante supériorité." Variations of the same comment were made ad infinitum about other actresses.

But Silvia is a delightful person in her own right, and fortunately at the turn of the century Mme. Bartet initiated the custom of playing Silvia for the role itself. Béatrix Dussane,[15] as a young actress, played Lisette to Bartet's Silvia, and Dussane reports that although Bartet was then in her fifties she endowed the role with the youthfulness that belongs to Silvia: "J'ai joué la pièce depuis lors avec bien des actrices de vingt ou trente ans, aucune n'a été aussi foncièrement *jeune* que l'était Bartet. . . . Bartet attaquait et conduisait ensuite la pièce avec une sorte de feu gracieux, un élan, un rythme que je n'ai vus qu'à elle, et qui entrainaient tous ses partenaires." Since that time performances have not been spoiled by overpersonalized acting.

Dramatic critics of the nineteenth century, except Geoffroy, held Marivaux in high esteem; and even Geoffroy,[16] in spite of an irrepressible antagonism toward him, interspersed words of praise among his hostile remarks. Apropos of *Le Jeu de l'amour et du hasard,* he says: "C'est, à mon gré, son chef-d'œuvre. . . . elle offre un fond sérieux et moral. . . . l'esprit, la délicatesse, le sentiment y dominent." Yet in the same article he contradicts himself: "Chez lui, l'esprit et le mauvais goût sont continuellement aux prises. . . . ses pensées les plus belles sont revêtues de haillons." (Few critics would agree with Geoffroy's last statement.) Duviquet,[17] who followed Geoffroy as dramatic critic on *Le Journal des débats* and

[14] Gautier, *Histoire de l'art dramatique en France depuis vingt-cinq ans* (Paris: Magnin, Blanchard et Cie, 1858–59), V, 340.
[15] *Reines de théâtre* (Lyon: H. Lardanchet, 1944), p. 217.
[16] *Le Journal des débats,* 9 fructidor, an 10 (August 1801).
[17] Pierre Duviquet, *Œuvres complètes de Marivaux* (Paris, 1830), IV, 180.

edited the works of Marivaux in 1830, wrote in his *jugement* of this play: "*Le Jeu de l'amour et du hasard* continue à embellir la scène française, et on l'y verra toujours avec plaisir, parce que la pièce satisfait à la double garantie d'un succès durable, l'agrément et l'utilité." Gautier's[18] admiration for Marivaux is well known; he spoke eloquently of *Le Jeu* and included this statement: "Les héroïnes de Marivaux ont une secrète parenté avec les femmes des comédies de Shakespeare; elles sont cousines des Rosalinde, des Hermia, des Perdita, des Béatrix." He added an interesting comment on Marivaux's modernness: "A travers l'œuvre ancienne, le caractère de l'époque moderne où on la représente se fait jour malgré tout. . . . là où nos pères riaient, nous nous attendrissons. . . . ce qui leur semblait charmant nous semble poétique." These words have been echoed by succeeding critics. Writing in 1881, Sarcey[19] called Marivaux "le plus aimable enchanteur du dix-huitième siècle," and he asked fondly: "Faut-il parler encore des *Jeux de l'amour et du hasard?* Tous les jeunes cœurs n'ont-ils pas fait ce rêve: être aimé pour soi-même? Où ce rêve fut-il jamais présenté sous une forme plus gracieuse et plus poétique?" Lemaître[20] had such high regard for Marivaux that he objected to the limited number of his plays in the repertory of the Théâtre Français: "Pourquoi ne joue-t-on, de Marivaux, que *le Jeu de l'amour et du hasard, les Fausses Confidences,* quelquefois *le Legs* et quelquefois *l'Epreuve?* Il y a pourtant, dans son théâtre, plusieurs autres comédies qui valent celles-là." He delighted in "la trame infiniment délicate du *Jeu de l'amour et du hasard,*" and he expressed the view that "Toute la poésie de la première moitié du XVIIIe siècle est dans Marivaux, comme toute la poésie de la seconde moitié est dans Jean-Jacques Rousseau."

The twentieth century has been prolific in revivals of *Le Jeu de*

---

[18] *Op. cit.,* V, 340. The article cited was written in 1848. For other comparisons with Shakespeare, see pp. 24, 37–38, 40–41, 148, 264.

[19] *Quarante ans de théâtre* (Paris: Bibliothèque des annales, 1900–2), II, 262.

[20] *Les Annales politiques et littéraires* (1892), II, 216.

l'amour et du hasard and concomitant criticism. Each generation of actors has produced new Silvias, new Dorantes, new Lisettes, new Arlequins; and each generation of critics has brought forth a plethora of reviews. In most cases the notices are laudatory for Marivaux as well as for the actors, as random samplings show. Adolphe Brisson,[21] in a favorable review of a new production of *Le Jeu* at the Théâtre Français in 1908, says of the Silvia role: "C'est une des figures les plus complexes, les plus riches, les plus délicates qu'il y ait au théâtre. Elle fait le désespoir et l'orgueil des comédiennes." Concerning Dorante, he makes a pointed comment: "il avance sur son siècle comme la plupart des personnages de Marivaux; il est moderne."

Louis Verneuil[22] reports the great success the play had at Geneva in 1918 when Georges Berr was invited to appear as guest star in performances of *Le Jeu* and *Les Précieuses ridicules.* "La troupe de Genève . . . répéta avec application sous la direction de Georges Berr et le 17 janvier, Marivaux et Molière furent acclamés par une salle comble."

Apropos of the debut of Pierre Fresnay as Dorante in 1920, Antoine[23] wrote: "Décidément, nous n'avons point fait à Marivaux la grande place à laquelle il a droit. . . . A chacune de ses réapparitions, il me semble que ce chef d'œuvre du *Jeu de l'amour et du hasard* s'éclaire de beautés nouvelles; on aperçoit qu'aucune comédie du XVIIIe siècle ne fut aussi contemporaine. . . . Silvia domine encore ses sœurs modernes." Antoine gives his press notice a curious ending; he was so delighted, he says, with *Le Jeu* that he did not want to spoil his pleasure by reviewing the *Phèdre* given on the same bill!

A series of *jeudis classiques* in the summer of 1926 included several Marivaux comedies, one of which was *Le Jeu.* Lucien Dubech,[24] always an ardent admirer of Marivaux, says: "La façon dont ce

21 *Le Temps,* September 14, 1908.
22 *Rideau à neuf heures* (Paris, 1944), p. 331.
23 Cited from clipping in *Dossier sur Marivaux,* Rf 11782, at the Bibliothèque de l'Arsenal.
24 *Candide,* August 19, 1926.

sentiment [l'amour] chemine dans le cœur de Silvia est une des fines merveilles du théâtre de tous les temps. . . . Une fois les deux jeunes gens embarqués, toutes les scènes qui les réunissent sont dignes des plus profondes analyses de Racine pour la maîtrise avec laquelle les cœurs sont mis à nu."

So many performances of Le Jeu were given from one season to the next that the bicentennial of the play in 1930 passed without special attention. Albert Thibaudet[25] regretted the fact that no theater in Paris observed the anniversary; he expatiates on "la plus parfaite pièce de Marivaux," saying: "Marivaux est le seul auteur du théâtre classique, avec Molière bien entendu, qui ait fondé un comique nouveau. Il a donné à la comédie un masque qui a pu faire une concurrence, aujourd'hui encore efficace, au masque imposé par Molière. . . . Et pourtant Le Jeu reste une comédie où l'on rit. Alors de quoi rit-on? Le secret est bien simple. Au lieu de rire de ce que sont les personnages, on rit de ce qu'ils disent. La pièce est une comédie non pas parce qu'ils sont comiques, mais parce qu'ils sont gens d'esprit. On ne rit plus contre eux, on rit avec eux et par eux. . . . Dans ce comique des mots, Marivaux est demeuré unique."

A dissident note in the general chorus of approval is sounded by Pierre Lièvre,[26] the drama critic of the Mercure de France in the 1930's. He is consistently hostile to Marivaux, his basic objection being that Marivaux is guilty of concealing untenable social doctrines and attitudes behind elegant personages and witty dialogue. He says: "Plus je vais, plus je m'étonne de la dureté cachée sous les aimables dehors des ouvrages de Marivaux. Derrière leur politesse exquise . . . s'abritent des pensées d'une rigueur et d'une inélégance qui surprennent. Des êtres extrêmement policés forment et exécutent des desseins à la fois inhumains et rudes." He especially chides Silvia for saying: "Je ne suis point faite aux cajoleries de ceux dont la garde-robe ressemble à la tienne" to the man she believes to be

---

[25] Les Nouvelles littéraires, artistiques et scientifiques, January 25, 1930.
[26] Le Mercure de France, Nouvelle Série, September 1, 1936.

Bourguignon, and he considers her haughtiness offensive when she exclaims: "Quel homme pour un valet!" as if in Marivaux's mind a valet could not have the decent qualities of other men. Of the actress who played Silvia, Lièvre says sarcastically: "Mme Maria Bell, qui a représenté pour nous une Silvia d'une heureuse et rare originalité, a merveilleusement fait sentir ce côté du rôle de son héroïne." He complains that "Marivaux continue à être jugé sur l'exquisité de ses apparences." All this savors of strong political and social prejudice, and it would seem that Lièvre is reading certain of his own personal grievances against modern society into Marivaux.[27]

In 1946 Gabriel Marcel,[28] already cited several times for his laudatory reviews of Marivaux, attended a program at the Théâtre Français comprising *Le Jeu de l'amour et du hasard* and *L'Epreuve.* In discussing the qualities of the plays Marcel says: "Il y aurait, je crois, pour un philosophe d'aujourd'hui, bien des richesses à exploiter dans l'œuvre de Marivaux."

Still more superlatives were poured forth on the occasion of Hélène Perdrière's debut as Silvia: "Cette représentation est au moins égale à celle des *Fausses Confidences* qui fut un des triomphes de J.-L. Barrault à Marigny et dans le monde entier. . . . Nous avons vu se réaliser devant nous cette rencontre toujours bouleversante d'un personnage et d'une interprète qui semble avoir été mise au monde pour l'incarner."[29]

The appeal of *Le Jeu* has spread beyond the borders of France. As the concluding program in a rich season of repertory in New York in 1955, the Comédie Française presented *Un Caprice* by Alfred de Musset and *Le Jeu de l'amour et du hasard* to delighted spectators. "Love leaped the language barrier last night in a Gallic gambol that brought bravos from the Broadway Theater audience," said Lois

---

27 For even more bitter attacks on Marivaux by Lièvre, see pp. 44, 212, 217, 238, 261.

28 *Les Nouvelles littéraires, artistiques et scientifiques,* February 21, 1946.

29 *Les Nouvelles littéraires, artistiques et scientifiques,* March 5, 1953.

Maxon.[30] Paul V. Beckley[31] applauded the "genteel artificiality" of Marivaux and the actors who performed it with their "customary brilliance." Herbert L. Matthews[32] dwelt at length on the play itself: "Marivaux in *Le Jeu,* as in nearly all his plays, gives us the battle of the sexes, a game of love played with exquisite subtlety by ardent, intelligent, elegant people. His lovers are never cynical or licentious. They fall in love at first sight and love with a serious, consuming passion." Comparing the comedy to a ballet, he said: "*Le Jeu* is like a quadrille. . . . The play was written in 1730, a time of good manners, of courtesy, sociability, breeding. The acting has to be delicate and subtle," and he praised the company for their "exquisite perfection."

And so the fame of *Le Jeu* grows. Like Marivaux himself, who explored *tous les sentiers du cœur,* the critics for the last two centuries have discovered undreamed of facets in this delightful comedy. On January 22, 1948, *Le Jeu de l'amour et du hasard* was given for the thousandth time at the Théâtre Français, thus surpassing by far the records of comedies by Destouches, La Chaussée, Gresset, Piron, and others considered superior to Marivaux in the eighteenth century. Its popularity continues unabated.

[30] *New York World Telegram,* November 16, 1955.
[31] *New York Herald Tribune,* November 16, 1955.
[32] *The New York Times,* November 16, 1955.

17 La Réunion des amours

[One act in prose. First presented at the Théâtre Français, November 5, 1731.]

EVER eager for renown at the Théâtre Français, Marivaux wrote his next comedy, *Les Serments indiscrets,* for that theater. The play was drawn from the same reservoir of dramatic content as *Le Jeu de l'amour et du hasard,* and the recent success of the latter at the Théâtre Italien undoubtedly moved Marivaux to use the formula for a piece that would bring him equal fame at the Théâtre Français. However, once again, the actors wrangled over the casting, as they had done in *La Seconde surprise de l'amour* in 1727, and almost two seasons elapsed before *Les Serments indiscrets* was produced. In the meantime, two other plays reached the boards ahead of it.

The first of these was *La Réunion des amours,* an allegorical fantasy that Marivaux wrote in the vein of two earlier plays, *L'Amour et la vérité* and *Le Triomphe de Plutus.*[1] The characters are mythological deities on Mount Olympus. The play opens with a scene between Love, herein depicted as the stolid, respectful god of sentiment and tenderness personified in seventeenth-century novels, and Cupid, shown as young and impudent, the god of passion and voluptuousness representative of the *libertinage* of the eighteenth century. Cupid chides Love for his timid and languorous manner and brashly recom-

[1] See Chapters 2 and 14.

mends amorous liaisons without any moral restraints. Jupiter has asked all the gods to assemble on Mount Olympus because "il veut que chacun d'eux fasse un don au fils d'un grand roi qu'il aime" (Sc. 1).[2] Cupid alone has not been invited, and he is determined to prove that he has a right to be admitted to the assembly. Goaded by Plutus, the little imp goes "chez Bacchus" to imbibe "du bon vin de Champagne" so that its aroma may lend eloquence to his arguments. Minerva is charged by Jupiter to determine which of the two, Love or Cupid, is to be responsible for the conduct of the Prince. "Quoi qu'il en soit, nous ne voulons point que le Prince ait une âme insensible" (Sc. 9). Love politely states his qualifications, which Cupid in turn ridicules. Minerva reserves judgment until Virtue can be consulted. Love pleads his case before Virtue by quoting time-honored clichés from *Cléopâtre;* Cupid rushes headlong into an amorous declaration that sweeps the goddess off her feet, and she has to flee to escape falling from grace. Virtue and Minerva decide against Cupid, but Jupiter intervenes to decree that Cupid and Love unite "pour former le cœur du Prince." So Love and Cupid embrace, with Cupid saying: "Je vous apprendrai à n'être plus si sot; et vous m'apprendrez à être plus sage (Sc. 14).

The play is essentially an exercise in witty dialogue and has little literary value, although the *Mercure*[3] thought it "ornée de traits fins et délicats. . . . cette vivacité de stile, secondée de la légèreté et de la grace a charmé egalement la cour et la Ville; . . . *La Réunion des amours* est un ouvrage à faire beaucoup d'honneur à son ingénieux Auteur." In the eighteenth century co-authorship of the play was credited to M. de la Clède, an obscure literary figure of the day who published *Histoire du Portugal* in 1734. However, the play is too thoroughly imbued with Marivaux's wit and style to make the

[2] This is obviously a reference to Louis XV, and it is the consensus of opinion that the play was written and presented as a flattering gesture to the monarch after the birth of the dauphin.

[3] October 1731, p. 2627–34.

theory of a helping hand plausible, and modern critics are inclined to reject M. de la Clède as collaborator.

In spite of its characters and theme, *La Réunion des amours* is not one of Marivaux's philosophical comedies. There is no moralizing. If the play teaches a lesson, it is to be found in the suggestion that the Prince should be sensitive and gallant, that he should show decency in his pleasures, and that his love should be approved by Virtue. These thoughts had been expressed ten years earlier by Marivaux himself in *Le Spectateur français,*[4] in which he berates men for their voluptuous appetites and condemns them for taking advantage of defenseless women.

Marivaux's long-hoped-for success at the Théâtre Français failed to materialize in *La Réunion des amours.* The play was fortunate in being billed with *Mithridate, Horace, Phèdre,* and *Le Cid* and had nine performances in two months in addition to one at court. At best, the comedy had only a minor success, with most of its popularity attributed to Mlle. Dangeville and Mlle. Gaussin as Cupid and Love. The moment was not entirely sterile in satisfaction, however. Marivaux had just published the first volume of his great novel, *La Vie de Marianne,* and this work received critical tribute.

La Réunion des amours was not played again at the Théâtre Français until September 28, 1957, when it was given a sumptuous production that belatedly compensated for its mediocre success in the eighteenth century. Upon witnessing the presentation, Robert Kemp[5] called the play "un exquis chef-d'œuvre de langage et d'intelligence"; he found that "Micheline Boudet, prédestinée à ce rôle [Cupid] de vif-argent, de volubilité, a été vraiment parfaite."

Thus still another Marivaux comedy, usually considered outmoded, has been given a successful and sparkling revival.

---

[4] See Feuilles 4 and 17.
[5] *Le Monde,* September 29, 1957.

18   Le Triomphe de l'amour

[Three acts in prose. First presented at the Théâtre Italien, March 12, 1732.]

WHILE Marivaux was impatiently waiting for the Comédie Française to produce *Les Serments indiscrets,* he wrote still another comedy, *Le Triomphe de l'amour,*[1] this time for the Théâtre Italien. Variously labeled *comédie héroïque* by Arland and Larroumet, *comédie romanesque* by Fleury, and *comédie fantaisiste* by Fournier and Bastide, it is one of those plays that defy the usual dramatic classifications, containing, as *Le Prince travesti*[2] had done eight years earlier, a curious combination of royal personages and stock characters from the Théâtre Italien. Silvia was again called upon to impersonate a young man, in a type of role not unfamiliar to her, for she had scored a personal triumph as the Chevalier in *La Fausse suivante*[3] eight years earlier.

Oddly for Marivaux, whose plays are often criticized for lack of movement, the exposition of *Le Triomphe de l'amour* is as complicated as a Crébillon tragedy. Twenty years before the action begins Léonidas had usurped the throne of the Spartan king Cléomène because the latter had kidnaped his mistress. Léonidas cast the king and

---

[1] Quinault and Lulli wrote an opera by the same title in 1681, but Marivaux borrowed nothing from it.
[2] See p. 53.
[3] For a discussion of this play, see Chapter 8.

Arlequin poli par l'amour as produced
by the Comédie Française in 1955.

Jean Desailly as Dorante, Madeleine Renaud as Araminte, and Jean-Louis Barrault as Dubois in *Les Fausses confidences*.

Xavier de Courville's productions of *Les Sincères* (above) in 1931 and *La Double inconstance* (below) in 1925 exemplify some of his pioneering innovations in staging Marivaux's comedies.

Mony Dalmès as Silvia, Maurice Escande as M. Orgon, Jacques Toja as Mario, and Jean-Louis Jemma as Dorante in the production of *Le Jeu de l'amour et du hasard* by the Comédie Française in 1955.

his wife in prison, where a son was born shortly before they died. The child was rescued and entrusted to the philosopher Hermocrate to raise. He is now living there as Agis until his loyal followers can find the opportune moment to seize the throne for him. The usurper died childless, and the crown went to his brother, who left a daughter Léonide, now the reigning princess. She has recently seen a young man in Hermocrate's garden and has fallen in love with him; and when she learns that he is the rightful heir, she determines to restore him to power.

At this point the play opens. Léonide and her *suivante* Corine, both disguised as men under the names of Phocion and Hermidas, come to the house of Hermocrate, ostensibly to study philosophy. Corine warns her mistress of the danger of exposure, but Léonide confidently states that she has devices to counterbalance the possible opposition of Hermocrate and of his spinster sister, Léontine. Almost immediately Arlequin overhears conversation that betrays the sex of the two visitors, but Léonide's liberality buys not only his secrecy but his co-operation. Her chance meeting with Agis is cut short when the suspicious gardener, Dimas, brings Léontine to chase the two youths. In order to be allowed to stay on the premises, Léonide pretends to be smitten with the withering spinster and makes love to her so effectively[4] that she wins her support. Hermocrate recognizes the supposed Phocion as a young girl he had seen previously in the neighborhood and accuses her of seeking to entice his ward Agis. To overcome this obstacle, Léonide says that her name is Aspasie; overwhelming the philosopher by declaring that it is he she loves and not the ward, she obtains his permission to remain. When Léonide finally contrives a moment with Agis, she first awakens *amitié* in him. He states that love, which had caused the misfortunes of his parents, would never enter his heart. Whereupon, Léonide confides to Agis that she is a young lady in disguise fleeing the persecution of the

---

4 Silvia had played a similar scene in *La Fausse suivante* (1724), in which, as a gay chevalier, she wooed a flighty countess.

reigning princess. Agis gallantly offers to aid the maiden in distress. Léonide has a field day carrying on a triple intrigue. In due course she presses her suit with Léontine, claiming to have made her portrait as a sign of her affection; then she uses the same trick on Hermocrate. At the same time she manages to win the heart of Agis without revealing her conquest to the others, in spite of the clumsy errors of Arlequin and Damis, who are always on the verge of giving away the secret. Léontine is ready to break with her brother and leave the household. Hermocrate confides to the supposed Aspasie that he will soon be free to marry, for his ward is actually the prince, and his friends are conspiring to overthrow the princess and put him on the throne. There ensues an amusing scene (III, 8) in which Hermocrate, Léontine, and Agis all discover that they are in love with the same person. Agis ruefully scoffs at Léonide for not giving him a portrait, too, but she calms him by answering: "Les autres n'auraient pas eu ce portrait, si je n'avais pas eu dessein de vous donner la personne" (III, 9), and she reveals that she is the princess. Hermocrate and Léontine are disenchanted as love passes them by. The imbroglio ends when the royal retinue arrives in the garden to accompany the prince and princess back to the palace.

Le Triomphe de l'amour is one of the few plays by Marivaux with some tangible sources. In its spirit of grandiose adventure, it descends from the romantic episodes of the seventeenth-century novel. The names Phocion, Aspasie, and Agis occur in L'Astrée. The travestissement of a young lady into a young man occurs in Marivaux's three early novels: Les Effets surprenants de la sympathie, Pharsamon, and La Voiture embourbée. Frédéric Deloffre finds that part of the plot and the denouement, as well as the characters of the philosophe and his sister, come from Socrate by Mme. de Villedieu. It should be pointed out, however, that the role of Hermocrate derives even more directly from the gouverneur found in several early eighteenth-century tragedies—a faithful follower who has raised a dispossessed child to manhood, like Phanès in Amasis by La Grange-

Chancel. Together, these fragments constitute a body of source material not usually found in Marivaux comedies.

Although the action takes place in the philosopher's garden, where one might expect to hear a flood of moralizing, the play contains not the slightest hint of philosophy. Arlequin, so often Marivaux's mouthpiece, does not utter one precept on social reform. Indeed, Arlequin's moments are few, and in this play they are wanting in the humor associated with the role. Characterization in other personages is superficial, and Marivaux does not treat the awakening of love in Agis as a "surprise de l'amour."

Le Triomphe de l'amour has no trace of *vraisemblance,* and eighteenth-century audiences found it lacking in *bienséance.* Although Léonide is called a "princesse de Sparte," people looked upon her as a princess of France or of Spain and considered her actions unworthy. They were shocked to see a princess pursue a young man and demean herself by tricking two older persons with the artifices of love. Léonide feels justified in punishing Hermocrate and Léontine, since they have spent their lives engendering hatred for the princess in the heart of Agis; she further absolves herself of guilt: "d'où vient tout le mal qu'ils me font? Est-ce parce que j'occupe un trône usurpé? Mais ce n'est pas moi qui en suis l'usurpatrice. D'ailleurs, à qui l'aurais-je rendu? Je n'en connaissais pas l'héritier légitime; il n'a jamais paru" (I, 1).

Eighteenth-century critics did not agree with Léonide's reasoning. The *Mercure de France*[5] thought that "cette intrigue auroit encore mieux convenu à une simple Bourgeoise qu'à une princesse de Sparthe." Le *Journal littéraire*[6] stated that "*Le triomphe de l'amour* n'est pas une des meilleures pièces de Monsieur de Marivaux," and pointed to similarities with the *Démocrite* of Regnard (1700). Desboulmiers[7] called Léonide's triple intrigue "une fourberie digne

[5] April 1732, pp. 778–82.
[6] 1734, Part II, p. 461.
[7] Cited from Marcel Arland, *Théâtre complet de Marivaux* (Paris: La Nouvelle revue française, 1949), p. 1509.

de Scapin." A run of only six performances pronounces the verdict against Marivaux.

Yet *Le Triomphe de l'amour* is not without merit in style, as attested by the very critics who condemn the plot: "une des mieux intriguées qui soient sorties de la plume de M. de Marivaux,"[8] "beaucoup de tour et du bon comique,"[9] "purement écrite et vivement dialoguée."[10] Jules Lemaître,[11] one of the few nineteenth-century critics who knew Marivaux's theater thoroughly, spoke glowingly of *Le Triomphe de l'amour:* "Cette fantaisie est, si je ne me trompe, un des plus aimables chefs-d'œuvre de Marivaux"; he considers the play worthy of comparison with Shakespeare: "Je vous assure que l'aile du caprice, qui emporte si haut et si loin le poète du *Songe d'une nuit d'été,* a pour le moins frôlé le front poudré de Marivaux. Il n'y a point un abîme entre *le Triomphe de l'amour* et *Comme il vous plaira,* mais seulement les différences de deux races, de deux époques et de deux esprits. . . . A côté de la fantaisie de Shakespeare, qui est excessive et débordante, celle de Marivaux paraît bien raisonnable et bien modérée." Since Lemaître's time more and more critics find resemblances between Marivaux and Shakespeare.[12]

A revival of *Le Triomphe de l'amour* took place in the spring of 1912 when it was staged by Xavier de Courville's troupe, La Petite Scène. The spectators who attended the few performances found the play and the production to their liking. Louis Joubert[13] of *Le Correspondant* says wistfully: "C'est la grâce et le sourire de la vieille France." Henri Bidou of *Le Journal des débats* exclaims: "Quel plaisir de voir enfin des personnages de gens du monde tenus par ceux-ci et de reconnaître les gestes, la voix, les sentiments véritables."

[8] *Le Mercure de France,* April 1732.
[9] *Le Journal littéraire,* 1734, Part II.
[10] Desboulmiers, cited in Arland, *op. cit.*
[11] *Les Annales politiques et littéraires,* April 3, 1892.
[12] See pp. 24, 37–38, 40–41, 136.
[13] This and the other citations in this paragraph are taken from clippings in the archives of La Petite Scène.

Touched by the elegant portrayal of "une société à demi réelle, à demi inventée," Rémi of the *Figaro* muses: "Je ne sais si quelques larmes d'attendrissement n'ont pas été l'hommage que nous rendions à une grâce d'autrefois, à une grâce qui n'est plus la nôtre." The artistic success of this revival showed that *Le Triomphe de l'amour* is a stageworthy piece in spite of its deficiencies.

Another proof of its theatrical value is the solid triumph won by the performances given at the Théâtre National Populaire in February 1956. Robert Kemp[14] exclaims: "Quelle surprise et quel ravissement!" If the words seemed cold to him in print, on the stage "le texte s'aère; les personnages, glacés sur les pages, s'en envolent. C'est la métamorphose en papillons. . . . En somme, l'exquis répertoire de Marivaux s'est enrichi hier soir d'une œuvre sur laquelle on ne comptait pas."

In the final analysis, however, the success of *Le Triomphe de l'amour* has been mediocre to date. Perhaps Marivaux himself gave the best judgment of the play in the eighteenth century when he wrote in the "Avertissement de l'auteur"[15] for the published version in 1732: "Le sort de cette pièce-ci a été bizarre. Je la sentais susceptible d'une chute totale ou d'un grand succès. . . . Je me suis trompé pourtant; et rien de tout cela n'est arrivé. La pièce n'a eu, à proprement parler, ni chute ni succès; tout se réduit simplement à dire

[14] *Le Monde,* February 26, 1956.
[15] A curious error was made in connection with the *avertissement.* Originally published with the first edition in 1732 and with the reprint in 1740, the *avertissement* was unintentionally placed as the "Préface" to *Annibal* in the *Œuvres complètes* of 1755, an error repeated in 1758 and thereafter consecrated in the definitive edition of 1781. It is odd that such a mistake could have been committed in both 1755 and 1758 when Marivaux was still living, but it is well known that he was totally indifferent to the printed versions of his plays. The *avertissement* contains no dates or titles or names to identify it readily with *Le Triomphe de l'amour;* yet it does contain statements not applicable to *Annibal.* The general lack of scholarship in the treatment of Marivaux's lesser plays has permitted this substitution to be perpetuated in most editions since 1781. Fournier and Bastide have recounted the history of this error and have restored the *avertissement* to its rightful place (*Théâtre complet de Marivaux* [2 vols.; Paris: Les Editions nationales, 1946], II, 6).

qu'elle n'a point plu." But we have not yet heard the end of *Le Triomphe de l'amour*. Two twentieth-century revivals have delighted the public. Modern spectators are not troubled by eighteenth-century conventions, and the critical climate is no longer hostile to Marivaux. The future holds bright promise for *Le Triomphe de l'amour*.

19   Les Serments indiscrets

[Five acts in prose. First presented at the Théâtre Français, June 8, 1732.]

AT last, after a delay of nearly two seasons, the Comédie Française finally staged *Les Serments indiscrets*—with most unhappy results! The spectators maltreated the play at a première that the *Mercure*[1] describes as "une des plus tumultueuses"; and Mlle. de Bar[2] reports "qu'on siffle depuis le commencement du second acte jusqu'à la troisième scène du cinquième." When the comedy was played again in 1738 the *Mercure*[3] said that it was "infiniment plus goûtée" than it had been in 1732. *Les Serments indiscrets* had nine performances in 1732 and another six in 1738, which marked the end of its professional career, except for a revival at Talma's theater on August 20, 1792. Etienne and Martainville,[4] recalling previous failures, report that the play "n'eut guère plus de succès malgré les efforts de Mlle Candeille, qui, ayant découvert un rôle assez agréable dans cette pièce, avait eu assez de crédit pour la faire remettre au théâtre." The dismal fate of *Les Serments indiscrets* must be counted with the other theatrical misfortunes Marivaux experienced at the Théâtre Français.

[1] See the June 1732 issue (pp. 1408–17) for the comments quoted here.
[2] Marcel Arland, *Théâtre complet de Marivaux* (Paris: La Nouvelle revue française, 1949), p. 1510.
[3] March 1738, p. 564.
[4] *Histoire du Théâtre-Français* (Paris: Barba, 1802), III, 12. They misnamed the play *Les Faux serments*.

This time the failure was not due to injudicious casting, as with *La Seconde surprise de l'amour* in 1727.[5] In fact, the *Mercure* reports quite the opposite: "on n'a guère mis au Théâtre Français de Pièce mieux joüée que celle-ci; le sieur Quinault l'aîné, la Dlle Quinault sa sœur, parfaitement secondée des Dlles Dangeville et Gaussin, et leurs autres camarades, y brillent à qui mieux mieux."[6] The real weakness of the play lies in its length: it does not contain enough action to fill five acts. The first act is good exposition, and the fifth act provides a well-written denouement, but the three intervening acts lack movement, and the complications are needlessly prolonged by rambling dialogue that critics have pointed out as illustrations of *marivaudage*. The *Mercure* said that "le plus grand deffaut qu'on trouve dans toute la Pièce, c'est de n'avoir pas assez d'action et trop d'esprit."

Another reason for the play's failure may be that it is too reminiscent of *Le Jeu de l'amour et du hasard*. Marivaux wrote *Les Serments indiscrets* in 1730, immediately after the triumph of *Le Jeu* at the Théâtre Italien, and he may have felt that he could duplicate its success at the Théâtre Français if he used similar material. Permeated with the spirit of *Le Jeu,* the new play lacks the inspired perfection of its predecessor.

The central figure of the new comedy is Lucile, in whose home the action takes place. Like Silvia in *Le Jeu,* Lucile fears that Damis, the man her father has chosen for her, will not be her ideal; therefore, even before she has seen him, she has sworn not to marry him.

[5] See p. 99.

[6] Larroumet made an incredible error when he attributed the failure of this play to Adrienne Lecouvreur. Apropos of a revival of *Le Jeu* in 1882, he wrote an extensive letter about Marivaux's plays at the Théâtre Français to Francisque Sarcey, a letter that the latter published verbatim in *Quarante ans de théâtre* (Paris: Bibliothèque des annales, 1900–2), II, 274. Larroumet said of Mlle. Lecouvreur: "celle-ci fit tomber deux de ses pièces, *la Seconde surprise de l'amour et les Serments indiscrets.*" Although it is true that Mlle. Lecouvreur's mannered acting contributed to the cool reception of *La Seconde surprise,* she could have had nothing to do with the failure of *Les Serments indiscrets*, since she died two years before it was performed.

Damis, like Dorante, is apprehensive about what the marriage may hold for him, and he arranges to arrive at the house in advance of his father to seek Lucile's opposition to the union. Through the intermediary of the *suivante,* Lisette, Damis announces that he plans to reject her mistress. Lucile, eavesdropping in the next room, confronts Damis angrily. Both young people catch their breath on first seeing each other, but their minds are so prejudiced that Lisette has no difficulty in having them take halfhearted vows never to marry. Almost immediately both realize that their "serments" have been "indiscrets"; yet pride will let neither of them recant.[7] Lucile's father, M. Orgon, and Damis' father, M. Ergaste, like the M. Orgon of *Le Jeu,* are indulgent toward their children, but they find it hard to understand this unexpected obstinacy. To save his honor and make amends to his friend, M. Orgon offers his younger daughter Phénice to Damis. Ergaste accepts the arrangement; Lucile and Damis, goaded by *dépit amoureux,* approve the project, too, even though they are genuinely in love by this time, and miserable at the prospect of the new marriage. Phénice is the only one who is not deceived by the pretenses of the couple: Damis' feckless wooing and Lucile's ill temper show her where their true feelings lie. Amused rather than hurt, Phénice puts Damis and Lucile through a few uneasy moments with her teasing, but finally brings them to confess that they love each other. When Orgon and Ergaste come to draw up the final contract between Phénice and Damis, they are bewildered to find that it is Lucile and Damis who are to be married after all. Phénice is happy in her sister's happiness. Lisette and Frontin, whose ministrations influenced the action, will marry like their masters.

For all the similarity between *Le Jeu de l'amour et du hasard* and *Les Serments indiscrets,* striking differences are noted: there are no *travestissements* in the latter; instead of posing as servants to observe each other, Lucile and Damis have predetermined their opposition

---

[7] This initial antagonism between Lucile and Damis recalls the mutual scorn between the Countess and Lélio in *La Surprise de l'amour* (see pp. 32–34).

to each other; the development and solution of the plot are entirely different. In the *avertissement* of the published version, Marivaux does not mention *Le Jeu,* but he goes to great pains to dismiss the suggestion of any resemblance between his new play and *La Surprise de l'amour.* In *La Surprise* the lovers "ignorent l'état de leur cœur, et sont le jouet du sentiment qu'ils ne soupçonnent point en eux; c'est là ce qui fait le plaisant du spectacle qu'ils donnent: les autres, au contraire, savent ce qui se passe en eux, mais ne voudraient ni le cacher, ni le dire, et assurément, je ne vois rien là dedans qui se ressemble." Marivaux explains why he thinks people associated the two plays: "c'est qu'on y a vu le même genre de conversation et de style; c'est que ce sont des mouvements de cœur dans les deux pièces; et cela leur donne un air d'uniformité qui fait qu'on s'y trompe."

The most original feature of *Les Serments indiscrets* is the character of Phénice. Younger sisters are extremely rare in the theater before Marivaux's time, the chief examples being Henriette in *Les Femmes savantes,* and Lisette, the younger sister of Flaminia, in *La Double inconstance.* Phénice is as refreshing as a breath of cool air. She is mature enough to understand the forces at play in Lucile and Damis and young enough not to be hurt by being cast aside in her sister's favor. She knows that her marriage lies in the future. If *Les Serments indiscrets* had continued in the repertory, young actresses would undoubtedly have prized the role of Phénice.

Les Serments indiscrets is the chief source of Alfred de Musset's *On ne badine pas avec l'amour,* as Edna Frederich[8] has pointed out. The two plays have the same type of opinionated heroine, whose vanity pits her against an equally proud suitor. Lucile and Damis are the prototypes of Musset's Camille and Perdican, except that Marivaux's characters reflect the suavity of the eighteenth-century drawing room, whereas Musset's characters are the product of the pessimism and intense emotions of the romantic period. In each play there is a third person who is a pawn in the struggle between the

8 "Marivaux and Musset," *The Romanic Review* (1940), pp. 259–64.

major parties: Perdican turns to Rosette to assuage his wounded pride just as Damis turned to Phénice. Phénice and Rosette serve the same purpose in the two plays, but they have little in common so far as character goes; and the tragic fate of Rosette differentiates her completely from Phénice. In a way, *Les Serments indiscrets* and *On ne badine pas avec l'amour* are expressions of the personal experiences of the two authors. Marivaux, leading a tranquil existence, gives his comedy the traditional happy ending; Musset, buffeted by a tempestuous life and afflicted with *mal du siècle,* brings his play to a tragic ending. Miss Frederich concludes: "By portraying life as it is, by allowing tragedy to mingle with comedy, perhaps even overshadow it, Musset renewed and transformed the classical play of Marivaux."

It is in connection with *Les Serments indiscrets* that Voltaire started a protracted but one-sided quarrel with Marivaux. Even before the play was produced, Voltaire wrote to M. de Fourmont: "Nous allons avoir cet été une comédie en prose du sieur de Marivaux, sous le titre *les Serments indiscrets.* Vous croyez bien qu'il y aura beaucoup de métaphysique et peu de naturel; et que les cafés applaudiront, pendant que les honnêtes gens n'entendront rien." The malice is obvious. But Marivaux, who loved peace as much as Voltaire relished a quarrel, never permitted himself to get involved with his adversary, on this occasion or others that followed frequently.

Les Serments indiscrets was one of Marivaux's favorite plays, and he never retouched it; but time has not been kind to it or given it belated prominence. It has had no modern revivals, and on evaluation it does not seem to have the qualities that would make it successful in the twentieth century.

20 L'Ecole des meres

[One act in prose. First performed at the Théâtre Italien, July 25, 1732.]

MARIVAUX was now in the midst of the most productive epoch in his career. Thoroughly skilled in the art of writing plays, well versed in the wiles of elegant drawing rooms, and inured against the deceptions of literary fortune, Marivaux was unhampered by inhibitions of a personal nature. After the success of *Le Jeu de l'amour et du hasard* in 1730, he busied himself with several projects: *Les Serments indiscrets* was written in 1730, though not produced until 1732; *La Réunion des amours* and the first volume of his monumental though unfinished novel, *La Vie de Marianne,* came in 1731; and after *Le Triomphe de l'amour* he produced a second play in 1732, *L'Ecole des mères.*

As if to compensate Marivaux for the recent failure of *Les Serments indiscrets* at the Théâtre Français, his friends at the Théâtre Italien made *L'Ecole des mères* one of his most notable successes[1]— partly because it provided Silvia with the type of role in which she excelled. It is written in a sprightly vein and contains elements of originality and distinction that entitle it to detailed consideration, though it is but a one-act play.

How should a mother treat her daughter's inclination toward marriage? It is a question that intrigued Marivaux on several oc-

---

[1] It was given fourteen times in its initial run and was frequently revived.

casions. As early as 1722–23, when he published *Le Spectateur français,* he sketched the portrait of a girl who expresses her bitterness at being too severely repressed by her mother (Feuille 12); she became the prototype of the Angélique of *L'Ecole des mères.* In 1732, as Marivaux was writing that play, he must have been thinking of his own daughter, Colombe, now fourteen years old and motherless since childhood. Three years later he returned to the question once more in *La Mère confidente,*[2] in which one senses a sort of personal concern on the part of Marivaux.

In *L'Ecole des mères* Mme. Argante, with egotistic arbitrariness, has decided to marry her daughter Angélique to the elderly wealthy Damis. Angélique, however, loves Eraste, a young man of her own age. When the play opens, Eraste is conniving with Lisette and Frontin to enter the Argante household in the livery of a *laquais.* It is the very evening when the marriage contract between Angélique and M. Damis is to be signed. Under the circumstances, Frontin recommends kidnaping the girl, but Eraste seeks only a rendezvous with Angélique away from the guests. Mme. Argante, entering unexpectedly, is pleased with the appearance of the prospective servant and permits him to stay. She then questions Lisette about Angélique's inclination toward the proposed marriage. Into each of Lisette's assertions that the girl is unhappy about the future, Mme. Argante reads some compliment to herself for the rigid training she has given her daughter, and she does not heed Lisette's warning that Angélique may not be of the disposition Mme. Argante supposes. Confronting Angélique herself, Mme. Argante is no less opinionated:

MADAME ARGANTE: Vous voyez, ma fille, ce que je fais aujourd'hui pour vous; ne tenez-vous pas compte à ma tendresse du mariage avantageux que je vous procure?

ANGÉLIQUE: Je ferai tout ce qu'il vous plaira, ma mère.

MADAME ARGANTE: Ne trouvez-vous pas qu'il est heureux pour

[2] See Chapter 24.

vous d'épouser un homme comme Monsieur Damis? . . . Allons, répondez, ma fille!

ANGÉLIQUE: Vous me l'ordonnez donc?

MADAME ARGANTE: Oui, sans doute. Voyez, n'êtes-vous pas satisfaite de votre sort? . . . je veux qu'on me réponde raisonnablement; je m'attends à votre reconnaissance. . . . je commence à vous entendre: c'est-à-dire, ma fille, que vous n'avez point de volonté?

ANGÉLIQUE: J'en aurai pourtant une, si vous le voulez.

MADAME ARGANTE: Il n'est pas nécessaire; vous faites encore mieux d'être comme vous êtes, de vous laisser conduire, et de vous en fier entièrement à moi. . . . Oui, grâce à mes soins, je vous vois telle que j'ai toujours souhaité que vous fussiez. . . . (Sc. 5)

Once free of her mother's domination, Angélique is at ease with Lisette, and shows herself to have more of a mind of her own than her mother suspects.

LISETTE: Vous épouserez donc Monsieur Damis?

ANGÉLIQUE: Moi, l'épouser! Je t'assure que non; c'est bien assez qu'il m'épouse.

LISETTE: Mais vous n'en serez pas moins sa femme.

ANGÉLIQUE: Eh bien, ma mère n'a qu'à l'aimer pour nous deux; car pour moi je n'aimerai jamais qu'Eraste. . . . tout ce que me dit Eraste est si touchant! on voit que c'est du fond du cœur qu'il parle; et j'aimerais mieux être sa femme seulement huit jours, que de l'être toute ma vie de l'autre.

LISETTE: Vous êtes d'une vivacité étonnante avec moi et vous tremblez devant votre mère.

ANGÉLIQUE: Tu as raison; mais quand ma mère me parle, je n'ai plus d'esprit. . . . Moi qui suis naturellement vertueuse, sais-tu bien que je m'endors quand j'entends parler de sagesse? (Sc. 6)

Lisette and Frontin manage to arrange a brief interview between Eraste and Angélique, during which the two young people confess their love with disarming candor:

ÉRASTE: Il m'a paru que vous m'aimiez un peu.

ANGÉLIQUE: Non, non, il vous a paru mieux que cela; car je vous ai dit bien franchement que je vous aime; mais il faut m'excuser, Eraste, car je ne savais pas que vous étiez là.

ÉRASTE: Est-ce que vous seriez fâchée de ce qui vous est échappé?

ANGÉLIQUE: Moi, fâchée? au contraire, je suis bien aise que vous l'ayez appris sans qu'il y ait de ma faute; je n'aurai plus la peine de vous le cacher. (Sc. 7)

The interview is cut short by the approach of a servant, but Lisette and Frontin promise the young lovers a longer rendezvous as soon as the masked ball gets under way. The servant, who has caught a glimpse of Eraste, heralds the arrival of M. Damis; but before he can explain the presence of Eraste to his master, Mme. Argante and Angélique come to greet the suitor. It is revealed that his name is really Orgon; he has adopted the name Damis because he knows that unequal marriages such as the one he is contemplating are frequently subject to cancellation at the last minute; furthermore, he thinks it wise to hide his plans from his son. After appropriate civilities, M. Damis asks to speak to Angélique alone. More experienced and worldly-wise than the young girl, he suspects that she has a suitor, and he has no difficulty in eliciting the admission that she is in love with another. When Frontin comes to escort them to the guests, M. Damis lags behind long enough to bribe the valet to tell him the truth of the situation. Frontin even explains that the young suitor is in the house and that the candles are to be extinguished for the imminent rendez-vous. For an additional bribe Frontin hides M. Damis in the room.

There follows one of those cleverly arranged imbroglios at which Marivaux was so adept. Eraste comes first. In the darkness he mistakes the unseen person for Angélique and makes an impassioned but respectful declaration. M. Damis recognizes the voice and realizes that he is his son's rival. Lisette brings in Angélique; Eraste, unaware that he has not been speaking to her all the time, continues his declaration. Frontin conducts Mme. Argante into the room unseen, so that both parents are the unsuspected witnesses of their children's lovemaking:

> ANGÉLIQUE: . . . je vais comme le cœur me mène, sans y entendre plus de finesse; j'ai du plaisir à vous voir, et je vous vois, et s'il y a de ma faute à vous avouer si souvent que je vous aime, je la mets sur votre compte.

> ÉRASTE: Que vous me charmez!

> ANGÉLIQUE: Si ma mère m'avait donné plus d'expérience, si j'avais été un peu dans le monde, je vous aimerais peut-être sans vous le dire. Mettez-vous à ma place; j'ai tant souffert de contrainte, ma mère m'a rendu la vie si triste! . . .

> ÉRASTE: Oui, ma joie, à ce que j'entends là, va jusqu'au transport! Mais il s'agit de nos affaires: j'ai le bonheur d'avoir un père raisonnable qui, j'espère, entrera volontiers dans nos vues.

> ANGÉLIQUE: Pour moi, je n'ai pas le bonheur d'avoir une mère qui lui ressemble. (Sc. 18)

Infuriated, Mme. Argante bursts out: "Ah! c'en est trop, fille indigne de ma tendresse! . . . Vous plaindre d'une éducation qui m'occupait tout entière! Eh bien, jeune extravagante, un couvent, plus austère que moi, me répondra des égarements de votre cœur." Frontin lights the candles to clear up the misunderstandings.

M. Damis accepts the situation with good will and, introducing the would-be *laquais* as his son, advises Mme. Argante to acquiesce also. Eraste gratefully throws himself at his father's feet: "Que je vous ai d'obligation, mon père!" and Angélique seeks her mother's pardon: "Puis-je espérer d'obtenir grâce?" (Sc. 19). Mme. Argante yields glumly to the inevitable and gives her consent. The entertainers hired for the masked ball are brought on to end the play with a *divertissement* typical of the Théâtre Italien.

There are certain aspects of *L'Ecole des mères* that recall Molière —this, in spite of Marivaux's avowed dislike for the type of play

Molière wrote. Even granting that Marivaux added his own inimitable touch, it seems improbable that he would have written *L'Ecole des mères* without the materials of *L'Ecole des femmes, L'Ecole des maris,* and *L'Avare.* Agnès and Isabelle are the ancestors of Angélique, and Marivaux goes so far as to describe his heroine in the words of Frontin as "une Agnès élevée dans la plus sévère contrainte" (Sc. 2). It must be stated, however, that Marivaux has brought Angélique up to date; Agnès is the innocent sheltered *jeune fille* of the seventeenth century, emboldened by love, whereas, Angélique, though innocent and sheltered, reveals a keen intelligence and an analytical mind not discernible in Agnès; to this she adds a flair for ruses characteristic of Isabelle and, like Isabelle, she revolts. Whatever the sources of the character, Angélique, who emerges as the focal personality in *L'Ecole des mères,* is endowed with an originality that places her among the most engaging characters in Marivaux's gallery.

It might be pointed out that when Mme. Argante coaches Angélique in the duties of a wife (Sc. 5), one is reminded of Arnolphe's "Maximes du mariage" (*L'Ecole des femmes,* III, 2). Her reproaches to Angélique duplicate the accusations of ingratitude heaped on Agnès by Arnolphe and on Isabelle by Sganarelle.

The Sganarelle-Arnolphe type of role (an elderly guardian who aspires to be the suitor of his ward) is divided between two characters in Marivaux: Mme. Argante and M. Damis. The former is the dominating parent, shrewish, *criarde,* disregarding her daughter's feelings. The children's comparison of their parents (Eraste: "j'ai le bonheur d'avoir un père raisonnable"; Angélique: "je n'ai pas le bonheur d'avoir une mère qui lui ressemble") only points up the harshness of Mme. Argante. Prior to this play Marivaux had depicted only two mothers: Claudine, the raucous peasant in *L'Héritier du village,* and Mme. Sorbin, the militant suffragette of *La Colonie,* both of whom are essentially caricatures. Mme. Argante is the first mother whose parental attributes come into play; she is an unpleasant woman, almost the opposite of the laudable fathers Marivaux has created. Several other mothers will appear in future Marivaux comedies, and each one (with the exception of Mme. Argante in *La Mère confidente*) will have some disagreeableness in her make-up. If it is hard to understand why Marivaux always presented his fathers as praiseworthy gentlemen—and now M. Damis must be added to the list—it is equally difficult to understand why his mothers possess so little of the devotion usually associated with motherhood. Mme. Argante is never affectionate enough to *tutoyer* her daughter, and in a moment of rage threatens to put the girl in a convent.[3]

M. Damis fulfills the other part of the Sganarelle-Arnolphe role, that of the elderly suitor. Though he earnestly wishes to marry Angélique, he yields without resentment to the claims of young love, and thereby saves himself from being ridiculous, as Molière's characters are. The father-son rivalry in *L'Ecole des mères* savors of the Harpagon-Cléante situation in *L'Avare*, except that Eraste is not disrespectful toward his father, as Cléante had been toward Harpagon.

In his article on Marivaux, Brunetière[4] words certain comments in such a way as to distort the relationship between Molière and Marivaux. For example, he says that Marivaux "a voulu refaire telles et telles pièces de Molière, et non pas *le Sicilien* ou *le Mariage forcé*, mais tout bonnement *l'Ecole des femmes* dans son *Ecole des mères* et *le Misanthrope* dans *les Sincères*." The verb "a voulu" seems inappropriate, for it implies that Marivaux set out deliberately to rewrite Molière's comedies in much the same manner as Voltaire tried to rewrite Crébillon's tragedies. Nothing could have been farther from Marivaux's mind. Our knowledge of his dislike for Molière's plays and his peaceful disposition forbids our attributing to him a churlish jealousy of Molière. Both plays deal with the recurrent

---

[3] This is the second time Marivaux has showed the use of a convent for disciplinary purposes. See *La Seconde surprise de l'amour*, p. 100.
[4] *Revue des deux mondes*, April 1, 1881, p. 675.

theme of a young girl enlightened by love, rebelling against parental or tutorial severity. If occasional facets of *L'Ecole des femmes* reappear in *L'Ecole des mères,* it is not necessarily by deliberate plagiarism, but rather because the two plays naturally revolve about certain common human verities. Furthermore, if Brunetière had wanted to prove Marivaux dependent on Molière, he should have cited *L'Ecole des maris* and *L'Avare* along with *L'Ecole des femmes.*

A little later Brunetière says: "C'est au moment précis qu'il quitte décidément les traces de Molière que Marivaux devient original. C'est alors qu'il entre dans une voie nouvelle." This statement, too, is misleading in that it suggests that as a young writer Marivaux was a disciple of Molière, like Dancourt, Regnard, Destouches, and La Chaussée, but that sometime in his maturity he developed a style of his own. Such an implication is the reverse of the truth. It is in his early and middle plays, *Arlequin poli par l'amour, La Surprise de l'amour, La Double inconstance, L'Ile de la raison,* and *Le Jeu de l'amour et du hasard,* that Marivaux is completely free of traditional influences. It is only toward the end of his career that he wrote the plays Brunetière associates with Molière.

It is regrettable that Brunetière was not familiar with all of Marivaux's theater and that he had so little sense of the chronology of the plays. In contrast, he was well acquainted with Molière. His judgments about Marivaux are valid when he is discussing a play he knows, but—not surprisingly—they are unsound when he does not stand on familiar ground.

Perhaps Edouard Fournier[5] resolved the Molière-Marivaux issue squarely when he wrote: "Marivaux, procédant comme un maître, ne s'est inspiré de Molière que pour ne pas l'imiter."

Eighteenth-century critics, strangely enough, did not make comparisons with Molière. The *Mercure de France* gave *L'Ecole des*

5 Cited from Marcel Arland, *Théâtre complet de Marivaux* (Paris: La Nouvelle revue française, 1949), p. 1511.

mères two notices: the first one[6] reported that "Le Public l'a reçuë
très favorablement," and the second[7] gave a long analysis without
critical comment. Desboulmiers[8] said: "C'est une des pièces que le
public a revues le plus souvent et avec le plus de plaisir," and
Lessing[9] looked upon it as one of Marivaux's best comedies. In none
of these reviews is there any mention of Molière.

The play had one important influence. La Chaussée wrote *L'Ecole
des mères* for the Comédie Française (April 27, 1744); he owes not
only the title but the character of the mother to Marivaux. La
Chaussée's Mme. Argant is as opinionated and inconsiderate as
Marivaux's Mme. Argante in that she is ready to squander her wealth
on a good-for-nothing son whom she favors over a virtuous daughter.
However, La Chaussée's play is in five acts in verse, which, from
the eighteenth-century point of view, gave it pre-eminence over
Marivaux's one act in prose. But if, as Arland has pointed out,
Marivaux would not have written his play without Molière, it is
equally true that La Chaussée would not have written his play
without Marivaux. When Marivaux's comedy was performed during the Revolution at the Théâtre de la République and in 1809 at
the Théâtre Français, it was called *La Petite école des mères* to distinguish it from La Chaussée's long play, which was given in 1781–
92 and again in 1807–8.

Mlle. Mars did not fare well as Angélique when *L'Ecole des mères*
was officially adopted by the Théâtre Français on April 11, 1809. For
all her brilliance, she performed the play only twice. Geoffroy,[10] who
constantly showed a lack of sympathy for Marivaux, found little to
commend in this "bagatelle": "l'on a prétendu apprendre aux mères
qu'une excessive sévérité dans l'éducation de leurs filles est encore

[6] July 1732, p. 1619.
[7] September 1732, pp. 2017–25.
[8] *Histoire anecdotique et raisonnée du Théâtre Italien depuis son rétablissement
en France jusqu'à l'année 1769* (Paris: Lacombe, 1769), III, 491.
[9] Cited from Arland, *op. cit.*
[10] *Le Journal de l'Empire,* April 14, 1809.

plus nuisible qu'une excessive indulgence. . . . Les mères ont un bien meilleur précepteur que Molière, que Marivaux, et que tous les faiseurs de comédies: c'est Fénélon."

On the other hand, a revival of *L'Ecole des mères* at the Odéon on December 18, 1878, had an exceptional success. The critics were entranced, not only with the freshness of the acting, but with the freshness of the play itself, and they paid tribute to Marivaux accordingly. Edouard Fournier,[11] who had published a splendid edition of Marivaux earlier the same year and was rather severe with *L'Ecole des mères* when he read it, reversed his opinion when he saw it on the stage and declared it "une merveille de naturel et d'esprit, de vivacité et de charme." Caraguel[12] asked: "Comment se fait-il que ce petit bijou dramatique soit resté enfoui si longtemps dans la poussière des bibliothèques?" Bertrand[13] detected the enjoyment of the spectators by "ces murmures unanimes de plaisir qui saluent au passage des détails fugitifs, mais de valeur exquise." Sarcey[14] qualified his praise of *L'Ecole des mères:* "Je l'ai vue avec plaisir; mais il faut bien l'avouer, c'est une des moindres œuvres de Marivaux." Even after comparing Marivaux with Molière, Sarcey admitted: "Ces réflexions n'empêchent point qu'on ne goûte un réel et vif plaisir à écouter ces fines et subtiles analyses du cœur féminin, par un homme qui a été l'un des plus ingénieux moralistes de ce temps."

A sparkling miniature in its day, equally enchanting in 1878, though rejected in 1809, *L'Ecole des mères* is too brief to be classified as one of Marivaux's best plays. But it contains the essential elements of his genius and can be read and performed with pleasure today.

11 *La Patrie,* December 2, 1878. Cited from G. Larroumet, *Marivaux: sa vie et ses œuvres* (Paris: Hachette, 1882), p. 217.
12 *Le Journal des débats,* December 23, 1878.
13 *La République française,* December 18, 1878.
14 *Le Temps,* December 23, 1878.

21   L'Heureux stratagème

[Three acts in prose. First presented at the Théâtre Italien, June 6, 1733.]

"CETTE pièce fut fort bien accueillie et jouée dix-huit fois. Puis elle tomba dans l'oubli. On regrette," complains Marcel Arland,[1] "que la Comédie-Française ne la reprenne pas." Arland's point is well taken, for *L'Heureux stratagème* is a superior eighteenth-century comedy—one of Marivaux's most successful; yet it is completely unknown to the public at large and, except for Marivaux specialists, even to students of French literature. It has never been performed since it faded from the Italian repertory in the mid-eighteenth century.

The total abandonment of *L'Heureux stratagème* is difficult to explain, for the play was hailed with enthusiasm at its première: "Les beautez qui sont repanduës dans cette Pièce ne sont peut-être pas à la portée de tout le monde; mais ceux qui accusent l'Autheur d'avoir trop d'esprit, ne laissent pas de convenir qu'il a une parfaite connoissance du cœur humain, et que peu de gens font une plus exacte Analise de ce qui se passe dans celui des femmes."[2] This praise was echoed and even amplified a few years later by Desboulmiers.[3]

---

[1] *Théâtre complet de Marivaux* (Paris: La Nouvelle revue française, 1949), p. 1512.

[2] *Le Mercure de France,* June 1733, pp. 1428–41.

[3] *Histoire anecdotique et raisonnée du Théâtre Italien depuis son rétablissement en France jusqu'à l'année 1769* (Paris: Lacombe, 1769), IV, 54.

L'Heureux stratagème has a certain importance in that it marks a new phase in Marivaux's writing for the theater. In this play the emphasis shifts from the portrayal of young hearts undergoing "la surprise de l'amour" to the exploration of love among adults in an atmosphere of high comedy (or to the examination of love from a philosophical point of view). This is a transition in which the stock features of Italian farce are subordinated to the spirit of drawing-room sophistication or to some moral precept. From the beginning of his Parisian career in 1716, Riccoboni, the leader of the Italian troupe, had sought scripts by Parisian dramatists, and by 1733 the repertory was largely French. In the same span Riccoboni's Italian actors had become adept at interpreting French comedy. To be sure, vestiges of the *commedia dell'arte* still appear in Marivaux's plays— his whole theatrical career was too closely associated with the Italian troupe for him ever to break completely with the genre—but henceforth "la surprise de l'amour" occupies less of his attention, and he injects some innovations of style or fresh ideas into each play (except *La Méprise* and *La Joie imprévue*.) Till the end Marivaux enlivened his theater with an originality that accounts for the sustained interest in his plays more than two centuries after he wrote them.

The basic situation in *L'Heureux stratagème* is a *chassé-croisé.* When the play opens Dorante is in love with the Countess and the Chevalier is attached to the Marquise. But it is evident that the frivolous young Countess is wearying of Dorante's stolid virtue and is carrying on a flirtation with the opportunist Chevalier; she seeks to lure him from the Marquise, just to satisfy her vanity. The Marquise, a bit older and more worldly-wise, views this with stoic good humor, feeling that all will right itself. Dorante is in despair at seeing himself rejected; likewise Arlequin, his valet, and Lisette, the *suivante* of the Countess, are chagrined at the prospect of having to forgo their marriage.

Lisette chides her mistress for abandoning Dorante: "Que vous avez le cœur inconstant! Avec autant de raison que vous en avez, comment pouvez-vous être infidèle? car on dira que vous l'êtes" (I, 4). To which the Countess replies: "Eh bien! infidèle soit puisque tu veux que je le sois; crois-tu me faire peur avec ce grand mot-là?"; and she goes on to justify her change of heart: "Bien loin que l'infidélité soit un crime, c'est que je soutiens qu'il ne faut pas hésiter un moment d'en faire une, quand on en est tentée, à moins que de vouloir tromper les gens, ce qu'il faut éviter, à quelque prix que ce soit." The Countess flouts marriage with men like Dorante: "avec ces Messieurs-là, voilà comment il faudrait vivre; si vous les en croyez, il n'y a plus pour vous qu'un seul homme, qui compose tout votre univers; tous les autres sont rayés, c'est autant de morts pour vous. . . . la sotte fidélité lui a fait sa part, elle lui laisse un captif pour sa gloire. . . . Quel abus, Lisette, quel abus."

Therefore, when Dorante demands an explanation of her conduct, the Countess mocks him: "Que vous auriez été un excellent héros de roman! Votre cœur a manqué sa vocation, Dorante" (I, 5). Lisette, won over for the moment by her mistress's twisted reasoning, rebuffs both Dorante and Arlequin: "La fidélité n'est bon à rien; c'est mal fait que d'en avoir; de beaux yeux ne servent de rien, un seul homme en profite, tous les autres sont morts" (I, 6).

But the Marquise, who has seen many coquettes in her day, conceives the idea of resorting to a stratagem to bring the Countess and Lisette to their senses. She proposes that she and Dorante pretend to fall in love; she will arrange to satisfy Arlequin by giving him Marton. They will assume, of course, that the Countess will marry the Chevalier and Lisette will marry his wily servant Frontin. The Marquise explains that if, as they both believe, the Countess is really in love with Dorante she will not go through with the marriage and Dorante can claim her for his own.

Dorante agrees with some misgivings. His first chore is to hint to the Chevalier that he is in love with the Marquise. The fickle Chevalier unhesitatingly relinquishes the Marquise and is delighted to know that Dorante no longer desires the Countess.

The stratagem bears fruit immediately. The Countess expects the Marquise to reproach her for stealing the heart of the Chevalier, and she is not a little abashed when the Marquise insinuates that she has found Dorante a suitable replacement for the Chevalier. At first the Countess thinks the Marquise is just being spiteful. But when Dorante himself addresses her unwittingly as "Marquise" and then seeks to avoid her presence, the Countess is piqued. She tells the Chevalier that she has decided to postpone their wedding because she does not want to hurt her friends. She cannot bring herself to admit that she has been rejected. The Chevalier answers that Dorante and the Marquise have already made their plans and there is no need for delay. A delightful subplot with the servants, whose fate is usually identical with their masters', only shows the Countess that Dorante no longer cares for her. As if to put Dorante to a final test, the Countess gives her hand to the Chevalier in the presence of Dorante. When he congratulates them, the Countess declares rashly that she will marry the Chevalier that very evening. Dorante is concerned about the outcome of the affair, but the Marquise re-assures him: "Toutes nos mesures sont prises; allons jusqu'au con-trat comme nous l'avons résolu; ce moment seul décidera si on vous aime. L'amour a ses expressions, l'orgueil a les siennes; l'amour soupire de ce qu'il perd, l'orgueil méprise ce qu'on lui refuse: at-tendons le soupir ou le mépris; tenez bon jusqu'à cette épreuve" (III, 4).

In the meantime, Lisette, who was corrected of her folly when she thought she had lost Arlequin, tries to show her mistress where her true feelings lie.[4] Reminded of her inconstancy, the Countess cries: "Eh bien, mon enfant, je me trompais; je parlais d'infidélité sans la connaître" (III, 6), and at the mention of Dorante's name the Countess admits ruefully: "je l'aime, et tu m'accables. . . . j'ai tort, un tort affreux! . . . Misérable amour-propre de femme! Misé-rable vanité d'être aimée!" (III, 6).

4 For a similar scene, see *La Surprise de l'amour* (III, 2), p. 34.

At this delicate juncture the gardener Blaise announces that a notary has arrived with contracts for Dorante and the Marquise as well as for the Chevalier and the Countess. The Countess is beside herself:

> LA COMTESSE: . . . Je suis accablée! Ils vont s'épouser ici si je n'y mets ordre. Il n'est plus question de Dorante, tu sens bien que je le déteste: mais on m'insulte.
>
> LISETTE: Ma foi, Madame, ce que j'entends là m'indigne à mon tour; et à votre place, je me soucierais si peu de lui, que je le laisserais faire.
>
> LA COMTESSE: Tu le laisserais faire! Mais si tu l'aimais, Lisette?
>
> LISETTE: Vous dites que vous le haïssez!
>
> LA COMTESSE: Cela n'empêche pas que je l'aime. (III, 7)

The impulsive Chevalier is eager to go through with the ceremonies, but in her bewilderment the Countess bluntly announces that she will not marry him. The rest of the parties assemble for the signing of the contracts. When the moment arrives for the Countess to witness the contract for Dorante and the Marquise, she sighs and faints in Lisette's arms. The proof the Marquise had hoped for is manifest, and Dorante and the Countess embrace happily. However, the Marquise is not so kindly disposed toward the Chevalier:

> LA MARQUISE: Quant à vous, Chevalier, je vous conseille de porter votre main ailleurs; il n'y a pas d'apparence que personne vous en défasse ici.
>
> LA COMTESSE: Non, Marquise, j'obtiendrai sa grâce; elle manquerait à ma joie et au service que vous m'avez rendu.
>
> LA MARQUISE: Nous verrons dans six mois. (III, 10)

This sort of *chassé-croisé,* in which the dramatic and comic substance comes from the interchange of two pairs of lovers who return to their original partners in the end, was a commonplace in the eighteenth century. Marivaux himself used the same pattern later in *Le Legs* (1736) and again in *Les Sincères* (1739). But in

L'Heureux stratagème—and here Marivaux's originality shows itself —only half the foursome find happiness at the final curtain. This was an innovation of striking audacity. The *Mercure*[5] said: "Ce dénouëment a paru un des plus interessans qu'on ait vûs au Théâtre." In an age when dramatists adhered strictly to the theatrical conventions, Marivaux dared give his play an unconventional ending.

Perhaps the characters and plot of *L'Heureux stratagème* are not too far removed from other comedies of the day,[6] but in style and form it is an excellent play. The action moves forward briskly, the dialogue is smart, the climax is well handled; on the whole, *L'Heureux stratagème* remains a splendid example of eighteenth-century light comedy.

The actor Lanoue copied much of *L'Heureux stratagème* for *La Coquette corrigée,* a five-act comedy in verse constructed on the classical pattern. The Comédie Française produced it in 1756 with the author himself in the leading role. Lanoue presents a flirtatious young widow in Julie, a stolid suitor in Eraste, a worldly-wise and coquettish aunt in Orphise, and a roué in the Marquis, all of whom are involved in a *chassé-croisé.* But Lanoue had a vulgar taste, and his comedy is indelicate to the point of coarseness; in style and wit it bears no resemblance to Marivaux's. At its première *La Coquette corrigée* was coolly received, although a brilliant revival of it by Mlle. Gaussin a few years later became the rage in Paris and made the play one of the secondary successes of the latter half of the eighteenth century. It was performed as late as 1836.

Both Grimm and La Harpe attacked Lanoue's comedy, the latter going so far as to say: "Je n'ai fait mention d'un si mauvais ouvrage que parce que son succès est un des scandales de nos jours."[7]

---

[5] June 1, 1733, pp. 1428–41.

[6] Jean Fleury (*Marivaux et le marivaudage* [Paris: Plon, 1881], p. 135) traces the ancestry of this type of play back to *El perro del hortelano* of Lope de Vega. Various *canevas* of the Italian troupe utilized the situation of a romantic foursome changing partners.

[7] Ch. Lenient, *La Comédie en France au XVIIIe siècle* (Paris, 1888), II, 16–19.

Today *La Coquette corrigée* has rightly been consigned to oblivion, whereas *L'Heureux stratagème* has finally been brought to light and, it is hoped, will join *Le Prince travesti* and *La Surprise de l'amour* as another Marivaux comedy worthy of modern presentation.

22   La Méprise

[One act in prose. First performed at the Théâtre Italien, August 16, 1734.]

ERGASTE is waiting with his valet Frontin in a garden where he hopes to have a rendezvous with a beautiful girl whose glove he found the day before. Although their conversation was short, the girl did not scorn his advances, and Ergaste hopes she will return. Frontin, in the wily manner of an eighteenth-century servant, has gotten to know the girl's *suivante,* and he warns his master that Clarisse has a twin, Hortense, that they are wealthy, and that they are both so happy single that they have renounced marriage.

Soon Hortense enters, masked. She had seen the young man approach her sister the day before, and she has come to the garden to break up a possible romance. She therefore rebuffs Ergaste, and he is disenchanted by the seeming change in the girl. It is not long after Hortense leaves that Clarisse enters and treats him with an encouragement that enraptures him. In the ensuing scenes, Hortense and Clarisse enter and leave alternately, bewildering Ergaste with their opposite reactions and giving him the impression of a weather-vane personality in the girl he loves. Finally he sees the two together, the confusion is explained, and Clarisse accepts Ergaste as her husband to be—over the haughty protests of her sister. Intervening scenes are taken up by the usual subplot involving Frontin and Lisette.

The source of this trivial comedy goes back to the *Menaechmi* of Plautus, although the subject had been treated on the French stage as recently as 1705 by Regnard in *Les Ménechmes,* and before that by Lenoble in *Les Deux Arlequins* (1691), by Boursault in *Les Nicandres* (1664), and by Rotrou in *Les Ménechmes* (1630?). In all these plays, as in Plautus (and also in Shakespeare's *Comedy of Errors*), the twins are male. Marivaux, with his mania for being different, used female twins, but neither this innovation nor a generous dose of wit enabled Marivaux to make his version a successful play. Written as a curtain raiser for a revival of *L'Heureux stratagème, La Méprise* was performed only three times and not repeated thereafter.

The action, oddly enough, takes place in Lyon. Ergaste is returning to Paris from one of his estates in Dauphiné, and in Lyon, as Frontin explains to Lisette, "deux paires de beaux yeux nous raccrochèrent hier, pour autant de temps qu'il leur plaira" (Sc. 2). Frontin feels his superiority over the provincial servants and takes pleasure in boasting of his worldly knowledge, much like Trivelin of *La Fausse suivante*.[1] Of particular interest is his observation on Paris: "Paris, c'est le monde; le reste de la terre n'en est que les faubourgs" (Sc. 13).

La Méprise was not reviewed by the journals at the time of its première, and few historians of the theater have bothered even to mention it. In the ensemble of Marivaux's work, *La Méprise* is of minor importance.

[1] See pp. 69–70.

23   Le Petit-maître corrigé

[Three acts in prose. First performed at the Théâtre Français, November 6, 1734.]

THE complaint Arland voiced about *L'Heureux stratagème*, "On regrette que la Comédie-Française ne la reprenne pas," could be applied with equal justice to *Le Petit-maître corrigé*, a play that has many outstanding merits in spite of the dismal failure it suffered at the Théâtre Français in the eighteenth century.[1] When one reads *Le Petit-maître corrigé* today, one is tempted to predict that it could weather critical inspection on the stage, for, if it lacks emotional force and poetry, it has dramatic impact. In general tone *Le Petit-maître corrigé*, like so many other Marivaux comedies, seems somewhat ahead of its day, savoring more of nineteenth-century social drama than of eighteenth-century comedy.

The *petit-maître* had become a commonplace character by Marivaux's time.[2] The expression probably originated during the Fronde (1648–53) to designate the young followers of Le Grand Condé, and at that time had a military connotation. Although military prestige was connected with the word down through the War of the

---

[1] *Le Petit-maître corrigé* had only two performances and no revivals. See *Le Mercure de France,* November 1734, p. 2502.

[2] F. Deloffre, in his critical edition of *Le Petit-maître corrigé*, cites scores of plays containing a *petit-maître*, from *Le Rendez-vous des Thuilleries* (1685) by Baron to *Le Fat dupé* (1837) by Deligne. Some thirty of them were written before 1734.

League of Augsburg (1689–97) and the War of the Spanish Succession (1702–13), an element of gallantry had been associated with it from the beginning; and during the Regency (1715–23) that element became more and more prominent and soon gave the word its major significance. In the eighteenth century *petit-maître* was applied loosely to the whole scale of "la jeunesse impertinente et mal élevée," to use Voltaire's term, from foppish youths entering the whirlpool of Parisian society to decadent roués. The word had a number of variants, *chevalier à la mode, chevalier d'industrie, homme à bonne fortune, esprit fort, blasé,* etc., which in modern times are included under the general heading of *petit-maître.*

On the stage the *petit-maître* became more or less typed in *L'Homme à bonne fortune* (1686) by Baron and in *Le Chevalier à la mode* (1687) by Dancourt. In the eighteenth century the fraternity of *petits-maîtres* may be looked upon as the nephews of Molière's *marquis,* tarnished by the corruption of the Regency.

Marivaux's *petit-maître* is a provincial nobleman, Rosimond, who has had his fling in Parisian society and is now brought home by his mother, the Marquise, to marry Hortense, who is the daughter of the Count, a family friend. While in Paris, Rosimond has adopted the sophisticated scorn for marriage called "le préjugé à la mode," and he regards his own marriage with levity. Frontin explains his master's attitude to Hortense's *suivante,* Marton: "il n'est pas de Paris comme de la province, les coutumes y sont différentes. . . . en province, par exemple, un mari promet fidélité à sa femme, n'est-ce pas? . . . A Paris, c'est de même, mais la fidélité de Paris n'est point sauvage, c'est une fidélité galante, badine, qui entend raillerie, et qui se permet toutes les petites commodités du savoir-vivre; vous comprenez bien?" (I, 3). Hortense has a real inclination for Rosimond in spite of his contempt for conjugal love and his flippant scorn for provincial people and manners. Like other Marivaux heroines, Hortense wants to marry for love; and when the young dandy, who is obviously enamored of her, refuses to say, "Je t'aime," and when he answers her question about setting a wedding date with a glib: "Que faisons-nous cet après-midi?" she startles him by suggesting that they post-pone the marriage.

Rosimond receives an unsigned letter from Dorimène, his Parisian mistress, in which she chides him for abandoning her and says disrespectful things about the provincial girl. He loses the letter, and Marton finds it; since she cannot read, she gives it to Hortense and the Count, so that they can return it to its owner.

At this point, Dorimène arrives with Dorante, a past master of Parisian gallantry, who has been responsible for giving Rosimond his veneer of sophistication. She has come for the sole purpose of breaking up the proposed marriage and snaring Rosimond for herself. Their arrival brings out the worst in Rosimond: in the presence of his Parisian friends he swaggers arrogantly and author-izes Dorante to make love to his future wife. Hortense seems to accept Dorante's advances, which sparks jealousy in Rosimond: for the first time his heart is touched.

In the course of events the Count and the Marquise deduce that the unidentified letter could have been written only by Dorimène to Rosimond about Hortense. Rosimond had previously persuaded Frontin to assume responsibility for the letter, and he blandly lies to his mother and the Count to protect Dorimène. However, when Hortense comes upon the scene she says she knows he is too honest to tell her a lie, and she demands the truth. Rosimond stutters with-out answering, but Marton and Frontin confess, whereupon the Marquise disowns her son and the Count breaks off the marriage, leaving the severely shaken young man to the mercies of his Parisian friends.

Rosimond now finds himself faced with the ugly necessity of marrying Dorimène, even though in his heart his affection for Hortense has grown with her faith in him. Dorante only increases his despair by proposing that he compensate Hortense for the loss of Rosimond by marrying her himself. At an opportune moment Rosimond, his flippancy tempered by a resurgence of his innate good nature, tries to tell Hortense how fond he is of her, but he cannot yet bring himself to admit that he loves her. Dorante busies himself to resolve the predicament: he persuades the Count to accept him as a son-in-law, and he elicits the consent of the Marquise for her son to marry Dorimène. These events make Rosimond realize where his happiness really lies. It is Frontin and Marton who convince him that he should abandon his foolish prejudices and tell Hortense simply what is in his heart. At the climax, when he is torn between his love for Hortense and what he looks upon as his duty to Dorimène, his veneer of sophistication gives way to his natural instinct: in the presence of Dorimène and Dorante, Rosimond, now *corrigé,* falls on his knees before Hortense:

> HORTENSE: Quoi, Rosimond, vous m'aimez?
>
> ROSIMOND: Et mon amour ne finira qu'avec ma vie.
>
> HORTENSE: Et vous n'aimez pas Dorimène?
>
> ROSIMOND: Elle est présente, et je dis que je vous adore. . . . Adieu, belle Hortense; ma présence doit vous être à charge. Puisse Dorante, à qui vous accordez votre cœur, sentir toute l'étendue du bonheur que je perds!
>
> HORTENSE: Arrêtez, Rosimond; ma main peut-elle effacer le ressouvenir de la peine que je vous ai faite? Je vous la donne.
>
> ROSIMOND: Je devrais expirer d'amour, de transport et de reconnaissance.

This confession regularizes the situation: Rosimond and Hortense will be happily married; Dorante and Dorimène leave for Paris, scoffing at the ridiculous sincerity of provincial manners.

One might cite two possible sources of *Le Petit-maître corrigé: Les Dames vengées* (1695) by Donneau de Visé and *L'Obstacle imprévu* (1717) by Destouches, in both of which a young man is predisposed against marrying a provincial girl. In both plays the hero is smitten with the girl as soon as he sees her, and there is some praise for the honesty and simplicity of country manners; the Donneau de Visé play also utilizes the episode of a lost letter. It goes without saying, however, that both plays are so inferior to *Le Petit-maître corrigé* in construction and development that they have fallen into even greater disregard than Marivaux's comedy.

Other authors, before and after Marivaux, treated the *petit-maître* as a glib show-off, a *farceur,* or a social parasite. Marivaux, on the other hand, does not make a caricature of Rosimond; rather, he analyzes the young man and traces his transition from a flippant dandy to an *honnête homme.* Not again until Alfred de Musset will the heart of the *petit-maître* be so thoroughly studied.

It is hard to explain why *Le Petit-maître corrigé* failed so miserably, for it is far superior from a dramatic and literary point of view to many contemporary comedies that enjoyed great success in their day. Certainly, one major explanation would seem to be premeditated opposition, probably inspired by Voltaire, Crébillon *fils*, and others who had petty reasons to belittle Marivaux. Mlle. de Bar[3] describes the disturbance that took place at the première: "Le parterre s'en est expliqué en termes très clairs et très bruyants; et même ceux que la nature n'a pas favorisés du don de pouvoir s'exprimer par ces sons argentins qu'en bon français on nomme sifflets, ceux-là, dis-je, enfilèrent plusieurs clefs ensemble dans le cordon de leur canne, puis, les élevant au-dessus de leurs têtes, ils firent un fracas tel qu'on n'aurait pas entendu Dieu tonner." In another passage[4] Mlle. de Bar gives her own reaction: "Le petit-maître a été traité et reçu comme un chien dans un jeu de quilles. . . . il n'y a ni conduite ni liaison, ni intérêt; au diable qui s'y trouve; il n'y a pas la queue d'une situation; on y voit trois ou quatre conversations à la Marivaux." This type of comment is hardly valid criticism of the values inherent in the play; it may be a reflection of what a spectator

[3] Cited by Marcel Arland, *Théâtre complet de Marivaux* (Paris: La Nouvelle revue française, 1949), p. 1513.
[4] Paul Chaponnière, *Piron: sa vie et son œuvre* (Genève, 1910), p. 175.

expected at the Théâtre Français in 1734; or, more likely, it is the expression of a personal antagonism against Marivaux.

Perhaps an injudicious assignment of roles among the actors had something to do with the failure, for the Comédie Française had made several unfortunate blunders in casting Marivaux comedies before this time.[5]

Still another reason for the failure may have been that the principal character is the *jeune premier* Rosimond instead of the *ingénue* Hortense. This is very unusual in Marivaux, for in most of his plays —and always in the "surprises de l'amour" and the *comédies de mœurs*—it is the young girl who occupies the center of the stage. Since Marivaux was less expert in portraying young men, the play suffers from the fact that he did not use his best talents. The ensemble of the play is excellent, but it lacks a memorable focal point.

The failure *Le Petit-maître corrigé* suffered in 1734 did not prevent Gresset in 1747 and Musset in 1836 from imitating it.

In *Le Méchant* Gresset did more than utilize similar situations: he borrowed characters, philosophy, whole segments of plot. The basic situation in Gresset's play is the same as in Marivaux's: Valère, a wellborn provincial youth, has just had a lengthy sojourn in Paris, where he has come under the influence of a certain sophisticate, Cléon. Valère is brought home to marry Chloé, and Cléon accompanies him. Cléon now becomes the major character in *Le Méchant*. He tries to disrupt the marriage and seduce both the girl and her mother. In the end Cléon is unmasked; Valère is cured of his affected manners and is quite willing to settle down to conjugal bliss in the provinces. As Marivaux had done before him, Gresset champions the superiority of provincial honesty over Parisian corruption. Gresset wrote his play in the classical formula of five acts in verse— some of the most polished verse in eighteenth-century dramatic literature. As had happened so often before, Gresset's play was hailed at the time as a masterpiece, while Marivaux's three acts in prose

[5] See pp. 29, 99.

were scorned. *Le Méchant* can still be read with pleasure as an example of good eighteenth-century comedy, but it has not been performed since 1835. Today it seems distinctly dated and less appropriate for staging than *Le Petit-maître corrigé*.

In *Il ne faut jurer de rien* Alfred de Musset has not indulged in such outright borrowing as Gresset. But the Hortense-Rosimond relationship is repeated by Cécile and Valentine; the two young people pass through the same evolutions of love; and the play has the same happy ending. Marivaux's spirit and tone are transmuted into Musset's roguish gaiety. Furthermore, it is worth noting that the title of the play may have been appropriated from Marivaux. Musset is known to have been fond of Marivaux, and a well-used copy of his plays was in the Musset library. "Il ne faut jurer de rien" occurs twice in Marivaux's works: the first time in *La Seconde surprise de l'amour*[6] when Lubin says: "Eh bien, tout coup vaille, il ne faut jurer de rien dans la vie, cela dépend des fantaisies" (I, 11); and the second time in *Le Paysan parvenu* when a coach passenger, who relates his unhappy marriage to Jacob, says: "Mon vœu me porta malheur; il ne faut jamais jurer de rien."

The actor Grandval, who created the role of Rosimond and always had a predilection for *Le Petit-maître corrigé,* frequently performed the play in private theaters, with great success. The play need not be blighted forever by the failure surrounding its première.

[6] See p. 104.

24 La Mère confidente

[Three acts in prose. First performed at the Théâtre Italien, May 9, 1735.]

NONE of Marivaux's comedies is more original from the point of view of dramatic evolution than *La Mère confidente*. In the theater of Marivaux—indeed, in the history of the French theater—*La Mère confidente* deserves a place apart. In the 1730's, when dramatists were groping hesitantly through the *comédie sérieuse* and the *comédie larmoyante* toward some new though as yet undefined form of theatrical expression, Marivaux unwittingly produced a play that was in reality a *drame bourgeois* some twenty years before the genre was crystallized by Diderot. The theme of *La Mère confidente* is the conflict between a mother and her daughter over the girl's marriage. Not that conflicts between parents and children had not been dramatized before this time: the French theater abounds with severe and even tyrannical parents who oppose the romantic inclinations of their children. As a rule, in Molière's comedies and those of his successors, the conflict is of secondary importance and is treated as comedy. However, Marivaux not only makes this conflict the focal point of the play, but he treats the subject with a sympathetic tenderness that was startlingly new on the French stage in 1735. Therefore, among the multiple facets of Marivaux's originality, one of the most notable is his position as the chief precursor of the *drame*.

That *La Mère confidente* is a play of unusual distinction has been recognized by critics. Petit de Julleville[1] called it "un petit chef-d'œuvre dans un genre un peu bâtard" and said that Marivaux "voulut y montrer le personnage tout nouveau d'une mère qui se fait l'amie de sa fille, et obtient, par la confiance et par la tendresse, plus que l'autorité ou le respect n'auraient jamais su obtenir." Sarcey[2] exclaims: "Quelle main ingénieuse, quel art discret ne fallait-il pas pour mener à bien une œuvre aussi délicate."

The public of 1735 liked *La Mère confidente:* witness an initial run of nineteen performances followed by a sustained period of popularity thereafter. The play needed the sympathetic interpretation of the Italian actors; they caught the spirit of the play and with their facile ingenuity did it justice. Had the play been presented at the Théâtre Français in 1735, it would undoubtedly have failed, as it did when revived there in 1810 and again in 1863, for it was entirely unsuited to the stylized acting of the Comédie Française at those periods. The Parisian public had to wait till the twentieth century for the troupe to assemble a group of actors free from traditional shackles and capable of portraying the Marivaux characters as the author conceived them.

Angélique loves a penniless young man, Dorante, whom she has met during a walk and with whom she has had several rendezvous arranged by her *suivante*, Lisette. True, Dorante is to inherit a fortune from his uncle, but the uncle is only thirty-five and about to marry, so that Dorante's chances of bettering his financial status are rather remote. Angélique is undismayed by Dorante's poverty, for she will gladly share her enormous fortune with him. Her mother, Mme. Argante, is distressed when she learns of her daughter's romance through a servant, Lubin, especially since she has promised the girl to one Ergaste, whom Angélique considers "glacé, taciturne, mélan-

---

[1] *Le Théâtre en France* (Paris: Nouvelle édition, 1923), pp. 277.

[2] F. Sarcey, *Quarante ans de théâtre* (Paris: Bibliothèque des annales, 1900–2), II, 261.

colique, rêveur et triste" (I, 8). Rather than force her will on Angélique, Mme. Argante aspires to understand the girl's feelings and guide her to a happy but proper marriage with Ergaste. She promises not to violate her daughter's inclination: "s'il ne vous accommode pas, vous ne l'épouserez pas malgré vous, ma chère enfant" (I, 8), but in return she asks Angélique to confide in her:[3]

> MADAME ARGANTE: . . . . Je n'ai point d'ordre à vous donner, ma fille; je suis votre amie, et vous êtes la mienne. . . . Viens donc que je t'embrasse. Te voici dans un âge raisonnable, mais où tu auras besoin de mes conseils et de mon expérience. . . . parle-moi à cœur ouvert, fais-moi ta confidente.
>
> ANGÉLIQUE: Vous, la confidente de votre fille?
>
> MADAME ARGANTE: Oh! votre fille; eh! qui te parle d'elle? Ce n'est point ta mère qui veut être ta confidente; c'est ton amie, encore une fois. (I, 8)

When Angélique hesitates to speak freely, Mme. Argante reproaches her tenderly: "Hum! Tu ne te fies pas à moi; j'ai peur que ce ne soit encore à ta mère que tu réponds" (I, 8). Little by little Angélique yields to her mother's tactful pressure and recounts her chance meetings with Dorante—Mme. Argante surmises Lisette's connivance. Reminded of the impropriety of giving her affections to a penniless stranger, Angélique accepts the advice of her mother and agrees to dismiss Dorante.

Angélique would keep her word, but Lisette (who is something of a temptress in this play) does not prevent her from accidentally meeting Dorante again. Halfheartedly, Angélique rebuffs him and he is crushed by her unwarranted severity. Without the resources that would entitle him to ask for her hand in the conventional manner, Dorante in his frustration suggests an elopement.

---

[3] In *La Princesse de Clèves* Mme. de Chartres shows concern for the influence of court intrigue on her innocent daughter and asks to be the girl's confidante. Marivaux, well versed in the seventeenth-century novel, probably borrowed this idea from Mme. de Lafayette.

Angélique refuses to consider such a proposal but, sensing that he spoke out of desperation rather than concupiscence, she is more deeply touched than ever by his love for her and determines to appeal again to her mother. In a scene (II, 12) filled with tenderness Angélique tells her mother she has obeyed her and said the things to Dorante that she ought to have said. When Mme. Argante congratulates her on her moral triumph and asks her if she has any other confidence to make, Angélique falters a moment, then falls in tears at her mother's feet: "Non, ma mère, je ne triomphe point; votre joie et vos tendresses me confondent, je ne les mérite pas." The suggestion of an elopement alarms Mme. Argante, but Angélique defends Dorante vigorously, saying that he does not seek to seduce her; rather, the elopement was, as she delicately puts it, "une ressource qu'il ne m'a proposée que dans la seule vue d'être à moi; c'est tout ce qu'il y a compris." To Mme. Argante's intimation that Dorante is aware of Angélique's wealth, the girl counters: "Il l'ignorait quand il m'a vue; et c'est ce qui devrait l'empêcher de m'aimer; il sait bien que quand une fille est riche, on ne la donne qu'à un homme qui a d'autres richesses, tout inutiles qu'elles sont; c'est du moins l'usage; le mérite n'est compté pour rien."[4] Yet, as a dutiful daughter, Angélique offers never to see Dorante again if her mother compels her to give him up; but she adds with ingratiating candor that she would lose "tout le bonheur de la vie. . . . ce n'est pas la quantité de biens qui rend heureuse. . . . j'en ai plus qu'il n'en faudrait avec Dorante. . . . je languirais avec un autre." Mme. Argante is perplexed, for she knows now that Angélique's love is no mere caprice; she is touched by the sincerity and turmoil of Angélique's feelings, yet she cannot see the girl's happiness in a seeming misalliance. The better to understand the two young people, Mme. Argante agrees to talk to Dorante in the guise of an aunt in whom Angélique has confided everything.

---

[4] This is a variation of Marivaux's oft-repeated theme that personal merit is as much an asset as high birth. See pp. 58, 131, 244–47.

To his surprise Dorante comes unexpectedly upon his uncle Ergaste. In explaining why he is there Dorante reveals how much Angélique loves him, although her mother has promised her to another man whom she detests. Thus enlightened, Ergaste confounds Dorante by explaining that he is the proposed husband. However, he urges Dorante to pursue his course, insisting that he keep their kinship secret. Knowing that Mme. Argante wants to conclude the marriage arrangements with Ergaste at once, Dorante again pleads with Angélique to elope with him while there is yet time. Firmly refusing, she pardons his impetuosity and says that they have one last resort in her aunt. Dorante goes away in utter despair.

Mme. Argante enters disguised as the aunt. Lisette, mistaking her for a chaperon in the employ of Dorante, tells Angélique not to have any scruples about eloping and urges her to flee with the woman. Furious, Mme. Argante discharges the maid and sends Lubin for Dorante. At first when the young man confronts Angélique's aunt, he is a bit arrogant, proclaiming that his birth "est égale à celle d'Angélique, mais la différence de nos fortunes ne me laisse rien à espérer de sa mère" (III, 11); he vindicates his proposal for eloping: "Un enlèvement n'est pas un crime, c'est une irrégularité que le mariage efface. Nous nous serions donné notre foi mutuelle, et Angélique, en me suivant, n'aurait fui qu'avec son époux." In answer to this specious argument the aunt shows him that such an action would dishonor Angélique in the eyes of society; she speaks with such telling conviction that Dorante is ashamed. He reproaches himself for having made an indecent proposal to Angélique, and his repentance is so sincere that Mme. Argante sees in him an *honnête homme*. Angélique appeals to him to try to understand the goodness of her mother; her eloquence touches Dorante, who exclaims: "Quel respectable portrait me faites-vous d'elle! Tout amant que je suis, vous me mettez dans ses intérêts mêmes. . . . oui, belle Angélique, vous avez raison. Abandonnez-vous toujours à ces mêmes bontés qui m'étonnent, et que j'admire; continuez de les mériter, je vous y exhorte; que mon amour y perde ou non, vous le devez; je serais au désespoir, si je l'avais emporté sur elle" (III, 11). After which Mme. Argante can do no less than agree with Angélique: "ma fille, je vous permets d'aimer Dorante."

Ergaste enters. He wishes to break his agreement to marry Angélique and offers in his stead "un jeune homme riche et estimé." But Mme. Argante already has other plans: "Mon parti est pris, Monsieur, j'accorde ma fille à Dorante que vous voyez. Il n'est pas riche, mais il vient de me montrer un caractère qui me charme, et qui fera le bonheur d'Angélique" (III, 12). The happiness of the young lovers is climaxed by the revelation to Mme. Argante and Angélique that Dorante is the nephew of Ergaste and will be the heir to his fortune.

All this is carried out in an atmosphere of realism tinged by poetic fantasy. Marivaux's gift for idealizing what otherwise might be a commonplace or improbable situation is brought to a peak of perfection in La Mère confidente. Act I, Scene 8, in which Mme. Argante adroitly persuades her daughter to confide in her; Act II, Scene 12, in which Angélique confesses the plan for elopement and defends Dorante for proposing it;[5] and Act III, Scene 11, in which Mme. Argante confronts Dorante, are written with restraint and beauty. These passages glow with an earnestness of feeling that is free from marivaudage. Sarcey[6] calls them "les chefs-d'œuvre d'un esprit ingénieux et d'une imagination tendre." The style of the whole play is characterized by simplicity and warmth instead of the affectation and wit so often associated with Marivaux. The special merit of La Mère confidente lies in the treatment of Mme. Argante, for she is an original type to appear on the French stage in 1735.

5 Larroumet (Marivaux: sa vie et son œuvre [Paris: Hachette, 1882], p. 307, n. 2) calls this duo de tendresse sheer inspiration. He says there is nothing like it in French literature except the scene in La Princesse de Clèves in which the heroine confesses her love for M. de Nemours to her husband and seeks his protection against herself.
6 Op. cit., II, 261.

While the mothers in Marivaux comedies are usually disagreeable persons,[7] Mme. Argante is always gracious, sympathetic, not far removed in charm and appeal from the Silvias of other comedies. She is more concerned with understanding her daughter than with dominating her. Whereas the Mme. Argante in *L'Ecole des mères* is tyrannical and wants to impose her will on her daughter, the Mme. Argante of *La Mère confidente* is loving and seeks to satisfy her daughter's inclination. It is interesting to note that at the time Marivaux was composing *La Mère confidente*, he was also in the process of writing Parts III and IV of his novel *La Vie de Marianne*, in which he creates Mme. de Miran, the noblewoman who adopts Marianne and lavishes great love and kindness on the orphan. One cannot say which character Marivaux conceived first, but it is obvious that both Mme. Argante of *La Mère confidente* and Mme. de Miran are cut according to the same pattern.

Angélique and Dorante, while amusing as young people experiencing their first brush with love, have no great depth of character. Angélique is not as complex a person as the Silvia of *Le Jeu de l'amour et du hasard* or the Lucile of *Les Serments indiscrets*, nor is this Dorante beset by considerations of sacrificing social prestige like his counterpart in *Le Jeu*. These lovers are interesting only so far as they are accessories to the mother-daughter conflict.

Perhaps one reason why *La Mère confidente* is such a delight to connoisseurs is the fact that both the leading characters are women. With his penchant for exploring the feminine heart, Marivaux provides this play with a double measure of one of his most enchanting qualities. It was among the plays, along with *La Double inconstance, La Surprise de l'amour,* and *Les Serments indiscrets,* that Marivaux himself preferred.

The mother-daughter conflict is what sets apart *La Mère confidente* and makes it a pre-eminent forerunner of the *drame*, for knowingly or not Marivaux injected into it most of the elements required later

[7] See *L'Ecole des mères, Les Fausses confidences, L'Epreuve, La Femme fidèle.*

by Diderot. The play is written in prose, and the subject is a family complication in a bourgeois household. The dramatic impact springs from the mother-daughter relationship rather than from the love affair (Angélique and Dorante are in love when the play begins and they remain so throughout; Marivaux gives their love no special analysis or development). There is some moralizing, though probably not as much as Diderot would require, and at that the moral is implied rather than spoken. Comic tricks are at a minimum (which is odd, since the play was written for the Italian troupe), and the usual subplot of the servants is lacking. The elimination of nobles and of a *caractère* in the Molière manner further removes *La Mère confidente* from the classical formula. To Marivaux should go the credit for writing the first successful *drame*. As Larroumet[8] put it: "seul, ou presque seul, au dix-huitième siècle, il réussit à faire un drame bourgeois simple et vrai, offrant, dans une juste proportion, ce mélange de comique et de touchant, qui est le procédé même de la nature."

Nor is *La Mère confidente* the only example of Marivaux's use of elements of the *drame;* other illustrations can be found elsewhere in his work. *La Femme fidèle,*[9] a play written in 1755 for the private theater of the Comte de Clermont and not performed professionally until 1894, is a typical *drame.* The scene in *La Joie imprévue*[10] in which Damon, after having lost his money gambling, appeals for his father's pardon is another example of tense dramatic action arising from family relationships. In *La Vie de Marianne*[11] the deathbed reconciliation between Mme. Dursan and her ne'er-do-well son in the presence of the family contains all the ingredients of a *drame.* This episode, although part of a novel, has a dramatic structure (as do so many episodes in Marivaux's novels) that makes it almost a

---

[8] *Op. cit.,* p. 302.
[9] See Chapter 32.
[10] See Chapter 27.
[11] Part X, published in 1741.

one-act play in itself; the scene offers a *tableau vivant* that would have been a worthy subject for Greuze.

But Marivaux's eighteenth-century contemporaries, save perhaps Voltaire, seem to have missed his connection with the *drame*. While Grimm, Collé, and d'Alembert debated the plays of La Chaussée and the theories of Diderot, they were unaware that some of Marivaux's comedies reflected the same doctrine; it was not until the nineteenth century that critics placed each author in his proper perspective. Some critics have tried to classify *La Mère confidente* as a *comédie larmoyante*[12] and make Marivaux a competitor or disciple of La Chaussée. Such an allegation is untenable, for the points of view of the two men, not to mention their styles, are so different as to exclude similarities. La Chaussée writes for the sole purpose of extracting every ounce of sentimentality and emotion out of each scene: it is obvious that he wants his audience to shed tears without restraint. On the other hand, Marivaux never indulges in emotional extravagances, and, if he arouses a wistful sympathy in the spectators, he goes no farther.

A touching eighteenth-century compliment was paid to Marivaux posthumously by Maria Theresa of Austria. On April 16, 1770, the day Marie Antoinette was affianced to the future Louis XVI of France, the empress had *La Mère confidente* performed before the court at Vienna. Two weeks later she wrote to the Comte de Mercy-Argenteau: "Le seul vrai bonheur en ce monde est un heureux mariage."[13]

The fortunes of *La Mère confidente* on the stage have been varied. When it was first presented at the Théâtre Italien in 1735, it was

[12] Lintilhac (*Histoire générale du théâtre en France,* Paris, 1909, IV, 320) mentions *La Mère confidente,* "qui est incontestablement une de ses comédies larmoyantes."

[13] Cited in Fournier and Bastide (*Théâtre complet de Marivaux* [2 vols.; Paris: Les Editions nationales, 1946], II, 158) from "Correspondance secrète entre Marie-Thérèse et le comte Mercy-Argenteau."

greeted enthusiastically. The *Mercure de France*[14] announced a new play "sous le titre de *la Mère confidente*, qui est très-goûtée et très-suivie," and the next month gave the play a long analysis, prefaced by a statement that the comedy "fut généralement applaudie, par le mérite de la Piece, et par le jeu des Acteurs; elle fait un extrême plaisir, et attire beaucoup de monde à l'Hôtel de Bourgogne."[15] Desboulmiers[16] called it "une des meilleures et des plus intéressantes qui soient sorties de la plume de M. de Marivaux. Le sujet en est honnête, le but moral & bien rempli."

La Mère confidente was advertised by various theaters during the French Revolution,[17] but with what success it is difficult to ascertain.

The nineteenth century saw two revivals at the Théâtre Français: one in 1810, which apparently was a failure, for it was given only twice, and another in 1863, which had only a mediocre success according to the press notices.[18] Paul de Saint-Victor labeled it "une froide et pâle comédie" (*La Presse,* September 21, 1863), and Edouard Fournier described *La Mère confidente* as "une apparition de revenant plus inattendu que demandé" (*La Patrie,* September 22, 1863). Théophile Gautier was somewhat ironical when he asked: "N'est-ce pas une chose utile que de montrer les côtés par où pèchent ces grands écrivains qu'on admire?" (*Le Moniteur universel*, September 28, 1863). Francisque Sarcey defended the play vigorously: "*La Mère confidente* est une des plus aimables comédies de Marivaux, et les amateurs . . . ont été charmés qu'on la leur rendît sur la scène" (*L'Opinion nationale*, September 28, 1863). If the production failed to attract audiences, it was partly because the Comédie Française had committed another fatal blunder of miscasting, as it

---

[14] May 1735, p. 990.

[15] June 1735, pp. 1187–95.

[16] *Histoire anecdotique et raisonnée du Théâtre Italien depuis son rétablissement en France jusqu'à l'année 1769* (Paris: Lacombe, 1769), IV, 140–41.

[17] For example, it was advertised in *Le Moniteur universel* for the Théâtre National, Rue de Richelieu et de Louvois, on September 30, 1793, and several times in the following weeks.

[18] The following quotations are cited from Larroumet, *op. cit.,* p. 320.

had done so often in the eighteenth century[19] when presenting Marivaux plays. Larroumet says: "C'est l'interprétation qui, malgré le talent de plusieurs artistes, nuisit au succès de la pièce; en effet, tous n'étaient point faits pour leurs rôles."

The twentieth century was kinder to *La Mère confidente* than the preceding century had been. So far, there have been three revivals, all of which have met with approval, if not enthusiasm, at the hands of critics. When it was played in 1907 with Mme. Duminil, Mlle. Bovy, and M. Dehelly in the leading roles, Adolphe Brisson[20] endorsed it wholeheartedly: "Ç'a été un régal d'écouter *la Mère confidente* à la Comédie-Française. . . . Elle contient des beautés très délicates, et présente, au point de vue de l'histoire des mœurs, le plus vif intérêt." He advises his readers to "aller voir *la Mère confidente* avant qu'elle ne quitte l'affiche. Vous en aurez un pur ravissement." In evaluating the play Brisson says: "L'ouvrage est court et de signification profonde, léger par le décor et le costume, grave par les sentiments exprimés; et il dépasse le temps où il fut écrit; il est de tous les temps, il est du nôtre. Marivaux est l'auteur classique le plus près de nous; son œuvre exhale un extraordinaire parfum de 'modernité'!" Jules Truffier,[21] too, caught the spirit of timeliness in *La Mère confidente:* "A mon humble avis, c'est justement par son postulat que vaut cette composition dramatique rêvée en ce dix-huitième siècle où le sentiment maternel n'était pas du tout ce qu'il est aujourd'hui. Cette pièce est . . . très près de nous"; in considering Mme. Argante and her daughter, he exclaims: "Ah! les fraîches et nobles créatures que nous esquisse cette pièce!" Though Henri Bordeaux[22] thought that *La Mère confidente* was only "un ouvrage agréable, fort éloigné de valoir *Le Jeu de l'amour et du hasard* ou *L'Epreuve*," he admitted that "on y découvre avec plaisir un opti-

---

[19] See pp. 29, 99, 180.

[20] *Le Théâtre* (1907–12), III, 277–84. Brisson was dramatic critic for *Le Temps.*

[21] *Les Annales politiques et littéraires,* December 1907, p. 525.

[22] *La Vie au théâtre* (1910–21), I, 57.

misme à la Capus et de jolies répliques qui éclatent comme de jeunes vers de Musset dans un fatras vieillot. La muse de Marivaux garde sa fraîcheur parmi les modes d'autrefois."

Performances of *La Mère confidente* in 1912 caused Robert de Flers[23] to write at length on "ses rares et délicieux mérites." He found "ces trois petits actes . . . tout à fait délicieux. Marivaux est parvenu à donner de la coquetterie à celui de tous les sentiments qui semblent le moins fait pour l'accueillir, à l'amour maternel. Oui, cette mère est en coquetterie avec sa fille, et elle ne cesse pas pourtant jamais d'être sincère et tendre." Flers imagines that Mme. Argante herself had an unhappy marriage (there is no reference of any kind to her past in the play) and that she was loved by an ideal suitor whom she dismissed in order to remain virtuous; he suggests that she is realizing her own unfulfilled happiness in making Angélique happy. Be that as it may, Flers praised *La Mère confidente* in the highest terms because "nous retrouvons dans cette comédie, si peu réelle dans les faits, mais si vraie dans les sentiments, tout l'art gracieux, délicat, féminin et nonchalant de Marivaux. . . . tout ce cortège de rares qualités que nous aimons, et de ces charmants défauts que nous aimons peut-être encore mieux."

Again in the summer of 1926 the Théâtre Français included *La Mère confidente* in a series of *jeudis classiques*. This time the staging and acting more nearly approached the style required for this play. According to Lucien Dubech,[24] "la jeune troupe de la Comédie-Française n'est jamais aussi excellente que dans les comédies d'analyse de Marivaux. . . . C'est que ces comédiens possèdent le secret indispensable pour pénétrer l'art du dix-huitième siècle français, une fine et ferme culture. . . . C'est une joie de l'esprit et des sens de voir . . . Mlle Bovy en Angélique de *la Mère confidente*."

Although *La Mère confidente* has long been recognized as one of

23 *Le Figaro*, April 13, 1912. A much longer article appeared on April 14, 1912.
24 *Candide*, August 19, 1926.

Marivaux's masterpieces and its exquisite delicacy has been appreciated by connoisseurs, it has still not had the culminating seal of an overwhelmingly successful professional production. *La Mère confidente* is perhaps the most refined of Marivaux's comedies. Without action or comic twists to capture the audience, a successful production must rely on some ineffable quality of spirit to create its effect. Each year the understanding of Marivaux grows, and periodically the presentation of one or another of his plays reaches new heights of effectiveness; take as examples the productions of *Le Prince travesti* by the Comédie Française in 1949, of *La Seconde surprise de l'amour* by Jean-Louis Barrault in 1949, and of *L'Ile de la raison* by the Compagnie de l'Equipe in 1950. Perhaps in time some troupe will strike that perfect balance of staging, acting, and interpretation that will do full justice to *La Mère confidente*.

25 Le Legs

[One act in prose. First presented at the Théâtre Français, June 11, 1736.]

ALTHOUGH Marivaux made a uniquely original contribution to the evolution of the *drame* in *La Mère confidente* and pointed the way for others to follow, he himself did not continue on that path immediately. Instead, for his next play he reverted to his most scintillating drawing-room manner to produce *Le Legs* for the Comédie Française. This frothy little comedy, a sort of *partie carrée* or *chassé-croisé* devoid of social or dramatic import but vastly entertaining, became, after an inauspicious première, the second most popular of Marivaux's comedies at the Théâtre Français, ranking next to *Le Jeu de l'amour et du hasard* in the number of performances to date.

Strangely, in spite of its many performances, a definitive text for *Le Legs* has been difficult to establish. The original edition contains twenty-five scenes, but subsequent versions vary from twenty-two to twenty-five. The prompter's copy at the Théâtre Français has twenty-three scenes, and it contains many variants and corrections, some of which are in the author's handwriting. Still other changes occur in a manuscript at the Bibliothèque de l'Arsenal for the role of the Countess, probably copied for Mlle. Gaussin when she played that part at the Comte de Clermont's private theater at Berny. Marivaux himself did not prepare what can be called his own final version. In compiling their complete edition of Marivaux's theater in 1946,

Fournier and Bastide have used the 1736 text and added notes giving the variants of the Théâtre Français and Arsenal manuscripts.[1]

Le Legs has no plot; it is merely a conversation piece between two couples and a pair of servants, in the course of which the marriage arrangements of all of them are straightened out. By the will of a distant relative the Marquis has inherited 600,000 francs on condition that he marry Hortense. If he does not wish to marry her, he must give her 200,000 francs of the legacy; if she refuses to marry him, she must forfeit any claim to the 200,000 francs. Hortense loves, and is loved by, the Chevalier, and they need the money to live properly. The Marquis, a bachelor of forty, loves the dominating Countess, a widow almost his own age, but being too timid to declare himself, he is on the verge of marrying Hortense as the will suggests. The problem for Hortense is to inveigle the Marquis into marrying the Countess of his own accord so that she can justly claim the 200,000 francs.

To this end she enlists the service of Lépine, the valet of the Marquis, and Lisette, the *suivante* of the Countess. Lépine is in love with Lisette, but he cannot marry her, according to eighteenth-century dramatic conventions, unless his master marries the Countess; he is therefore interested in accepting Hortense's bribe. Lisette, on the other hand, is a perverse little wench who believes that she and her mistress are better off in their present state; she therefore refuses to co-operate with Hortense and Lépine and sets out to thwart their plans. Much of the comedy springs from the battle of wits between Lépine and Lisette.

Once these preliminaries have been established, the interplay moves forward briskly. Lisette so discourages the Marquis from hoping for a favorable response from her mistress that the timorous fellow, much to Lépine's consternation, immediately concedes that the

---

[1] For a more detailed statement of the difficulties involved, see Fournier and Bastide, *Théâtre complet de Marivaux* (2 vols.; Paris: Les Editions nationales, 1946), II, 182–83.

Countess does not love him. The Countess is aghast at Lisette's impertinence, for she would like nothing better than to become the wife of the Marquis. But the damage is done, and when the Marquis faces the Countess he talks in riddles. She does her utmost to entice him into saying the words he really means, but he becomes more befuddled than ever in his timidity, and what started out to be a proposal to the Countess sounds more like a declaration in favor of Hortense. Hortense enters and in the presence of the Countess not only spurns a settlement of 100,000 francs but traps the Marquis into an unwilling proposal. She accepts on the spot and urges the Marquis to send for his notary at once. Lépine uses hilarious excuses for refusing to ride to Paris, whereupon Lisette with insolent gaiety offers to find another servant to go. The Countess, exasperated, further delays matters by declining to permit the marriage to take place in her home. The Marquis, caught in the crossfire of these divergent interests, writhes in uneasiness. Lépine takes his master in hand and connives with the Countess in the arrangement of still another interview with the Marquis. Lisette, realizing that Lépine is outwitting her, decides to make the best of the situation before it is too late and work for the marriage, too; she even persuades the Countess to go farther than feminine modesty permits to extract a proposal from the Marquis. At last the Countess and the Marquis are brought together again. That diffident gentleman finds it hard to believe that the Countess still does not have an aversion to him; she is almost unable to convince him of the contrary:

LA COMTESSE: Vous allez voir. Tenez, vous dites que vous m'aimez, n'est-ce pas? Je vous crois. Mais voyons; que souhaiteriez-vous que je vous répondisse?

LE MARQUIS: Ce que je souhaiterais? Voilà qui est bien difficile à deviner! Parbleu, vous le savez de reste.

LA COMTESSE: Eh bien! ne l'ai-je pas dit? Est-ce là me répondre? Allez, Monsieur, je ne vous aimerai jamais, non jamais.

LE MARQUIS: Tant pis, Madame, tant pis; je vous prie de trouver bon que j'en sois fâché.

LA COMTESSE: Apprenez donc lorsqu'on dit aux gens qu'on les aime, qu'il faut du moins leur demander ce qu'ils en pensent.

LE MARQUIS: Quelle chicane vous me faites!

LA COMTESSE: Je n'y saurais tenir. Adieu.

LE MARQUIS: Eh bien! Madame, je vous aime; qu'en pensez-vous? Et encore une fois, qu'en pensez-vous?

LA COMTESSE: Ah! Ce que j'en pense? Que je le veux bien, Monsieur; et, encore une fois, que je le veux bien; car, si je ne m'y prenais pas de cette façon, nous ne finirions jamais.

LE MARQUIS: Ah! vous le voulez bien? Ah! je respire! Comtesse, donnez-moi votre main, que je la baise. (Sc. 24)

Having at last assured himself of the Countess's heart, the Marquis is only too willing to give Hortense her share of the inheritance. Lépine and Lisette, too, will marry:

LISETTE [*à Lépine*]: Maraud! je crois en effet qu'il faudra que je t'épouse.

LÉPINE: Je l'avais entrepris. (Sc. 25)

Le Legs[2] demonstrates perhaps better than any of Marivaux's plays his unique ability to spin out highly polished and clever dialogue in a situation where no action exists. The positions of the four leading characters are clearly stated at the beginning, and they do not change in the course of the play. The timidity of the Marquis is the factor that gives the play its *raison d'être*. Although *Le Legs* is in twenty-five scenes, it could well have ended after five, or less, had the Marquis spoken his mind in the first place.

Le Legs has always been an actors' play, one of those comedies

---

[2] Deloffre (*Mélanges d'histoire littéraire offerts à M. Paul Dimoff*, Annales Universitatis Saraviensis, Philosophie-Lettres, 1954, Vol. III) notes a possible source for *Le Legs* in *Le Testament* (1731) by Fontanelle (never performed and published only in 1751), which Marivaux may have read in manuscript or heard discussed in the drawing rooms he frequented.

that finished artists find a sheer joy to perform. The sharply contrasted characters offer each actor a splendid opportunity to shine in his role. The timorous middle-aged Marquis, the brusque but frustrated Countess with her *grande dame* manners, the aggressive Hortense, the amorous Chevalier, the imperturbable Lépine, and the tart Lisette—all these parts blend into a harmonious whole that becomes incandescent in the hands of skilled performers. Over the years *Le Legs* has been a favorite vehicle for Préville, Mlle. Contat, Molé, Mlle. Mars, Mme. Arnould-Plessy, Mlle. Brohan, Mme. Bartet, and Mme. Cerny.

The inauspicious première mentioned earlier—there seems little doubt that the cabal of Voltaire and his friends chilled the atmosphere of the first showing—hardly gave a clue to the extraordinary vogue the play was to have over the next two centuries; the inadequate performance was in line with the usual treatment given Marivaux's comedies at the Théâtre Français during his lifetime. Marivaux must have felt uncertain about the play's reception, for he did not acknowledge authorship at its première. The most that can be said for *Le Legs* in 1736 is that it was not a complete failure.[3] It was received with mixed feelings by the critics of the day and had only ten performances in its *nouveauté*. In a review that was very long for a one-act play, the *Mercure de France*[4] said of *Le Legs:* "On en a jugé diversement; cependant tout le monde convient que cet Ouvrage est plein d'esprit et très-bien écrit. . . . Au reste, cette Pièce est parfaitement bien joûée." Unfortunately the *Mercure* does not give the distribution of the roles. According to this review, the amount of money involved is 400,000 livres, and the valet is called Frontin instead of Lépine, which further points up the difficulties involved in determining a definitive text. One of the diverse opinions referred

[3] D'Alembert attributes a famous quip to Marivaux on the occasion of the cool reception of *Le Legs.* "Comme on objectait à Marivaux le jugement du public: Le public! le public! dit-il, combien faut-il de sots pour faire un public!" Cited by Jean-Bernard in *Commedia,* January 11, 1930.

[4] July 1736, pp. 1700–7.

to by the *Mercure* is that of Dubisson:[5] "Elle a paru, à la représentation, plus longue qu'une [pièce] de cinq actes, et je doute, quand on
l'élaguerait de moitié, qu'on pût la rendre bonne." While not criticiz-
ing the play itself, *La Bibliothèque française*[6] chided Marivaux for his
overuse of wit: "Tous les personnages de cette Pièce regorgent
d'esprit. Il y a longtemps qu'on fait ce reproche aux Ouvrages de cet
Auteur. Il est des défauts favoris, dont l'amour-propre s'applaudit. Si
celui-ci est de ce nombre, on a lieu de craindre que M. de M—— ne
s'en corrige pas si tôt."

Revived with great success by Préville in 1749, *Le Legs* was a
perennial favorite thereafter. It is interesting to note that during the
Revolution, while *Le Legs* was being played regularly at the old
Théâtre Français (now called the Théâtre de la Nation), it was also
given with unusual frequency not only by the Théâtre de la République (conducted by Talma and the dissident group of former
Comédiens), but by various new theaters that sprang up in the wake
of revolutionary freedom: the Théâtre du Marais, Théâtre de la Rue
Feydeau, and Théâtre National de Molière. One is tempted to wonder
what sort of productions these inexperienced troupes were capable of
giving a play like *Le Legs,* which requires consummate skill on the
part of the actors.

In its long span of popularity critical comments have appeared
only infrequently. The play was performed so often that critics passed
it by, especially since it contains no moralizing or ideas of a kind to
incite discussion in each generation. Allard[7] quotes from *La Pandore*
(November 1, 1823), which called the author "jargonneux Marivaux" and stated that "*Le Legs*, comme ses autres pièces, était du plus
mauvais genre." Such abusive comment hardly represents public
opinion, or the play would never have maintained its popularity. A
more accurate estimate is probably found in the words Lucien

[5] Marcel Arland, *Théâtre complet de Marivaux* (Paris: La Nouvelle revue
française, 1949), p. 1515.
[6] Vol. XXV, p. 178 (1737).
[7] Louis Allard, *La Comédie de mœurs* (Cambridge, 1923), II, 121.

Dubech[8] wrote after witnessing a performance of *Le Legs* in 1930: "Au sortir d'un Marivaux excellent, comme celui du *Legs*, on se dit que les jeux d'Octave et de Marianne sont débauchés, ceux de Perdican et de Camille indiscrets. Il y a dans *Le Legs* une finesse aérienne de propos, une subtilité de trame qui sont bien au nombre de réussites exceptionnelles de l'art."

Once again Marivaux supplied inspiration to Alfred de Musset. In *Le Legs*, which is one of the sources of *L'Ane et le ruisseau*,[9] there is no question of Musset's using a vague idea of Marivaux's: he actually made a replica of the four characters and literally rewrote several scenes of *Le Legs*. *L'Ane et le ruisseau* deals with the same situation and develops the same emotions as *Le Legs*. The servants, so amusing in *Le Legs*, are omitted in *L'Ane et le ruisseau*, since they were not a necessary part of a comedy in Musset's day, as they were in the eighteenth century. *L'Ane et le ruisseau*, however, is one of Musset's lesser works and distinctly inferior to *Le Legs*.

Le Legs has been given less frequently in the twentieth century than in the eighteenth and nineteenth, having had only fourteen performances since 1920. It is devoutly to be hoped that this delightful comedy will not be dropped from the repertory, for there are few like it that can give such keen pleasure to both actors and audience.

8 *L'Action française*, February 21, 1930.
9 Another source is *L'Amant malgré lui* by Carmontelle. The Biré edition of Musset (1942) indicates only Carmontelle as the inspiration for both *L'Ane et le ruisseau* and *Il ne faut jurer de rien* and does not mention Marivaux at all.

26   Les Fausses confidences

[Three acts in prose. First presented at the Théâtre Italien, March 16, 1737.]

MARIVAUX was at the peak of his career. His last two plays, *Le Legs* and *La Mère confidente,* were notable successes in line with *Arlequin poli par l'amour, La Surprise de l'amour, L'Ile des esclaves,* and *Le Jeu de l'amour et du hasard,* and at the same time installments of *La Vie de Marianne* and *Le Paysan parvenu* were adding to his popularity as a novelist. His creative power was at its height. In such an aura of literary effulgence Marivaux composed *Les Fausses confidences.* This comedy, the ethics of which have been questioned, has a cast of seriousness that has made it less popular to date than *Le Jeu;* nevertheless, it occupies a place of pre-eminent importance in Marivaux's theater, and its popularity in the twentieth century bids fair to make it vie with *Le Jeu* as his most highly regarded work.

When the Théâtre Italien first staged *Les Fausses confidences* in 1737, the play was apparently something less than a success, in spite of Gueullette's[1] terse comment: "Cette pièce qui est de M. de Marivaux est excellente." The *Mercure de France*[2] announced the new play in March 1737 and stated that a long review would be printed in one of the forthcoming issues. However, the long review never ap-

---

[1] *Notes et souvenirs sur le Théâtre-Italien au XVIIIᵉ siècle* (Paris: E. Droz, 1938), p. 123.
[2] Pp. 576–77.

peared. The next mention of *Les Fausses confidences* came over a year later when, in connection with the review of another play, the *Mercure*[3] explained: "elle avoit été donnée dans sa nouveauté au mois de Mars de l'année passée, & n'avoit eu qu'un très-médiocre succès. Le public a rendu, à la reprise de cette ingénieuse piece, toute la justice qu'elle mérite, ayant été representée par les principaux Acteurs dans la plus grande perfection." The new revival obviously hit the proper stride, for some years later Desboulmiers[4] wrote: "on l'a revue depuis avec un nouveau plaisir." Since then, *Les Fausses confidences* has had a long history of successes down to the present day.

The cast, somewhat more diversified than in the usual Marivaux comedy and lacking most of the stock characters of the Théâtre Italien, consists of Araminte, a wealthy young widow, bourgeoise by birth but eligible to marry a count or baron by virtue of her charm and wealth; Mme. Argante, her arrogant mother, who has aristocratic aspirations for her daughter; Marton, Araminte's *suivante,* who is more a companion than a servant; Dorante, a handsome though penniless young man of respectable ancestry; Dubois, his former valet, now in the employ of Araminte; M. Remy, Dorante's uncle, who is also Araminte's attorney; the Count, a nobleman held in tow by Mme. Argante as a husband for her daughter; Arlequin, included in the play to satisfy the spectators at the Théâtre Italien; and various other servants. With these characters Marivaux has fashioned a comedy of more than ordinary worth, which has—and this is rare in Marivaux—challengeable ethics.

The plot, which is complex in the extreme, turns on the most finely drawn shades of feeling. Dorante has fallen passionately in love with Araminte, although he has never met her. He is in despair, for he feels his indigence creates an insurmountable barrier between

---

[3] July 1738, p. 1620. The other play was *La Joie imprévue.* See Chapter 27.
[4] *Histoire anecdotique et raisonnée du Théâtre Italien depuis son rétablissement en France jusqu'à l'année 1769* (Paris: Lacombe, 1769), IV, 285.

them. Dubois, who sees nothing reprehensible in Dorante's position, cunningly sets about concocting a plot that will enable Dorante to marry Araminte. He answers the young man's complaint of poverty by saying: "Point de bien! votre bonne mine est un Pérou. . . . voilà une taille qui vaut toutes les dignités possibles, et notre affaire est infaillible, absolument infaillible: il me semble que je vous vois déjà en déshabillé dans l'appartement de Madame" (I, 2). Dubois arranges with the unsuspecting M. Remy to place Dorante in Araminte's employ as the business manager of her estate. M. Remy suggests to his nephew that he cultivate Marton with an eye to marriage since both are much above the servant class; and when Marton enters he even goes so far as to pronounce a sort of informal engagement between them. Both Dorante and Marton are overwhelmed—but for different reasons—by the unexpectedness of M. Remy's forthright scheme.

Araminte, charmed by Dorante's fine appearance and flattering speeches, accepts him without considering another man her mother and the Count have suggested. The arrival of Mme. Argante suddenly complicates the situation: she is displeased with Dorante because she feels he is too young and handsome to be a good manager. Mme. Argante intends to persuade her daughter to marry the Count in order to end a litigation between the families.[5] Furthermore— and most of all—she wants the satisfaction of calling herself the mother of the Countess Dorimont. To attain this end she directs Dorante to advise Araminte that she will lose if she insists upon suing. Dorante points out the dishonesty of such a procedure, whereupon Mme. Argante highhandedly orders him to deceive Araminte.

When Araminte talks to Dorante about some business affairs, an immediate accord springs up between them. Dubois interrupts their conversation, ostensibly to deliver an urgent message to Araminte,

[5] In *Le Méchant* (1747), Gresset uses the same device when Géronte wants to conclude a marriage between Valère and Chloé to terminate a protracted lawsuit.

but in reality to make the first of his "fausses confidences." Dubois tells Araminte that the young man is afflicted with a severe mental disorder. He cleverly traces the cause of the derangement to an incurable passion for none other than Araminte herself. Surprised at first, she shows little glints of satisfaction as Dubois expatiates on Dorante's adoration for her. He reassures her that Dorante will never speak of his love: enough for him to worship her in silence. Thus, far from dismissing Dorante, Araminte determines to help him and brave the disfavor of her mother and the Count.

In the interval between acts Dorante has gone over the business papers, and he now reports to Araminte that her legal position in the litigation is excellent and that if her only motive for marrying the Count is to avoid losing the case, she can sue with assurance. M. Remy arrives to demand that Dorante resign at once in order to take advantage of a marriage offer from a wealthy widow. To M. Remy's consternation and Araminte's delight, Dorante refuses on the ground that his heart is irrevocably given elsewhere. Signs of "la surprise de l'amour" are visible in Araminte as she sighs: "Il me touche tant, qu'il faut que je m'en aille" (II, 2). Marton, too, is touched by what she believes to be a sign of his affection for her, while Dorante himself is chagrined at his predicament.

At this point a new twist to Dubois' machinations takes place: the episode of the portrait. He arranges for a messenger to bring a box containing a portrait that is to be delivered only to a young man whom he does not name. According to eighteenth-century conventions the possession of a portrait is tantamount to a declaration of love. The Count, assuming it to be a portrait that Araminte has given to some other man, is irked and seeks an explanation; but Marton jumps to the conclusion that Dorante has had her portrait made. Therefore, when Araminte and the Count come with Mme. Argante to settle the argument, Marton refuses to open the box, but under pressure she confesses that it is her portrait. Araminte cannot believe it, and she demands to see the box, which Marton proudly hands over. The Count opens it—and there is Araminte's portrait! Marton is crestfallen, but Araminte, like Silvia of *Le Jeu de l'amour et du hasard,* cannot suppress the exclamation: "Et moi, je vois clair" (II, 9). In her mortification Marton relates how M. Remy had misled her about Dorante's inclination.

When Araminte is left alone at last, Dorante comes to seek her protection from the persecution of Mme. Argante. She takes delight in probing his feelings toward her by declaring that she has resolved to marry the Count; she is pleased to see that Dorante is more than a little perturbed. Continuing in a vertiginous mood of provocation, she produces the mysterious portrait in the box. Dorante throws himself at her feet to beg forgiveness for his impertinence, but Araminte is not the least displeased: "Dorante, je ne me fâcherai point. Votre égarement me fait pitié; revenez-en, je vous le pardonne" (II, 15). Marton, at the behest of Dubois, steps into the doorway. The intrusion of a third person, a rival, takes the enchantment from this blissful moment, and Araminte is disgusted at the point to which her giddiness has brought her.

Dorante fears that all is lost, but Dubois has other "fausses confidences" to set things to rights; he is determined to finish the plot while Araminte is still bewildered by the unexpected turn of events, because "elle ne sait plus ce qu'elle fait" (III, 1). When Dorante complains that Araminte in her anger called him "insupportable," Dubois reasons: "Voulez-vous qu'elle soit de bonne humeur avec un homme qu'il faut qu'elle aime en dépit d'elle? Cela est-il agréable? Vous vous emparez de son bien, de son cœur, et cette femme ne criera pas!" (III, 1).

As a new device to ensnare Araminte, Dubois asks Dorante to write a certain letter that he contrives to have fall into the hands of Marton. Mme. Argante has sent for M. Remy, demanding that he remove his nephew from the household, and they engage in an amusing spat. During the quarrel Araminte enters. When she learns that

Mme. Argante has discharged Dorante and brought along a replacement, she calmly defies her mother and vows to retain Dorante.

In the presence of all Marton gives the letter to the Count to read. In it Dorante tells a friend that because of the hopelessness of his passion he wants to leave the country. Araminte is not too confused to be deeply touched by these new signs of his adoration, but she is irritated by the snide remarks of the others: "il y a dans tout ceci des façons si désagréables, des moyens si offensants, que tout m'en choque" (III, 8). Alone at last, she is approached by Dubois, who has come to play his trump card; he deliberately boasts of planting the letter solely to discredit Dorante. Araminte is furious at him for having subjected her and Dorante to the humiliating scene just ended.

Arlequin begs Araminte to grant Dorante one last interview. There follows what Marcel Arland[6] calls "le plus bel instant de ce théâtre." Dorante wants to turn over some papers, but soon their enkindled feelings turn the conversation to love:

> DORANTE [*plaintivement*]: De tout le temps de ma vie que je vais passer loin de vous, je n'aurais plus que ce seul jour qui m'en serait précieux.
>
> ARAMINTE: Il n'y a pas moyen, Dorante; il faut se quitter. On sait que vous m'aimez, et l'on croirait que je n'en suis pas fâchée.
>
> DORANTE: Hélas! Madame, que je vais être à plaindre!
>
> ARAMINTE: Ah! Allez, Dorante, chacun a ses chagrins.
>
> DORANTE: J'ai tout perdu! J'avais un portrait et je ne l'ai plus.
>
> ARAMINTE: A quoi vous sert de l'avoir? Vous savez peindre.
>
> DORANTE: Je ne pourrai de longtemps m'en dédommager; d'ailleurs, celui-ci m'aurait été bien cher! Il a été entre vos mains, Madame.
>
> ARAMINTE: Mais vous n'êtes pas raisonnable.

[6] *Le Théâtre complet de Marivaux* (Paris: La Nouvelle revue française, 1949), p. li.

DORANTE: Ah, Madame, je vais être éloigné de vous; vous serez assez vengée; n'ajoutez rien à ma douleur.

ARAMINTE: Vous donner mon portrait? Songez-vous que ce serait avouer que je vous aime?

DORANTE: Que vous m'aimez, Madame! Quelle idée, qui pourrait se l'imaginer?

ARAMINTE [*d'un ton vif et naïf*]: Et voilà pourtant ce qui m'arrive.

But Dorante's rapture is not complete: it is spoiled by the tricks and false secrets of Dubois; he confesses the whole plot to Araminte:

DORANTE: . . . cette joie qui me transporte, je ne la mérite pas, Madame; vous allez me l'ôter; mais n'importe, il faut que vous soyez instruite.

ARAMINTE [*étonnée*]: Comment! que voulez-vous dire?

DORANTE: Dans tout ce qui se passe chez vous, il n'y a rien de vrai que ma passion, qui est infinie, et que le portrait que j'ai fait. Tous les incidents qui sont arrivés partent de l'industrie d'un domestique qui savait mon amour. . . . il voulait me faire valoir auprès de vous. Voilà, Madame, ce que mon respect, mon amour et mon caractère ne me permettent pas de vous cacher. . . . J'aime mieux votre haine que le remords d'avoir trompé ce que j'adore.

ARAMINTE [*le regardant quelque temps sans parler*]: Si j'apprenais cela d'un autre que de vous, je vous haïrais sans doute; mais l'aveu que vous m'en faites vous-même, dans un moment comme celui-ci, change tout. Ce trait de sincérité me charme, . . . et vous êtes le plus honnête homme du monde. Après tout, puisque vous m'aimez véritablement, ce que vous avez fait pour gagner mon cœur n'est point blâmable. . . . (III, 12)

The Count and Mme. Argante enter. The Count understands that Araminte has given her heart to Dorante, but Mme. Argante is unrelenting; she rails: "Ah! la belle chute! Ah! maudit intendant! Qu'il soit votre mari tant qu'il vous plaira; mais il ne sera jamais mon gendre" (III, 13). Araminte, happy in her new love, is gentle toward her mother: "Laissons passer sa colère, et finissons." Dubois takes credit for the success of this dubious venture: "Ouf! ma gloire m'accable. Je mériterais bien d'appeler cette femme-là ma bru."[7]

Les Fausses confidences, distinctly original for its day, was without tangible sources and without influence in the theater, unless one can make the general observation that perhaps more than any other play by Marivaux it foreshadows the social drama of the nineteenth century. *Les Fausses confidences* is the least Italian of the plays Marivaux wrote for the Riccoboni troupe. It has little comedy; even Arlequin's brief appearances are lacking in his usual *lazzi,* and his role could be omitted altogether without weakening the play. Mme. Argante, with her aristocratic pretensions and her belligerent bickerings with Araminte and M. Remy, becomes the comic figure of the play. There is no parallel subplot for the servants, since the nature of the circumstances precludes this sort of appendage to the main action.

This is the first play in the French theater that ends by a marriage that cuts across social lines. It is true that by birth Araminte and Dorante spring from the same class. In the nineteenth century and later their marriage might have been frowned on by a few, but it would not have been considered a misalliance; by eighteenth-century standards, however, it was a violation of the social code, for Araminte's wealth placed her out of reach of Dorante. In 1737 the arguments of a Mme. Argante, ridiculous as they seem in the play, would have prevailed. That Marivaux contrived to bring about his denouement is a *tour de force* in the eighteenth-century theater.

Araminte is undoubtedly one of the most ingratiating characters created by Marivaux, one of the roles most prized by fine actresses. She is the Silvia of *Le Jeu de l'amour et du hasard* grown lovelier and

---

[7] Larroumet (*Marivaux: sa vie et ses œuvres* [Paris: Hachette, 1882], p. 227 n 1) says that Dubois' last line, too strong for the spectators of 1881, was suppressed. The play ended with Araminte's kindly remark about her mother.

less complicated after some seven or eight years of maturity.[8] Larroumet[9] places her in the highest rank of amiable women in the French theater, along with the Elmire and the Henriette of Molière. She is a dignified yet utterly delightful person, kindly disposed toward everyone, with no trace of rancor or spite, even toward those who despitefully use her. One aspect of Araminte's character is left obscure by Marivaux: the experience of her first marriage. We are never told whether it was a happy one or not. As René Lalou[10] has pointed out: "nous ignorons ce que son mariage avait représenté pour cette jeune veuve. Est-elle à demi naïve encore ou bien à demi avertie déjà quand elle accepte Dorante pour son intendant?" Knowing Mme. Argante's views, we can assume that her daughter's first marriage was one of convenience, and since her husband was a wealthy financier we can also assume that he was much older than Araminte. But from Araminte herself, never an expression either of grief or joy in connection with her first marriage. Apparently, the "surprise de l'amour" that Dorante awakens in her is her first taste of love, and it is all the more charming in that it comes to her when she is no longer a *jeune fille*. Marivaux has never portrayed this awakening with greater skill, with more exquisite beauty. That he should also subject her to the humiliation of Dubois' plot shows a vein of cruelty that will come to light again in *L'Epreuve*.

Dorante has all the gallant grace, all the appealing passion of other Marivaux heroes. As an impecunious young man whose love leads him to seek marriage into a wealthy family,[11] he creates much sympathy; and the sincerity of his affection only underscores his admirable traits. But he presents something of an enigma in that he allows his judgment and the course of his romance to be con-

---

[8] It is interesting to note that most actresses who have excelled as Silvia have later acted Araminte with equal success.

[9] *Op cit.*, p. 214.

[10] *Les Nouvelles littéraires, artistiques et scientifiques*, December 17, 1953.

[11] O. Feuillet copied Dorante for the hero (Maxime) of *Le Roman d'un jeune homme pauvre* (1858).

trolled by Dubois; it is hard to pardon him, as Araminte did so generously, for yielding to Dubois' insidious advice at every step.

One cannot discuss Dorante without considering Dubois, too, for the latter is the mainspring of the action. As a personality, Dubois is a transition figure between Scapin and Figaro. He is closer to Figaro than to Scapin, for his tricks have less of the buffoonery of Scapin and more of the calculating reason of Figaro. He is another of Marivaux's creations that served as a prototype for Beaumarchais' immortal figure. In 1737 Dubois did not possess the revolutionary bitterness of his famous descendant, but in all other respects the valet who knew no moral restraint in his plotting embodies the roguish chicanery of Figaro.[12]

In fact, the ethics of *Les Fausses confidences* have been subject to much criticism. Is Dubois justified in subjecting his benefactress to so much cruelty and humiliation? Is Dorante worthy of winning Araminte's love if he resorts to deceitful tricks? Dubois looks upon his artifices with urbane self-righteousness, and he even believes Araminte has acted in bad faith when she chooses—as is certainly her right in such an intimate matter—to conceal her feelings about Dorante from him. But Dubois is offended by her secrecy ("Ne voyez-vous pas bien qu'elle triche avec moi?"), and he does not hesitate to use unfair tactics to punish her ("Ah! je lui apprendrai à me souffler mon emploi de confident pour vous aimer en fraude"). His rampant mendacity has little justification. Dorante, too, for all his gallant sincerity, is not a suitor of unalloyed candor. To be sure, he loves Araminte deeply, he is an unwilling or hesitant partner in Dubois' tricks, and in the end he does not accept her love until he has humbly confessed his part in the plot; but still he does not restrain Dubois from carrying out his deceptions. From Araminte's point of view—and therefore from Marivaux's and that of the eighteenth century in general—Dorante is not guilty: "il est permis

[12] For other manifestations of the Figaro character in Marivaux plays, see pp. 46–47, 67–68, 81–82, 85, 246.

à un amant de chercher les moyens de plaire, et on doit lui pardonner lorsqu'il a réussi" (III, 12).

But if the eighteenth century was indulgent toward Dubois' trickery and Dorante's part therein, the nineteenth and twentieth centuries have been less so. Edouard Thierry[13] condemns the point of view that condones an impudent intriguer's mistreatment of such an honorable woman as Araminte. And when Dubois cries: "point de quartier. Il faut l'achever pendant qu'elle est étourdie," Thierry rebels. He says: "Quelle que soit mon admiration pour Marivaux, j'avoue que celui-là me gâte toute la pièce." Pierre Lièvre[14] flays Marivaux unmercifully. In speaking of Les Fausses confidences he says: "C'est peut-être celui des ouvrages de l'auteur où la laideur morale s'étale le plus largement et avec le plus d'inconscience. . . . Marivaux représente des actions méchantes et même perverses sans paraître remarquer qu'elles le sont." Lièvre believes that these traits are camouflaged by an exquisite style, and "c'est là le miracle du marivaudage, mais aussi l'énigme de Marivaux."

In all these arguments no one has given any attention to Marton, who was as much wronged as Araminte, although the stakes were not so high in her case. She is perhaps only an injured bystander, but to herself her wounds are as sore as those of her mistress; her heart is twisted and her pride is hurt, perhaps more deeply than Araminte's. At least in the end Araminte's love is fulfilled, whereas Marton is left disenchanted, with no hope of marriage in sight.

These moral problems, however, have not spoiled the enjoyment of the play for the average spectator, and Les Fausses confidences has fared well on the stage. It was the first of Marivaux's Italian comedies to be officially inscribed in the records of the Comédie Française.[15] The play was given at the Théâtre de la Nation, June 15, 1793, and

13 La Revue de France, March 15, 1881.
14 Le Mercure de France, Nouvelle Série, May 1, 1937.
15 Since June 15, 1793, nine comedies from Marivaux's Italian repertory have been revived at the Théâtre Français.

won exceptionally fine notices in the midst of the Revolution.[16] *Le Moniteur universel,*[17] probably sated with the clumsy doctrinaire plays of the day, found the wit of *Les Fausses confidences* refreshing: "mais cet esprit, tout fin qu'il est, ne va point jusqu'au faux esprit dans lequel se sont jettés depuis les auteurs dramatiques qui ont travaillé dans ce genre. Marivaux a peint des nuances délicates, mais des nuances vraies." As for the actors, "Cette pièce est jouée avec un ensemble et une perfection qui ne laisse rien à désirer." *Le Journal de Paris*[18] likewise gave extravagant praise to the play and added that "le Public . . . s'y est porté en foule. . . . L'enthousiasme excité par le jeu des Citoyennes Contat et Joly & des Citoyens Fleury et Dazincourt a été porté à son comble." Arlequin was renamed Lubin when the play was transferred to the Comédie Française.

Although Etienne and Martainville,[19] writing some years later, said: "nous aimerions mieux admirer le Talent de Mademoiselle Contat, de Fleury, de Dazincourt dans les chefs-d'œuvre des pères du Théâtre Français," they admitted with respect to *Les Fausses confidences:* "Il n'est peut-être aucune pièce qui soit encore aujourd'hui mieux jouée que celle-là."

Geoffroy,[20] with characteristic hostility toward Marivaux, viewed this play with disfavor: "Il y a peu d'ouvrages de théâtre dont le fonds soit plus extravagant et plus romanesque que celui des *Fausses Confidences.* . . . Il n'y a point d'exemple d'un caprice aussi brusque." He was even less kind to Mlle. Contat as Araminte: "elle se fait applaudir, lors même elle n'est pas dans le sens du rôle. . . . Il

---

[16] Previously, Talma had revived *Les Fausses confidences* at the Théâtre de la République, July 24, 1791, and it may have been a successful production, for it was given with great frequency. On the other hand, it is possible that the staging left something to be desired, for when the Comédie Française performance was reviewed by *Le Journal de Paris* (July 22, 1793) the critic said: "Le Public a vu réellement pour la première fois une bonne représentation de cet ouvrage."

[17] June 25, 1793.

[18] July 22, 1793.

[19] *Histoire du Théâtre Français* (Paris: Barba, 1802), III, 85–86.

[20] *Le Journal des débats,* 13 floréal, an 10 (May 1799).

faut jouer Araminte en femme qu'on subjugue, et Mlle Contat joue souvent en conquérante." Geoffroy also deplored the influence of Marivaux on young writers: "Ce genre précieux, maniéré, romanesque, est celui qu'on cultive aujourd'hui de préférence, et nous avons une foule de petits Marivaux très habiles dans l'art d'imiter les défauts de leur modèle." That Geoffroy and his contemporaries had little appreciation of Marivaux's qualities is evident throughout the dramatic criticism of Napoleonic days. Geoffroy's unfriendliness seems to have abated a few years later, for in 1808 he said: "Je regarde *Les Fausses confidences* comme le chef-d'œuvre de Marivaux."[21] He had a sort of predilection for this play because in his youth it was the first theatrical production he ever saw.

Throughout the nineteenth century critics who reviewed *Les Fausses confidences* rarely mentioned the play itself; rather, they focused their attention on the actress playing Araminte. Mlle. Mars so dominated the role for thirty-five years that it was foolhardy for another actress to undertake the part, and Pierre Duviquet,[22] who succeeded Geoffroy on *Le Journal des débats,* felt that the comedy should be withdrawn if she ever left the theater. A few years later, when Jules Janin took over Duviquet's post on the same paper, he carried on the tradition of idolizing Mlle. Mars. For him any other actress who played Silvia or Araminte merely evoked the memory of the great comedienne: "Nous aimons Marivaux parce que les beaux rôles de Silvia et d'Araminte ont été ressuscités par Mlle Mars, et parce que, même absente, on la retrouve en ces mièvreries. . . . Si vous voulez revoir Mlle. Mars, vous qui l'avez vue, allez voir jouer par une autre comédienne *les Fausses confidences* ou *le Jeu de l'amour et du hasard.* Aussitôt l'ombre évoquée arrive à vos regards charmés: soudain vous retrouverez la magicienne."[23] When Mme.

21 *Cours de littérature dramatique* (Paris, 1825), III, 221.
22 *Œuvres complètes de Marivaux* (Paris, 1830), V, 177.
23 F. Sarcey, *Quarante ans de théâtre* (Paris: Bibliothèque des annales, 1900–2), II, 300.

Allan wanted to revive *Les Fausses confidences* in 1848, there were cries of sacrilege. Théophile Gautier[24] protested this "culte de souvenirs," and asked: "Chaque acteur célèbre, en rentrant dans l'ombre de la retraite ou de la mort, doit-il emporter avec lui les pièces du répertoire où il a brillé? A ce compte, on finirait par ne plus avoir de répertoire du tout." Not touching on the substance of the play, Gautier made his review a disquisition on the way great actresses, both tragic and comic, distort the author's conception of a particular role. According to Sarcey,[25] Mme. Arnould-Plessy acted Araminte in the tradition of Mlle. Mars, "mais l'Araminte que nous présente Mme Brohan n'est pas cette personne hautaine et impatiente." Sarcey himself preferred the Arnould-Plessy interpretation.

Although the fortunes of *Les Fausses confidences* were at a rather low ebb toward the end of the nineteenth century, the play has shown enduring vigor in the twentieth century. Critics, while not unmindful of the actors and the quality of their performances, are interested primarily in the play itself and its author. In the first decade, when the status of *Les Fausses confidences* was still uncertain, Adolphe Brisson[26] analyzed the play and labeled it only "un demi chef-d'œuvre." After witnessing a superb performance he wrote: "Une sorte de vague tristesse enveloppe la pièce, pèse sur l'auditoire," and he predicted: "la pièce, après une dizaine de représentations disparaîtra. Elle ne communique pas à la foule une joie pure." It is gratifying to report that Brisson misjudged the public, for since his day *Les Fausses confidences* has had a spectacular career, and his low evaluation of the play soon gave way to a more enthusiastic attitude.

During the First World War, when the Germans were close to Paris, the proximity of the enemy seemed to give critics[27] an even

---

[24] *Histoire de l'art dramatique en France depuis vingt-cinq ans* (Paris: Magnin, Blanchard et Cie, 1858–59), V, 235.

[25] *Op. cit.*, II, 305.

[26] *Le Temps*, October 11, 1909.

[27] The following quotations are from clippings in the *Dossier sur Marivaux*, Rf 11829, at the Bibliothèque de l'Arsenal.

keener appreciation of Marivaux.[28] "La Comédie-Française vient de reprendre avec éclat (c'est le mot, car au cours de la matinée on entendit plusieurs fois le canon à longue portée) *Les Fausses confidences* de Marivaux" (Guillot de Saxe); "goûter ce miracle de délicatesse psychologique, de finesse, de mesure, tandis que retentissait à la cantonade la voix brutale des modernes barbares, ce fut une volupté de l'espèce la plus rare et un réconfort souverain" (Gustave Fréjaville). The danger of bombardment did not prevent the critics from savoring the beauties of the text: "Marivaux sut mettre à propos les principales situations avec une rare adresse et dans ce style fameux que certains jugent contourné et trop écrit. . . . ce que nous appelons marivaudage était le naturel de son temps" (Guillot de Saxe); "L'immoralité ne choque pas Marivaux: à peine en a-t-il notion. . . . A la représentation le public ne s'en aperçoit guère, parce que le dialogue est à cent lieues d'être violent et brutal" (Paul Souday); "Et tout cela est d'une originalité, d'une nouveauté qui nous étonnent encore aujourd'hui" (Louis Schneider).

When the Comédie Française revived several of Marivaux's comedies[29] in 1926, *Les Fausses confidences* was included in the list. Lucien Dubech thought the company especially adept at interpreting Marivaux. In the course of reviewing several plays he compared *Le Jeu de l'amour et du hasard* with *Les Fausses confidences.* His considered judgment led him to bestow higher praise on *Les Fausses confidences:*[30] "*Le Jeu de l'amour et du hasard* contient donc le rôle le plus profond qu'ait tracé Marivaux, et cependant la pièce, en son ensemble, est moins bien venue, moins d'une coulée et moins parfaite que *Les Fausses confidences.* Ici, plus rien qui ne soit d'une perfection soutenue."

But Marivaux has not always been without detractors. Periodically

[28] It is curious to note that during the German occupation of Paris in the Second World War Marivaux's plays were exceptionally popular at the Théâtre Français.

[29] See pp. 137, 193.

[30] *Candide,* August 19, 1926.

some critic disturbs the current of generally laudatory comment. One such was Pierre Lièvre,[31] who uttered stinging tirades against *Les Fausses confidences* in 1937. He was equally venomous in the same review toward Marivaux himself, attributing to him "une sorte de dureté de cœur, ou tout au moins un manque de délicatesse. . . . Qu'était-il donc, cet écrivain singulier, qui savait placer tant de séductions auprès du mal qu'il ne désavouait point? N'était-ce pas simplement un homme un peu bête, un peu épais . . . ?" As if to answer Lièvre, —although there is no connection between the two critics—Gabriel Marcel[32] characterized Marivaux in 1946 in precisely opposite terms, once again apropos of the same play: "Il serait en vérité inconcevable que l'homme qui a écrit *Les Fausses confidences* n'ait pas été doué d'une bonté qui relève de la grâce bien plus qu'elle n'est une vertu."

At the time, Marcel was writing about the radiant production of *Les Fausses confidences* given in November 1946 by Jean-Louis Barrault's newly organized company, with Madeleine Renaud as Araminte. "*Les Fausses confidences,* à Marigny, sont un délice pour les yeux autant que pour l'esprit. Je songe à la fois au décor . . . et aux costumes dont chacun correspond à une nuance de la pensée. . . . La pièce est ravissante." As many critics have mentioned before, Marivaux's writing often evokes the imagery of music: "La musique seule, je pense, nous propose ici des points de comparaison, et je songe bien entendu à Mozart plus qu'à tout autre." Strangely, in place of the lack of rapport between actor and audience that Brisson deplored in 1908 ("Elle ne communique pas à la foule une joie pure"), Marcel found the exact opposite: "L'attendrissement ne dépasse pas ici le diapason du soupire, de l'exclamation aussitôt réprimée, et voilà pourquoi il se communique au spectateur."

In addition to enjoying sustained popularity in Paris—Barrault reports—*Les Fausses confidences* has been the company's "calling

---

[31] *Le Mercure de France,* Nouvelle Série, May 1, 1937.
[32] *Les Nouvelles littéraires, artistiques et scientifiques,* November 7, 1946.

card" on tour; the play also met signal success in South America (May–June 1950), in London (October–November 1951), in Italy (March 1952), and in Canada and the United States (November–December 1952).

Language barriers notwithstanding, Marivaux, as performed by the Renaud-Barrault troupe, elicited unqualified praise from New York critics. Brooks Atkinson[33] said: "the performance of *Les Fausses confidences* is a thorough delight, and unlike anything we have here except ballet." William Hawkins[34] found that "in the art of this company, the specific words and the details of complications make not the slightest difference. The players are so explicit, and so uncompromisingly honest, that any child could appreciate each situation. . . . Renaud is a breathtaking central figure. . . . Her quiet subtle elegance imbues the piece with rare quality." Walter Kerr[35] summarized his eulogies thus: "The company is uniformly impeccable, the sheen on the production endlessly glittering."

Robert Kemp,[36] inveterate theatergoer and learned critic of Marivaux's plays, reviewed a presentation of *Les Fausses confidences,* "pièce enchanteresse, et qui se passe de louanges," in which Eliane Bertrand made her debut as Araminte. Having attended many performances of the play in his lifetime, he recalled the luminous sets he had seen in other productions and found fault with the dull *décor* the Théâtre Français provided for this occasion. "Soyez ingénieux, ou précieux, ou ridicules, là-dessus, tant que vous voudrez. Je vous défie de trouver que le théâtre de Marivaux soit café au lait."

So much laudatory criticism has been written about *Les Fausses confidences* that one is tempted to ask: Is not this rather than *Le Jeu de l'amour et du hasard* Marivaux's masterpiece? It is the repetition of an old question in literary history: Is *Phèdre* greater than *Athalie?*

[33] *The New York Times,* November 13, 1952.
[34] *New York World Telegram,* November 13, 1952.
[35] *New York Herald Tribune,* November 13, 1952.
[36] *Le Monde,* December 11, 1953.

Polyeucte than *Le Cid? Le Misanthrope* than *Tartuffe?* There is no single answer to these questions. Each era brings forth new actors and new critics who put new values on a particular play. Sarcey[37] explains these ever-changing estimates by a metaphor: "les chefs-d'œuvre sont des urnes ciselées où chaque génération verse son esprit. Le vase est toujours le même, mais la liqueur change." Most of Marivaux's plays, like those of Racine, Corneille, and Molière, have so many sterling qualities that the appraisal of one play as superior to another must be accounted a mere reflection of individual taste. Geoffroy and Dubech prefer *Les Fausses confidences;* Larroumet and Marcel, *Le Jeu de l'amour et du hasard;* La Harpe, *Arlequin poli par l'amour;* Gautier, *La Surprise de l'amour;* and others, *La Double inconstance.* Suffice it to say that *Les Fausses confidences* emerges as one of the very fine plays of the classical theater in France.

[37] *Op. cit.,* II, 302.

27 La Joie imprévue

[One act in prose. First presented at the Théâtre Italien, July 7, 1738.]

WHEN the Théâtre Italien decided to restage *Les Fausses confidences,* Marivaux prepared a curtain raiser to fill the bill, just as Molière had been obliged to do when he wanted to produce *Le Misanthrope.* The curtain raiser Molière created was a minor masterpiece, *Le Médecin malgré lui;* the one Marivaux wrote was one of his weakest comedies, *La Joie imprévue.*

Two weeks before the action begins, M. Orgon sent his son Damon to Paris with his valet Pasquin to buy a position[1] and establish himself in the capital. At the hotel where he lives, Damon met the Chevalier, who took the young man to a neighboring dance hall and gambling resort. There the Chevalier won half the money Damon's father had entrusted to him. Damon has also met the charming Constance, chaperoned by her *suivante* Lisette, in a near-by garden, and they have fallen in love. But there is a cloud on the horizon: Constance is promised to another.

When the play begins Damon is on his way to his banker to draw the remaining half of his money, which he intends to gamble against the Chevalier in the hope of recouping all he has lost. The young man is now intent on buying a good office and marrying Constance. As Pasquin watches his master leave for the bank, M.

[1] In the eighteenth century public offices were sold by the government to provide a source of revenue.

Orgon enters from the other direction: he has followed his son to Paris and knows of his escapade and financial plight. He reveals to Pasquin that Constance is the girl he has chosen for his son to marry—Mme. Dorville, Constance's mother, has agreed to the match —but first he wants to teach his son a lesson. Bidding Pasquin prevent the Chevalier from arriving on time, M. Orgon plans to wear a yellow domino like the Chevalier and gamble with his son.

A little later the gambling takes place and Damon loses all his money. Upon leaving the gambling hall conscience-stricken, Damon sees the Chevalier, and he demands the identity of the stranger. Without unmasking, the man appeals to Damon to abandon gambling:

MONSIEUR ORGON: . . . vous me paraissez un jeune homme plein d'honneur, n'altérez point votre caractère par une aussi dangereuse habitude que l'est celle du jeu, et craignez d'affliger un père, à qui je sais que vous êtes cher.

DAMON: Vous m'arrachez des larmes, en me parlant de lui; mais je veux savoir avec qui j'ai joué. Etes-vous digne du discours que vous me tenez?

MONSIEUR ORGON [se démasquant]: Jugez-en vous-même.

DAMON [se jetant à ses genoux]: Ah! Mon père, je vous demande pardon. (Sc. 21)

M. Orgon forgives his son and punishes him only with new signs of paternal tenderness rather than angry reproaches. Damon cries out in repentance:

Eh bien! mon père, laissez-moi encore vous jurer à genoux que je suis pénétré de vos bontés, que vos moindres volontés me seront desormais sacrées; que ma soumission durera autant que ma vie, et que je ne vois point de bonheur égal à celui d'avoir un père qui vous ressemble. (Sc. 21)

Mme. Dorville and Constance arrive. When it turns out that the young man to whom Constance is promised is none other than Damon, "une joie imprévue" reigns. A divertissement ends the play.

La Joie imprévue shows Marivaux at his most commonplace. Once again he has written a play in which the young man is the central figure, as he had done in *Le Petit-maître corrigé*,[2] and with similar mediocre results. It is not that the play has any weakness in style or dramatic content; rather, it lacks the spark to lift it out of the prosaic. Constance is a most ordinary *jeune fille*, and without a spirited heroine Marivaux is not at his best. Constance appears only briefly, and her one scene with Damon contains little talk of love. The courtship between Pasquin and Lisette is much more lively than the romance of Damon and Constance.

The one detail of distinction in an otherwise colorless play is the scene (Sc. 21) in which Damon throws himself on his father's mercy. M. Orgon's magnanimous understanding of his son's folly and Damon's spontaneous gratitude, both depicted with simple sincerity, create a family tableau worthy of the *drame*. The play as a whole could never be classified as a *drame*, but as in several other of Marivaux's works one can find elements of the *drame* developed to various degrees.[3]

Admirable fathers have appeared so frequently in Marivaux's comedies up to this point[4] that this M. Orgon, exemplary as he is, adds little to the composite picture built up along the way. To be sure, he comes to grips with his son in a situation a little more serious than other fathers have been placed in, but one senses that the M. Orgon of *Le Jeu de l'amour et du hasard* or the M. Damis of *L'Ecole des mères* would have been equally generous with their sons in the same circumstances. On the other hand, Mme. Dorville follows the pattern of other uncongenial mothers in Marivaux's comedies; she opposes her daughter's inclination until she realizes that the young man in question happens to be the son of her old friend.

[2] See Chapter 23.
[3] For further discussion of this subject, see *La Mère confidente*, pp. 188–90, 250, 260.
[4] See *Le Jeu de l'amour et du hasard*, Chapter 16; *Les Serments indiscrets*, Chapter 19; *L'Ecole des mères*, Chapter 20.

The gambling theme is not highlighted, and Marivaux offers no moralizing on the evils of the game. It is merely treated as one of the vices of the day. Unlike Valère in *Le Joueur* by Regnard (1696), who sacrifices the love of his fiancée, his money, and the respect of his father to his mania, Damon repents of his error, wins the girl he loves, and gains his father's respect.

The exact number of performances of *La Joie imprévue* is not known, for the records of the Théâtre Italien at this time are fragmentary. However, it does not seem to have been one of Marivaux's more popular plays. Strangely, the notice in the *Mercure de France*[5] announcing the play is devoted almost entirely to extolling the brilliant revival of *Les Fausses confidences*. Furthermore, Riccoboni wrote an exceptionally fine *divertissement* for *La Joie imprévue,* and Marivaux's share in the program seems to have gone unnoticed.

[5] July 1738, p. 1620.

28 Les Sincères

[One act in prose. First presented at the Théâtre Italien, January 13, 1739.]

A mixed foursome, another *chassé-croisé* with a pair of crafty servants, provided Marivaux with the characters for his next comedy, *Les Sincères*. Written with consummate skill, *Les Sincères* is so vastly amusing that Sainte-Beuve[1] said of it: "Cette petite comédie des *Sincères* est une des plus agréables à lire de Marivaux."

The Marquise, who boasts of her inflexible sincerity, is about to cast aside the faithful Dorante because she has become infatuated with Ergaste, another *sincère*. Ergaste believes he has found his soul mate in the Marquise, and therefore is on the verge of jilting Araminte. All might have gone well had not this shift in affections been contrary to the inclination of Lisette, the *suivante* of the Marquise, and Frontin, the valet of Ergaste. These two servants had previously been pledged to their corresponding numbers under Dorante and Araminte, but now that their masters have changed partners it is incumbent upon the servants to follow suit. This, Frontin and Lisette are unwilling to do, and they reassure each other that their hearts are engaged elsewhere:

> LISETTE: Monsieur le fat, j'ai votre affaire. Dubois, que Monsieur Dorante a laissé à Paris, et auprès de qui vous n'êtes qu'un magot, a toute mon inclination; prenez seulement garde à vous.

[1] *Causeries du lundi* (Paris, Garnier, s.a.), IX, 372.

FRONTIN: Marton, l'incomparable Marton, qu'Araminte n'a pas amenée avec elle, et devant qui toute soubrette est plus ou moins guenon, est la souveraine de mon cœur. (Sc. 1)

Whereupon they join forces to thwart the plans of their masters.

As long as the Marquise and Ergaste apply their sincerity to their friends (the Marquise does a series of portraits reminiscent of Célimène's in *Le Misanthrope*, II, 4), they seem compatible enough; but when Frontin pointedly asks Ergaste, in the presence of Araminte and Dorante, whether he considers the Marquise the most beautiful woman in the world, the trouble starts. Ergaste replies: "Non, qu'est-ce que cette mauvaise plaisanterie-là, butor? La Marquise est aimable et non pas belle" (Sc. 8), and he even goes on to explain how much more beautiful Araminte is.

The remark reaches the Marquise. Her vanity not permitting her to believe the gossip, she questions Ergaste herself:

LA MARQUISE: . . . à qui de nous deux, amour à part, donneriez-vous la préférence? ne me trompez point.

ERGASTE: Oh! jamais, et voici ce que j'en pense: Araminte a de la beauté; on peut dire que c'est une belle femme.

LA MARQUISE: Fort bien. Et quant à moi, à cet égard-là, je n'ai qu'à me cacher, n'est-ce pas?

ERGASTE: Pour vous, Marquise, vous plaisez plus qu'elle. (Sc. 12)

The Marquise is piqued, and when Ergaste continues to tell her frankly what her faults are, she in turn reveals what defects she finds in him—all in elegant *précieux* verbiage. By the time they have finished, their friendship is ruined, and they are happy to return to their original partners. A notary is summoned to draw up the marriage contracts. The Marquise laughs off the whole episode: "Ah! ah! ah! nous avons pris un plaisant détour pour arriver là"[2] (Sc. 21). And

---

2 Sainte-Beuve said of this remark: "Ce mot pourrait servir d'épigraphe à toutes les pièces de Marivaux." *Ibid.*, IX, 373.

Frontin can exclaim joyfully to Lisette: "Enfin nous voilà délivrés l'un de l'autre" (Sc. 21).

Various critics have indicated three possible sources for details of *Les Sincères:* a scenario by Riccoboni himself, *Les Sincères à contretemps,* was enacted at late as 1727 and may have stuck in the back of Marivaux's mind; the scene of the verbal portraits probably came from *Le Misanthrope,* although Marivaux would probably not have admitted it; and the character of Ergaste is undoubtedly the enlargement of a sketch Marivaux drew in his journal, *L'Indigent philosophe* (1728). But the source for most of it—for the best of it—is to be found in Marivaux's inventiveness. No one else could have supplied the endless flow of crisp dialogue and sparkling wit that gives the play its merit. Scene 1 between Lisette and Frontin, in which they reverse the usual amorous subplot between servants and conspire to take the marital fortunes of their masters into their own hands (Lisette: Grâce au ciel, nous voici en état de nous entendre pour rompre l'union de nos maîtres; Frontin: Oui, ma fille: rompons, brisons, détruisons; c'est à quoi j'aspirais) is one of the most novel in all of Marivaux's theater.

This hilarious tidbit has few of Marivaux's characteristics except a scintillating wit. There is no love in the play (just *amour-propre*), no searching analysis, no thoughts of social or philosophical import. Like *Le Legs,* it has no action whatsoever, and eighteenth-century critics took Marivaux to task on this point. But the situation in *Le Legs* is based on human relationships, whereas *Les Sincères* is a conceit that must rely on pure cleverness to make its point. *Le Legs* has much greater appeal for the public in general and has surpassed *Les Sincères* in the number of performances. It should be added that *Les Sincères,* like *Le Legs,* is a gambol for finished actors to perform.

The exact fate of *Les Sincères* in its *nouveauté* is obscure, for the records of the Théâtre Italien are missing for this period. The play was favorably received at its première when the author was not named, but it was hooted at the second performance. How often it was given thereafter is not known, but it seems to have been rather popular for some years.

Eighteenth-century critics stressed the overabundance of wit in *Les Sincères* and the lack of action. The *Mercure*[3] said: "Cette pièce a été applaudie à la première représentation, et ne l'auroit pas moins été dans les suivantes, s'il ne falloit que de l'esprit pour faire une Comédie; . . . rien ne lui a fait plus de tort que le manque d'action." Reviewing the printed edition of the play, *La Bibliothèque française*[4] derided Marivaux because "elle n'a presque rien de théâtrale. C'est plutôt un ingénieux Dialogue, qu'une Comédie. Dans une Comédie il faut une action, il faut une intrigue, un nœud & un dénoûment. M. de Marivaux a crû pouvoir négliger de s'asservir de cette règle." Writing in 1769, Desboulmiers[5] complained that "Cet auteur abusait quelquefois de son esprit," but praised the originality of the servants: "Ce qu'il y a de singulier, c'est que ni le Valet, ni la Suivante n'ont aucun intérêt à la brouillerie, & qu'au lieu que dans la plupart des autres, Comédies, les Domestiques veulent marier leur maîtres pour être plus portés à se marier eux-mêmes, ceux-ci commencent par s'assurer entre eux d'une indifférence récipoque."

For some hundred and fifty years after its eighteenth-century run *Les Sincères* disappeared from the stage, but it has had three revivals in modern times: one in 1891 at the Odéon, one in 1931 by Xavier de Courville's Petite Scène, and one in 1950 by the Comédie Française.

A revival of *Les Sincères* at the Odéon on April 26, 1891, ran for thirty-one performances that season, which would indicate that it was a presentation of high order. It was used as a curtain raiser for the première of *Amoureuse* by Porto-Riche, whose play created such a sensation that critics overlooked *Les Sincères*. Even Jules Lemaître, whose dramatic columns had long advocated the revival

---

3 February 1739, pp. 343–51.
4 Vol. XXIX, p. 160 (1739).
5 *Histoire anecdotique et raisonnée du Théâtre Italien depuis son rétablissement en France jusqu'à l'année 1769* (Paris: Lacombe, 1769), IV, 386–94.

of more of Marivaux's comedies, did not mention this one in *Le Journal des débats.*

Xavier de Courville gave *Les Sincères* an impeccable production when his troupe presented it, March 2, 1931. Gérard d'Houville[6] called it "un des plus jolis spectacles de la Petite Scène"; the originality of the staging struck his fancy: "Au lieu d'un salon de rigueur . . . les personnages des *Sincères* évoluent autour d'un beau vieux puits. . . . ils se penchent au-dessus de l'eau noire où, nous l'a-t-on appris, se cache la Vérité. Aimable idée, ironique symbole qui donne à ce petit acte toute sa valeur poétique et sa saveur de raillerie si juste, si divertissante, et si familièrement humaine." Paul Chauveau,[7] while delighted with de Courville's staging, had reservations about Marivaux's play: "C'est une de celles où sa manière s'affirme avec une maîtrise qui va parfois jusqu'à ce point où elles commencent à devenir des travers."

Les Sincères was finally given at the Théâtre Français,[8] September 12, 1950—the latest of Marivaux's plays to be produced in the Salle Richelieu—as a vehicle for Mme. Véra Korène, who won unanimous plaudits for her performance as the Marquise. Renée Saurel[9] reports that "*Les Sincères* ont été chaleureusement accueillis mardi soir comme ils le furent à leur création," and was entranced by the language of Marivaux: "Ce qu'on est convenu de nommer 'marivaudage' brille ici de mille feux. . . . *Les Sincères* s'expriment en une langue admirable et l'on prend à les entendre un plaisir délicat. Mais terriblement superficiel . . ." Robert Kemp[10] considers Marivaux's play "une suite du *Misanthrope*," with the Marquise a Célimène grown a few years older and Ergaste a second Alceste. However, he

---

[6] *Le Figaro,* March 6, 1931.

[7] *Les Nouvelles littéraires, artistiques et scientifiques,* March 21, 1931.

[8] Mlle. Mars had tried in vain to have the Comédie Française adopt *Les Sincères* so that she could take the role of the Marquise.

[9] *Combat,* September 15, 1950.

[10] *Le Monde,* September 15, 1950.

agrees that "C'est un acte que seul Marivaux pouvait écrire, mais où il n'y a pas un de ses soupirs charmants. Oh! la fine curiosité littéraire. . . . un parfait régal pour les amateurs." J. B. Jeener[11] takes the opportunity to gibe at Marivaux's style: "jamais, sans doute, Marivaux ne nous offrit en si peu de mots tant de conversations et d'imparfaits du subjonctif," but after witnessing Mme. Korène in the portrait scene, he feels recompensed: "L'affaire en valait la peine pour une scène comme celle-ci." René Lalou[12] cannot resist succumbing to the charm of the play: "bien sûr, en fanatique de Marivaux, je me suis senti délicieusement chatouillé par la virtuosité de ce texte qu'il écrivit, dirait-on, pour aller jusqu'à l'extrême d'une de ses tendances." But then an afterthought occurs to him and he asks: "comment ne pas s'avouer qu'un tel tissu arachnéen de tirades et de reparties conduirait, s'il était pris pour modèle, à la totale négation de l'art du théâtre?"

And therein lies the crucial point about *Les Sincères*. Perhaps the style is no more than an exercise in fine language; perhaps the characters are no more than fragile figurines. Is it not part of Marivaux's genius that he can go to the extreme and still stay within bounds? No other writer of his day was so nimble in the use of glib repartee, all the while keeping his equilibrium with nonchalant assurance. Compared to plays with the solid values of *La Surprise de l'amour, La Mère confidente, L'Ile des esclaves,* and *Les Fausses confidences, Les Sincères* is sheer escapist entertainment, without depth in characterization or poetic tenderness in the style. It is the *non plus ultra* of refined eighteenth-century chitchat, which Voltaire again may have had in mind when he said: "Marivaux s'amuse à peser des œufs de mouche dans les balances de toiles d'araignée."

Labiche used the basic premise of *Les Sincères* in *Le Misanthrope et l'Auvergnat* (1853). The characters, however, are entirely dif-

---

11 *Le Figaro*, September 14, 1950.
12 *Les Nouvelles littéraires, artistiques et scientifiques*, September 28, 1950.

ferent, Labiche using a water carrier and a Parisian bourgeois instead of aristocrats. According to Larroumet,[13] Labiche's play is superior in that it is as amusing and entertaining as Marivaux's is cold and lagging in action.

[13] *Marivaux: sa vie et ses œuvres* (Paris, 1882), p. 182.

29   L'Epreuve

[One act in prose. First presented at the Théâtre Italien, November 19, 1740.]

THE last play Marivaux wrote for the Théâtre Italien, *L'Epreuve,* is one of the most beloved in his whole theater, one into which he poured the essence of his genius. With nothing of the superficial gloss of *Les Sincères,* which preceded it, *L'Epreuve,* in its poetic evocation of young lovers' feelings, its tender probing of their fears and desires, and, by way of contrast, the deft comedy of the servants, is a work of superb artistry.

With its felicitous role for Silvia,[1] *L'Epreuve* was a fitting climax to Marivaux's career as purveyor to the Italian actors. Yet, strangely, the play shows no trace of the old Italian influences. In the twenty years since Marivaux submitted *Arlequin poli par l'amour* to Riccoboni, he drew less and less on the *commedia dell'arte,* and his writing evolved to such a point that none of his last eight plays, except *Les Fausses confidences,* contain even a minor part for Arlequin.

From the beginning *L'Epreuve* endeared itself to the public, and each generation since has shown a fondness for it that betokens its

[1] In the printed edition the heroine's name is Angélique, but the *Mercure* (December 1740, pp. 2926–29) calls her Marianne. It is likely that in many of the performances the Italian troupe used Silvia as if the role and the actress were inseparable. In 1749 Mme. Favart, later the star of the Opéra Comique, made her debut in the role of Angélique at the Théâtre Italien.

merits. Immensely popular at its première,[2] and played throughout the eighteenth century, it became on July 20, 1793, the second play of the Italian repertory to be adopted by the Théâtre Français, where it has never ceased to be in the active repertory. It ranks next to *Le Jeu de l'amour et du hasard* and *Le Legs* in the number of performances given it by the Comédie Française, and it is also played with great regularity at the Odéon.

Lucidor, a wealthy young bourgeois, fell ill while visiting an estate he had just bought, and he was nursed back to health by the *concierge,* Mme. Argante, and her daughter Angélique. Mme. Argante comes of a bourgeois family also, but financial reverses have forced her to accept a position on the estate. During his convalescence Lucidor has fallen in love with Angélique. Now that he is well enough to return to Paris he wants to declare himself, but he fears that Angélique might marry him for his money. In order to be sure that she loves him for himself alone, he wishes to test her:[3] hence the title of the play. When his valet, Frontin, points out to Lucidor that he is in a position to make a fine marriage, Lucidor argues: "Il est vrai qu'Angélique n'est qu'une simple bourgeoise de campagne, mais originairement elle me vaut bien et je n'ai pas l'entêtement des grandes alliances" (Sc. 1), and he explains the restrained quality of their love: "il n'a pas encore été question du mot d'amour entre elle et moi; je ne lui ai jamais dit que je l'aime, mais toutes mes façons n'ont signifié que cela; toutes les siennes n'ont été que des expressions du penchant le plus tendre et le plus ingénu." Lucidor has had Frontin come from Paris garbed as a debonair young blade and plans to offer him to Angélique as a husband. Lucidor also commissions the country bumpkin Blaise to court Angélique.

[2] The initial run had seventeen performances.
[3] In *Le Curieux impertinent* (1710) by Destouches, Léandre, seeking to test the fidelity of Julie, asks his friend Damon to make love to her. Damon courts her so expertly and Julie is so irked at Léandre's trick that she marries Damon in the end.

When Angélique learns through Lisette that Lucidor has arranged a marriage for her involving "un mari distingué . . . un établissement considérable" (Sc. 6), Angélique is sure in her heart that Lucidor means himself. In an idyllic love scene Lucidor describes the husband he has picked out for her:

ANGÉLIQUE: . . . Ah ça, ne me trompez pas, au moins, tout le cœur me bat; loge-t-il avec vous?

LUCIDOR: Oui, Angélique, nous sommes dans la même maison.

ANGÉLIQUE: Ce n'est pas assez, je n'ose encore être bien aise en toute confiance. Quel homme est-ce?

LUCIDOR: Un homme très riche.

ANGÉLIQUE: Ce n'est pas là le principal. Après?

LUCIDOR: Il est de mon âge et de ma taille.

ANGÉLIQUE: Bon: c'est ce que je voulais savoir.

LUCIDOR: Nos caractères se ressemblent: il pense comme moi.

ANGÉLIQUE: Toujours de mieux en mieux. Que je l'aimerai!

LUCIDOR: C'est un homme tout aussi uni, tout aussi sans façon que je le suis.

ANGÉLIQUE: Je n'en veux point d'autre.

LUCIDOR: Qui n'a ni ambition, ni gloire, et qui n'exigera de celle qu'il épousera que son cœur.

ANGÉLIQUE [*riant*]: Il l'aura, Monsieur Lucidor, il l'aura; il l'a déjà; je l'aime autant que vous, ni plus ni moins. (Sc. 8)

Lucidor offers her a jewel in honor of her imminent marriage, which she accepts with a pretty compliment: "il ne fallait point de bijoux: c'est votre amitié qui est le véritable." Lucidor goes to get the future husband.

As Angélique waits in ecstasy, she confides her hopes to Lisette; Lisette cannot imagine that Lucidor is proposing himself, but Angélique is starry-eyed: "Si tu savais comme nous nous sommes parlé, comme nous nous entendions bien sans qu'il ait dit 'C'est moi!', mais cela était si clair, si clair, si agréable, si tendre!" (Sc. 9).

Lucidor returns with Frontin and introduces him as the husband to be. Angélique is stunned. In hurt silence she returns the jewel to Lucidor and excuses herself without looking at Frontin.

Left alone, Frontin and Lisette indulge in one of Marivaux's fine comic scenes: Lisette recognizes in Frontin a valet she had known when she was in service in Paris, but the brash valet carries out his impersonation to the discomfiture of the incredulous *suivante:*

> LISETTE: . . . mais j'avoue que je vous ai pris pour Frontin, et il faut que je me fasse toute la violence du monde pour m'imaginer que ce n'est point lui.
>
> FRONTIN: Frontin! mais c'est un nom de valet.
>
> LISETTE: Oui, Monsieur; et il m'a semblé que c'était toi . . . que c'était vous, dis-je.
>
> FRONTIN: Quoi! toujours des tu et des toi! Vous me lassez à la fin.
>
> LISETTE: J'ai tort; mais tu lui ressembles si fort! Eh! Monsieur, pardon. Je retombe toujours. Quoi! tout de bon, ce n'est pas toi? . . . Je veux dire, ce n'est pas vous? . . . Je sais garder un secret. Monsieur, dites-moi si c'est toi. . . . (Sc. 12)

Mme. Argante, mortified that her daughter has refused what seems to be a fine match, asks Lucidor and Frontin to excuse the girl on the ground that "elle est si jeune et si innocente! . . . regardez-la, dans cette occasion-ci, comme une enfant" (Sc. 14). Having sent for Angélique, Mme. Argante reproaches her with the callousness of another Mme. Argante in *L'Ecole des mères:*[4] "Comment? étourdie, ingrate que vous êtes!"; and she fulminates: "qu'elle l'accepte, ou je la renonce" (Sc. 15). Angélique is humiliated at this disclosure of her feelings before Lucidor.

Once her mother has left, Angélique dismisses Frontin politely and chides Lucidor for presenting her with a husband she did not ask for, repeating that her heart is already pledged. At this point

4 See Chapter 20.

Blaise enters as planned, and Angélique is subjected to still another test. Blaise proposes, and when Angélique refuses him, he hints it is because of Lucidor. Outraged, Angélique vehemently denies this to Lucidor: "Comment? Ne le croyez pas; vous ne seriez pas un homme de bien de le croire. M'accuser d'aimer, à cause que je pleure. ... Quoi! un homme qui ne songe point à moi, qui veut me marier à tout le monde, je l'aimerais, moi!" (Sc. 18). When Lucidor forces her to name the man she loves, Angélique points in exasperation to Blaise. Lucidor offers them a wedding gift of 20,000 francs and goes to get Mme. Argante's consent. Angélique sighs as Lucidor leaves: "Je crois que cet homme-là me fera mourir de chagrin" (Sc. 18), and she warns Blaise that she will not marry him if he accepts the gift, whereupon Blaise, free of his commitment to Angélique, becomes engaged to Lisette. Lucidor returns with Mme. Argante's consent, and when he learns of Lisette's and Blaise's engagement, he gives them his blessing.

Hurt and angry, Angélique wants to wash her hands of the whole affair. Lucidor, now convinced of her love and fidelity, tenderly asks the right to make her happy and lays bare his own heart: "Quand vous auriez pensé que je vous aimais, quand vous m'auriez cru de l'amour le plus tendre, vous ne vous seriez pas trompée. Et pour achever de vous ouvrir mon cœur, j'avoue que je vous adore, Angélique" (Sc. 21). Lucidor has no desire to return to Paris:

> LUCIDOR: Et si je restais, si je vous demandais votre main, si nous ne nous quittions de la vie?
> ANGÉLIQUE: Voilà du moins ce qu'on appelle parler, cela.
> LUCIDOR: Vous m'aimez donc?
> ANGÉLIQUE: Ai-je jamais fait autre chose?
> LUCIDOR: Vous me transportez, Angélique.

Mme. Argante cannot disapprove of this marriage. Lucidor calls in the villagers, and the play ends with a *divertissement*.

Angélique is one of Marivaux's most enchanting heroines. Tender in her love, poignant in her suffering, she is not angry at Lucidor for having subjected her to the tests. She is glad to give these proofs of her love, and seeks no retaliation. Lucidor, for all his cruelty, is an engaging young lover, willing to give up the glamour of Parisian society to marry Angélique. But at least one critic, Gabriel Marcel,[5] fears for the future of this young couple: "Lucidor m'est toujours apparu comme un tortionnaire qui annonce les dangereux expérimentateurs de Curel et surtout de Porto-Riche. . . . rien ne nous prouve que Lucidor ne sera pas un mari exécrable." Mme. Argante, in her brief scene, reveals what is worst in other mothers in Marivaux's theater. But these are peripheral considerations, which do not reflect on the outstanding qualities of *L'Epreuve:* the poetic beauty of the love scenes, the subtle probings of the heart, the bouncing gaiety of the servants—all blending into "un bien surprenant chef-d'œuvre."[6]

The *Mercure de France,*[7] with its customary recognition of Marivaux's plays, wrote: "Cette pièce a été très bien reçue du Public. On l'a trouvée pleine d'esprit, simple en action & élégamment dialoguée." Desboulmiers[8] paid glowing tribute to the play, but he dispensed with writing his usual synopsis because "Pour peu qu'on se livre à rapporter un seul mot du dialogue, on se trouve nécessairement obligé de transcrire toute la Scène: & conduit d'épigramme en épigramme, plein de sel & de vivacité, au lieu d'un extrait, on a souvent fait une nouvelle édition de la Piece."

For the opening of his new Théâtre de la République on April 27, 1791, Talma chose *L'Epreuve* as the *petite pièce* to accompany M. J. Chénier's *Henri VIII.* In contrast to the enthusiastic response accorded Chénier's tragedy, an unfortunate reception greeted Marivaux's comedy. *Le Journal de Paris*[9] says laconically: "l'Epreuve, de

---

[5] *Les Nouvelles littéraires, artistiques et scientifiques,* February 21, 1946.
[6] *Ibid.*
[7] December 1740, pp. 2926–29.
[8] *Histoire anecdotique et raisonnée du Théâtre Italien depuis son rétablissement en France jusqu'à l'année 1769* (Paris: Lacombe, 1769), IV, 537–38.
[9] April 29, 1791.

Marivaux, Pièce qu'on voit avec plaisir au Théâtre depuis plus de cinquante ans, & qu'on a voulu donner ensuite, n'a pu aller plus loin que la quatrième scène." The details of this rout were given some years later by Etienne and Martainville,[10] who attended the performance: "Si la tragédie était montée au nouveau théâtre de manière à dompter la cabale, il n'en était pas de même de la comédie. . . . les ennemis du nouveau théâtre se vengèrent-ils amplement sur la comédie, de n'avoir pu obtenir qu'un demi-succès contre la tragédie. Il fut impossible aux acteurs . . . de faire entendre deux phrases de suite. . . . enfin on fut obligé de baisser la toile sans achever la pièce." It was obvious that the antagonism was not against the play so much as against the dissident faction that had deserted the traditional Théâtre Français a few weeks earlier. Once the première was over and the opposition had vented its spite, Talma repeated L'Epreuve[11] frequently in the succeeding months, and several other new theaters added it to their programs.

It was on July 20, 1793, that L'Epreuve was first played by the Comédie Française, in competition with their erstwhile associates now at the Théâtre de la République. Le Journal de Paris,[12] which reviewed plays only spasmodically, took this occasion to bestow belated encomiums on the brilliant revival of Les Fausses confidences a month earlier and went on to state: "l'Epreuve n'a pas eu moins de succès." The acting of Fleury as Lucidor and Mlle. Petit as Angélique appealed to the spectators. "Le public a témoigné sa satisfaction par les applaudissemens multipliés & qui probablement se renouvelleraient à toutes les représentations." It was given repeatedly during the next few months before the arrest of the troupe, and it was revived again shortly after the reunion of the scattered actors in 1799.

[10] *Histoire du Théâtre-Français* (Paris: Barba, 1802), II, 81–83.
[11] The play was usually called *L'Epreuve nouvelle* at this time to distinguish it from *L'Epreuve réciproque, L'Epreuve villageoise,* and others of similar title that have vanished from the stage.
[12] July 22, 1793.

Since then *L'Epreuve* has enjoyed uninterrupted popularity through the nineteenth and twentieth centuries at the Théâtre Français and elsewhere. Like *Le Legs,* it has become such a standard item of programing that critics seldom mention it, although Sarcey[13] was moved to exclaim: "Quelle jolie œuvre, quel bijou exquis que cette *Epreuve nouvelle!* Alfred de Musset, avec toute sa poésie, n'a rien écrit de plus frais, de plus aimable. . . . Je plains ceux qui ne goûtent pas le charme fin et mesuré de ces conversations."

Jules Lemaître[14] gave *L'Epreuve* an odd sort of notoriety when he "discovered" *la cruauté de Marivaux.* "J'ai fait, un jour, à l'Odéon, une découverte: celle de la cruauté de Marivaux. Je ne raille point. . . . il y a dans *L'Epreuve* un moment où le cœur se serre comme si c'était une tragédie. . . . à certaines minutes, Racine et Marivaux c'est presque la même chose. . . . Cette petite comédie est douloureuse, vraiment douloureuse, pendant cinq minutes." This strain of cruelty in the treatment of love is perhaps one of the influences of the drawing rooms Marivaux frequented, where love was one of the chief topics of conversation. For example, Mme. de Lambert,[15] in whose home Marivaux was a caller every week, wrote in her *Réflexions sur les femmes:* "Il y a toujours une sorte de cruauté dans l'Amour. Les plaisirs de l'Amant ne se prennent que sur les douleurs de l'Amante. L'Amour se nourrit de larmes." Since Lemaître's time one critic or another has repeated the theme. Pierre Lièvre[16] is even virulent against Marivaux. He condemns *La Double inconstance*[17] for the infidelity the Prince would force on Arlequin and Silvia; then he turns to *L'Epreuve:* "*L'Epreuve* est abominable. On ne conçoit pas qu'un homme l'impose à une fille qu'il aime, ni que cette fille

---

[13] *Le Temps,* January 26, 1874. Cited by G. Larroumet, *Marivaux: sa vie et ses œuvres* (Paris: Hachette, 1882), p. 221.
[14] *Les Annales politiques et littéraires* (1890), XV, 120.
[15] *Œuvres de Mme la marquise de Lambert* (Paris, 1761), I, 363.
[16] *Le Mercure de France,* Nouvelle Série, May 1, 1937.
[17] See p. 44.

continue d'aimer après l'avoir subie." But Jacques Lemarchand,[18] like so many others, has grown weary of the excessive talk about *la cruauté de Marivaux*, and he would have it done with. So far as he is concerned, "il n'y a pas trace de cruauté chez Marivaux." The cruelty, such as it is, is an integral part of *L'Epreuve*, just as Dorante's and Dubois' cruelty to Araminte in *Les Fausses confidences*. Without it there could be no play in either case. In the long run, neither public nor critics have found anything so repellent in *L'Epreuve* and *Les Fausses confidences* as to spoil these plays for them on the stage.

Gabriel Marcel[19] credits Marivaux with revealing a trace of Sartre's thinking in the way he projects Lucidor: "La vérité est qu'il veut se voir, se sentir divinisé; c'est là sans doute le moyen qu'il a découvert pour se justifier à ses propres yeux—et ici la psychologie sartrienne a gain de cause."

[18] *Combat*, February 7, 1949.
[19] *Les Nouvelles littéraires, artistiques et scientifiques*, February 21, 1946.

30   La Dispute

[One act in prose. First presented at the Théâtre Français, October 19, 1744.]

IN December 1742 Marivaux was elected to the Académie Française, triumphing over Voltaire,[1] among other candidates. Thereafter Marivaux wrote plays for the Théâtre Français only, in spite of the ill treatment he had always received there. It is likely Marivaux felt that as an "Académicien" it was beneath his dignity to write for the Théâtre Italien, and Bastide and Fournier suggest that some estrangement developed between him and his friends at the Théâtre Italien. More likely, perhaps, is that age was taking its toll. Marivaux had been creating plays for twenty years, and now his inspiration was ebbing. At the Théâtre Italien, too, time was working ravages: Silvia had passed the age of forty and was no longer the embodiment of the lovely heroines she had been depicting for two decades. Furthermore, Thomassin, the incomparable Arlequin of Marivaux's most popular comedies, had died the year before.

Marivaux actually wrote six more one-act plays, only two of which were produced professionally; two others were submitted to the Comédie Française but never performed: one was given at the private theater of the Comte de Clermont and the other (whose authenticity is disputed) was published without any attempt at

---

[1] Naturally this defeat only added to Voltaire's animosity toward Marivaux.

production. After his election Marivaux's literary activities consisted, for the most part, in giving papers before the Académie.[2] He never finished either of his novels, *La Vie de Marianne* (1731–41), which he abandoned after the eleventh volume, or *Le Paysan parvenu* (1735–36), which he did not continue beyond five volumes.[3]

La Dispute is a play that is hard to judge by the usual dramatic criteria. Arland has classified it as a *comédie d'amour,* Fournier and Bastide as a *comédie romanesque,* Fleury as an allegory, and Larroumet as a *comédie héroïque.* Perhaps it has some of the characteristics of all those types. Marivaux has already revealed himself as an author of unconventional talent, and in *La Dispute* he has written one of his most original and baffling pieces. For spectators in 1744 it was an enigma.

Imagine still another mythical kingdom, this time with an oriental flavor. The Prince has invited his *amante* Hermiane to witness a fête that is about to take place. Nineteen years earlier his father had isolated four infants, two boys and two girls, each to be raised without the knowledge of any other human being except the guardians Carise and Mesrou. On this day they are to be brought into society, and it is hoped that their actions will reveal which sex first introduced inconstancy and infidelity in love. From a balcony overlooking the garden the courtiers can see and hear what happens. Eglé is the first to be brought out, and as she looks at her image in a pool she is overwhelmed by her beauty. When Azor enters, he falls in love with Eglé and swears eternal constancy. Then Adine, the other girl, appears; she scoffs at Eglé's beauty, and each girl boasts that she can take away the other's lover. Mesrin sees Adine and is smitten with her. In time the two young men meet and immediately become friends, without quarreling as the girls had just done. Yet when they meet Eglé

---

2 These treatises have never been collected. F. Deloffre has made a start at organizing this mass of material in articles appearing in *Revue des sciences humaines* (1954).

3 Some authorities also attribute a spurious sixth volume to Marivaux.

and Adine, each succumbs to the charm of the other's girl, and a *chassé-croisé* is in the making. Eglé and Adine regret the loss of their lovers and want them back.

At this point Hermiane exclaims that she has had enough. The Prince proclaims that the experiment shows neither sex has cause to reproach the other; vices and virtues are equally distributed between them. How these cloistered young people can have so many of the foibles of eighteenth-century Parisian society, Marivaux does not bother to explain.

La Dispute is less a play than a philosophical, symbolic dialogue. With its implausible premise, exotic characters, and oriental setting, its curious features outweigh its tangible dramatic substance. If it can be considered a play at all, it is two hundred years ahead of its time. It is more akin to the symbolic fantasies of Giraudoux, Pirandello, or T. S. Eliot. It is a sort of premature, unwitting thrust toward the philosophical play of the twentieth century, completely out of place in 1744, when the *comédie larmoyante* of La Chaussée was at the height of its vogue. Little wonder, then, that "Cette nouveauté n'ayant pas été goûtée du Public, l'Auteur l'a retirée après la première représentation."[4]

La Dispute remained in obscurity until it was presented on a program with *L'Age ingrat* and *Le Fanal* on April 26, 1938. Few critics mentioned the revival, but Robert Kemp[5] commented: "Le spectacle s'égaye de *la Dispute,* de Marivaux, fin treillis de phrases symétriques, artificieuses, de prouesses de style agaçantes et jolies." Lucien Dubech[6] spoke of his great pleasure at witnessing *La Dispute* and promised to write on it at length in his next column; but he left Paris for several weeks, and the review never appeared.

La Dispute was given nine times in 1938, twice in 1939, and revived again for twelve performances in 1944 during the German

---

[4] *Le Mercure de France,* October 1744, p. 2259.
[5] *Le Temps,* April 27, 1938.
[6] *L'Action française,* May 13, 1938.

occupation. Fournier and Bastide[7] say: "On ne s'étonne guère que *la Dispute* . . . ait été sifflée à la première représentation et retirée par son auteur, et l'on reste plutôt surpris que la Comédie-Française l'ait reprise en 1938." On the other hand, Marcel Arland[8] calls Marivaux's *La Dispute* "son œuvre la plus folle et par instants la plus exquise," and elsewhere: ". . . cette comédie puérile et précieuse, légère et profonde, l'une des plus surprenantes que Marivaux ait écrites. Elle n'était pas à sa place au Théâtre Français; il faudrait pour la jouer une troupe jeune et vive, sans tradition, une scène de hasard, un décor de deux sous, nulle recherche, simplement de l'esprit et de la fraîcheur. C'est demander un miracle."

An odd play, with limited possibilities for production at best, with little chance of popular support because of its highly specialized wit, *La Dispute* will probably never be more than a connoisseur's delight.

[7] *Théâtre complet de Marivaux* (2 vols.; Paris: Les Editions nationales, 1946), II, 283.

[8] *Théâtre complet de Marivaux* (Paris: La Nouvelle revue française, 1949), pp. xxiii, xliii.

31   Le Préjugé vaincu

[One act in prose. First presented at the Théâtre Français, August 6, 1746.]

FOR his last play, Marivaux returned to his old love: a "surprise de l'amour" mingled with moralizing on *le préjugé de la naissance*.[1] To the end, Marivaux never lost his refreshing touch in the treatment of young love, nor did he ever assume a conservative, old-age attitude in his social thinking. The elements that make up *Le Préjugé vaincu* are derived almost entirely from previous comedies; Edouard Fournier,[2] on the occasion of its revival in 1868 (which turned out to be its last), called it "un radotage de ce joli talent." The remark is not entirely fair, for it overlooks the sparkling style and nimble wit that pervade the play and made it a favorite in the eighteenth century.

Once again Marivaux, now that he was a member of the Académie, wrote for the Comédie Française. Gone are Arlequin, Lélio, and Silvia and their companions from the Théâtre Italien. Instead, there are Angélique, Dorante, and the Marquis. When the curtain rises, the servants Lépine and Lisette are on the stage, Lépine to announce the imminent arrival of Dorante, who is to seek the hand of Angélique.

---

[1] This theme occurs throughout Marivaux's theater, especially in *La Double inconstance, Le Jeu de l'amour et du hasard, Les Fausses confidences,* and *L'Epreuve.*

[2] Marcel Arland, *Théâtre complet de Marivaux* (Paris: La Nouvelle revue française, 1949), p. 1521.

He forthwith declares his love to Lisette. She rebuffs him on the ground that she is above him, "la fille du procureur fiscal," to which he counters that his own position will soon equal hers, since Dorante has promised to promote him to a managerial post on his estate. Just as Dorante enters, their conversation turns to Angélique and her overwhelming pride of birth. Lisette discourages him from court-ing Angélique because, even though he is a fine match in all other respects, he is of bourgeois origin. Dorante decides to woo her, using the device of pretending to speak for a friend. When Angélique comes, she finds she can talk to Dorante with the utmost friendliness; delighted, she listens to him expound the virtues of the proposed husband, and she is unaware that it is "la surprise de l'amour" that makes her reject Dorante's "friend" in favor, she claims, of her cousin the Baron. Upon hearing her decision, her father, the Marquis, ac-cepts it as binding, and hopes to do justice to Dorante by offering him his younger daughter. This only sharpens the suffering both of Dorante and of Angélique, who is now dismayed at the prospect of marrying the Baron. Dorante plans to leave immediately, and Angélique seeks a reason for detaining him at the château. She conceives the idea of arranging a marriage for Lisette and Lépine and prevails on Dorante to remain for the wedding. She overcomes her prejudice enough to hint that it was not Dorante but his "friend" that she was rejecting earlier. Dorante is overjoyed at the suggestion and falls on his knees to offer her his love. The Marquis is surprised at this unexpected turn of events, but Angélique readily admits that her pride is now a "préjugé vaincu," and all ends happily for them, as well as for Lisette and Lépine.

Throughout, the dominant characteristics of earlier Marivaux comedies appear in *Le Préjugé vaincu*. Angélique is reminiscent of Silvia. Like Silvia, she dreads a misalliance[3] and sets too much store by the prerogatives of birth. The Marquis has a much more liberal at-titude than his daughter. He allows Angélique complete liberty in

[3] Cf. Silvia in *Le Jeu* and Lucile in *Les Serments indiscrets.*

choosing her husband,[4] and he does not attempt to use his *autorité de père* to make her marry Dorante. The offer of a younger daughter to the rejected suitor recalls a similar situation in *Les Serments indiscrets*. For servants, Lépine and Lisette are somewhat out of the ordinary. Lisette is more of a companion than a *suivante* to Angélique,[5] although her lack of education is evident in her provincial dialect. Lépine, an ambitious fellow, is slated to become the *concierge* of Dorante's château and later his *bailli;* there is much of the Figaro complex[6] in his make-up, without the bitterness, however. In many respects *Le Préjugé vaincu* resembles *L'Epreuve,* but the emotions are much less poignant. It is as well constructed as *Le Jeu de l'amour et du hasard* and, in a miniature way, as good. It contains not only "la surprise de l'amour" but also a conflict between love and prejudice, in which love, of course, wins.

Though there were only seven performances of *Le Préjugé vaincu,* its success seemed complete from the critical point of view. The *Mercure de France*[7] gave a rapturous account of it: "Quoi qu'elle eût été bien reçue, l'Auteur a jugé à propos d'y faire quelques changemens qui ont fait redoubler les applaudissemens & l'affluence des spectateurs. . . . On peut dire qu'on trouve dans cette pièce la vivacité du dialogue, l'abondance de pensées fines & l'art d'intéresser le spectateur."

At court the actors in Marivaux's comedy had an even greater success. Louis XV was so pleased with the production that he added 500 livres to the royal pension already accorded to Mlle. Gaussin, who played Angélique, and Mlle. Dangeville, who played Lisette.

Voltaire, much as he scoffed at Marivaux, was not above appropriating the idea of *Le Préjugé vaincu* for his *Nanine* three years

[4] Cf. M. Orgon in *Le Jeu,* M. Damis in *L'Ecole des mères,* and M. Orgon in *La Joie imprévue.*

[5] Cf. Marton in *Les Fausses confidences.*

[6] See Trivelin in *La Fausse suivante* (pp. 67–69), Dubois in *Les Fausses confidences* (p. 211). See also pp. 80–82.

[7] August 1746, pp. 141–57.

later, and he used Marivaux's title as the subtitle of his play. But what Voltaire could not appropriate was the special charm of Marivaux; and though *Nanine* had a longer life at the Théâtre Français, it is generally judged inferior to *Le Préjugé vaincu* from a literary point of view.

Several nineteenth-century dramatists have pursued the path Marivaux hewed with respect to prejudice of birth: Jules Sandeau in *Mademoiselle de la Seiglière* (1851), Emile Augier in *Le Gendre de M. Poirier* (1854), and Ernest Legouvé in *Par droit de conquête* (1855). These writers, however, approach the problem after the marriage has taken place.

Since *Le Préjugé vaincu* ends Marivaux's career as a professional dramatist, it is fitting that the play should contain his most noteworthy qualities. A person reading only this play of Marivaux's would get an accurate impression of the author. But in the ensemble of Marivaux's dramatic production, *Le Préjugé vaincu* has the softness of afterglow rather than the radiance of bright sunlight.

32   Plays Not Performed in the Professional Theater

IN his productive years from 1720 to 1740, Marivaux usually wrote at least one play each year, sometimes two or even three. After *L'Epreuve* in 1740 greater intervals occurred between plays: *La Dispute* appeared only in 1744 and *Le Préjugé vaincu* in 1746. Then nine more years elapsed before he produced his next play, *La Femme fidèle*. By this time Marivaux had outlived his creative genius, and his last four plays have the weakness of a talent that has long since passed its peak.

La Femme fidèle

[One act in prose. Performed only in the private theater of the Comte de Clermont at Berny, August 24 and 25, 1755.]

A curious circumstance about *La Femme fidèle* is that its existence was unknown to literary critics until 1867, when Jules Cousin was preparing a study on the life and loves of the Comte de Clermont. The Count, the son of one of Louis XIV's illegitimate children and the great-grandson of Le Grand Condé, was an amateur actor with a private theater in his château, where he presented comedies especially written for him, occasionally enlisting the aid of professional performers from Paris. In his research at the Bibliothèque de l'Arsenal, Cousin came across a bundle of manuscripts that contained among other things some fragments of conversation. Upon examination they turned out to be cue sheets for four of the eight characters in a comedy by Marivaux. The complete manuscript of *La Femme fidèle* has never been found, but the cue sheets have enabled several writers to reconstruct the action and fill in enough dialogue to make a coherent play. The most noteworthy attempt was that of Larroumet's friend, Julien Berr de Turique, whose version was performed with considerable success at the Odéon in 1894 under the title of *Les Revenants*. However, he took so many liberties with the text and added so many scenes of his own that *Les Revenants* turned out to be rather far removed from *La Femme fidèle*. On the other hand, Fournier and Bastide[1] have scrupulously re-established the original text, retaining only the authentic fragments, with sufficient additional dialogue to permit fluent reading.

The manuscript of the four roles supplies enough information to outline the plot clearly. Ten years before the action takes place, the Marquis d'Ardeuil and his valet Frontin have been seized by Algerian pirates and are presumed to be dead. During these years Mme. Argante, the mother of the Marquise, has urged her daughter to marry Dorante. Until recently the Marquise has refused to be unfaithful to her husband's memory, but now she has reluctantly yielded to the insistence of her mother and suitor. The Marquis and Frontin, bearded and disguised as escaped captives, return to the château on the very day the marriage is to take place. The Marquise welcomes

---

[1] *Théâtre complet de Marivaux* (2 vols.; Paris: Les Editions nationales, 1946), II, 311–22.

them eagerly in the hope that they have some word from her husband. Lisette is less anxious for news from Frontin, since she has long
since considered herself free and has already given her love to Jean-
not. In spite of Mme. Argante's objections, the Marquise insists on
accepting the stranger's suggestion that he talk alone with her. The
stranger begins his interview by handing the Marquise a letter purported to have been written by her husband on his deathbed. Evidence
of the devotion of the Marquise to her husband is so sincere and
heartrending that the Marquis is assured his wife is still "une femme
fidèle." Hopefully, he insinuates that the husband may not be dead
after all; as the Marquise glows with fervent anticipation, he prepares her little by little to confront the man she believes dead. At
the crucial point he tears off his beard and reveals his true identity—
to the inexpressible joy of his wife. Lisette accepts Frontin's re-
suscitation as a dour necessity.

The special virtue of this little episode lies in the treatment
Marivaux gives it. Swinging completely into the framework of the
drame here,[2] he is still two years in advance of Diderot's theory. It is
the first and only time Marivaux depicted conjugal love on the stage,
and he did it in the manner of a social drama. Some critics have designated *La Femme fidèle* as a *comédie larmoyante* in imitation of La
Chaussée. Although the climactic scene of recognition (which
fortunately is preserved intact) verges on the tearful, the general
tenor of the play places it more appropriately within the framework
of the *drame*. If Marivaux followed his usual pattern, he also included
comic scenes (unfortunately not preserved) between Frontin and
Lisette, as a contrast to the emotional scenes between the Marquis
and the Marquise.

Judging from the extant fragments, Marivaux achieved in *La
Femme fidèle* a happy combination of the amusing and the serious—
the final flare-up of a fading genius.

---

[2] For previous examples of the *drame* by Marivaux, see pp. 188–90, 222.

Félicie

[One act in prose. Published in *Le Mercure de France,* March 1757.]

Félicie has been endowed with all the gifts of beauty and grace by the fairy Hortense. The young girl likes to display her charms in spite of the admonitions of Modesty and of Diana, who, strangely in this play, incarnates virtue. When a troop of hunters, among them the gallant Lucidor, passes her sylvan retreat, Félicie starts flirting with him. Lucidor in turn so plies Félicie with amorous declarations that she all but succumbs to his advances. The fairy intervenes in time to save the young coquette.

Félicie joins the list of mythological *féeries* Marivaux had already composed in *Le Triomphe de Plutus* and *La Réunion des amours.* It was submitted to the Comédie Française in March 1755 and accepted for production in its turn. However, the actors cannot have been enthusiastic about the play, for Marivaux withdrew it almost immediately and published it in the *Mercure de France* within the same month. Perhaps he realized that *Félicie* would not hold up on the stage. As a play it has little dramatic value: it is no more than a pretty dialogue.

It is interesting to note that the archives of the Comédie Française show that Marivaux submitted another play, *L'Amante frivole,* to the troupe in May 1755. It, too, was accepted to be presented in its turn, but its turn never came. The text was never published, and there remains no trace of the manuscript now.

Les Acteurs de bonne foi

[One act in prose. Published in *Le Conservateur,* November 1757.]

Marivaux conceived a startling new idea as the premise for *Les Acteurs de bonne foi:* a group of personages rehearse a play that so closely resembles their own situation that they become confused between comedy and life.[3] The aim of the play differs essentially from *L'Impromptu de Versailles* in that in Molière's play, which is a plea for naturalness on the stage, the actors give a picture of backstage life, whereas in Marivaux's play the characters come face to face with their own problems.

Merlin, the clever valet of Eraste, plans to present a play in celebration of the marriage of his master to Angélique. Instead of using a comedy with dialogue, he has only a scenario in the manner of the *commedia dell'arte* and allows the personages to supply words that come naturally. It becomes evident in the course of the rehearsal that Colette, although betrothed to Blaise, has a real inclination for Merlin, which in turn disturbs the latter's sweetheart, Lisette. These revelations threaten to break up the performance until Mme. Amelin, Eraste's aunt, insists that the play go on with the aristocrats of the household in the roles. This almost breaks up the marriage of Eraste and Angélique, but all ends happily by the final curtain.

Somehow, the main idea of the play is never fully realized, and *Les Acteurs de bonne foi* emerges as a less brilliant comedy than the subject warrants. The comedy is said to have been performed at the Théâtre Français on September 16, 1755, but the theater was closed that day, and there is no reference to the performance of *Les Acteurs de bonne foi* either in the archives or in the periodicals of the day. It is unlikely that the actors would have risked staging a play based on such complicated subtleties. As Blaise complains: "ils font semblant de faire semblant" (Sc. 13). The Marivaux touch is occasionally evident in the style, but his ability to construct a successful comedy was evidently waning.

[3] This is exactly the premise of *La Répétition* by Jean Anouilh (1950). Anouilh even uses a Marivaux comedy as the play his characters are rehearsing. See p. 51.

La Provinciale

[One act in prose. Published in *Le Mercure de France,* April 1761.]

Mme. La Thibaudière has just arrived in Paris from the provinces with her *suivante* Cathos. Unversed in the vices of the city, she falls into the clutches of Mme. Lépine, who connives with the Chevalier de la Trigaudière and the valet La Ramée to seduce and fleece the newcomer. The plot might have succeeded had not Mme. La Thibaudière's cousin, M. Lormeau, unmasked the rascals in time to spare her humiliation and grief.

As the play stands, it provokes a curious assortment of comparisons. The names are derived from the classical comedies of Molière and Dancourt; Marivaux had never used any of them before. The action resembles that in *Les Bourgeoises de qualité* or *La Femme d'intrigue,* comedies that depict the dissolute society of the early part of the eighteenth century. If M. Lormeau bears some resemblance to the kindly M. Remy of *Les Fausses confidences,* the Chevalier de la Trigaudière is akin to his debauched counterpart of *Le Chevalier à la mode* or the Marquis of *L'Ecole des bourgeois.* The amorality of the Parisians savors of the knaves Lesage portrayed in *Turcaret.* Least of all, *La Provinciale* resembles the thirty-odd comedies Marivaux had written previously.

La Provinciale was published anonymously in the *Mercure de France* in 1761 with a note stating merely that it was by "un auteur connu par plusieurs pièces justement applaudies." Since that time the identity of the author has been the subject of intermittent disputes. It is known that Marivaux wrote a play entitled *La Provinciale,* for he submitted one by that name to the Comte de Clermont. Fleury[4] and Chaponnière[5] have analyzed the play to show that it contains

4 *Marivaux et le marivaudage* (Paris: Plon, 1881), pp. 246–49.
5 "Une Comédie inconnue de Marivaux," *Revue de Genève,* 1922.

elements characteristic of Marivaux. In addition, when *Le Conservateur* published *Les Acteurs de bonne foi* anonymously in 1757, it said that there was in the same packet of manuscripts another comedy with the title: *La Provinciale.*

On the other hand, Larroumet[6] and Arland[7] argue that since *La Provinciale* was not performed professionally, another author could have used the same title. They further believe that this play is so lacking in the delicacy and wit of Marivaux that he could not have written it, even in his old age.

Fournier and Bastide[8] have published the text of *La Provinciale* in their edition of Marivaux, but they do not take sides on the question of authorship. In any event, until more concrete evidence is found one way or the other, the problem must remain in the realm of uncertainty where it now stands.

[6] *Marivaux: sa vie et ses œuvres* (Paris: Hachette, 1882), p. 618.
[7] *Théâtre complet de Marivaux* (Paris: La Nouvelle revue française, 1949), pp. 1527–30. These pages contain a detailed summary of the arguments pro and con.
[8] *Théâtre complet de Marivaux* (2 vols.; Paris: Les Editions nationales, 1946), pp. 345–64.

Conclusion

MARIVAUX, then, was the most original French dramatist of the eighteenth century. In his theater as a whole and in the details of the individual plays, in experimentation with new themes and in the expression of philosophical ideas, his originality stands out.

Perhaps the most salient feature in Marivaux's complete theater is his break with the classical tradition. Though it cannot be said that Marivaux is entirely free of the influence of inherited dramatic material, still the special flavor he gives old subjects sets him apart from his contemporaries. If he derived an occasional idea from a comedy by Molière, from the *canevas* of the *commedia dell'arte,* or from a seventeenth-century novel, what he borrowed consisted at most of a fragment; he so revitalized the idea that his own contribution became the major element in the play. At the same time his theater is peppered with the *philosophie* of the early eighteenth century. Not only are some of his plays based entirely on a philosophical thesis, but most of his comedies—even those written in a tone of sophisticated badinage—contain stimulating precepts and unexpected bits of philosophizing. His style, too often stigmatized by the epithet *marivaudage,* has a freshness that differentiates it from the uninspired versification and stilted prose of his contemporaries. His own inventiveness led Marivaux into heretofore unexplored realms and placed him outside—perhaps one should say, ahead of—the main current of the evolution of the theater in the eighteenth century.

When one applies these generalizations to the individual plays, the originality in detail is even more evident. Perhaps the best-known trait in Marivaux's theater is his depiction of awakening love—"la surprise de l'amour"—and many of his best and most enduring comedies turn on this theme. He already shows a well-developed conception of the "surprise" in *Arlequin poli par l'amour,* and two years later the conception emerges full-blown in *La Surprise de l'amour:* a new formula of comedy has come into being. From then on each comedy of this type[1] has a mainspring of its own, usually based on the protagonists' resistance to falling in love, and Marivaux creates ingenious ways of probing the hearts of his various personages. In all his "surprises" Marivaux leads his young lovers through the enchanting mysteries of *l'amour naissant,* subjects them to tender and heart-searching trials, and leaves them rapturous on the threshold of avowed love.

Voltaire has said of Marivaux: "Il a connu tous les sentiers du cœur sans trouver la grande route." If Marivaux did not re-tread the broad highways of the heart in the classical tradition—which in his day had fallen to the level of hackneyed sterility—it was not for want of understanding, for on occasion Marivaux could probe to profound depths.[2] It was rather that he found newness in exploring byways of the heart that his predecessors had shunned. With his infinite resources of analysis, Marivaux could have prepared a *carte du tendre* with detailed topography unmatched before his time. In developing "la surprise de l'amour" Marivaux made a distinctive contribution to the *fonds dramatique* of the French theater. He introduced into comedy the type of psychological analysis of love that

---

[1] See *La Double inconstance, La Seconde surprise de l'amour, Le Jeu de l'amour et du hasard, Les Serments indiscrets, Les Fausses confidences,* and *L'Epreuve.*
[2] See *Annibal* and *Le Prince travesti.*

Racine had achieved in tragedy, and in the realm of comedy Marivaux attained a peak of perfection equal to that of Racine in tragedy.

But "la surprise de l'amour," typifying as it does the special quality associated with Marivaux, represents only one aspect of his theater, only one of the many facets of his originality. From the whimsical fantasy of *Arlequin poli par l'amour*, in which the scene changes four times and thereby breaks the classical unity of place, to the enigmatic conceit of *La Dispute*, a plotless philosophical dialogue with subtle beauties, almost each play contains some new element. The creation of new types of character in comedy (*Le Prince travesti*, *La Mère confidente*), novelty of staging (*L'Ile de la raison*), the multiplication of disguises into a four-way *travestissement* (*Le Jeu de l'amour et du hasard*), and the reversal of the usual subplot of the servants (*Les Sincères*) are all departures from the past. While Marivaux's whole theater is imbued with *philosophie*, certain plays give new impetus to the ideas circulating in the *bureaux d'esprit* (*L'Ile des esclaves*, *L'Ile de la raison*, and *La Colonie*). For the first time in eighteenth-century comedy, Marivaux dares assign royalty a prominent place (*Le Prince travesti*). He also looks forward to the *drame* (*La Mère confidente* and *La Femme fidèle*) and to nineteenth-century drawing-room social drama (*L'Heureux stratagème* and *Les Fausses confidences*). Marivaux's turn of mind rarely permitted him to lag in the area of the commonplace.

One of Marivaux's most obvious qualities is his versatility. He composed comedies of love, philosophical comedies, allegories and fantasies, farces, comedies of manners, *drames*, heroic comedies, and a tragedy—all with equal literary and dramatic skill. Critics have classified his plays according to different systems,[3] but any classification is arbitrary, for so many of the plays contain elements that

---

[3] G. Larroumet, *Marivaux: sa vie et ses œuvres* (Paris: Hachette, 1882), p. 157; Jean Fleury, *Marivaux et le marivaudage* (Paris: Plon, 1881), p. 61; Marcel Arland, *Théâtre complet de Marivaux* (Paris: La Nouvelle revue française, 1949), p. xi; Jean Fournier and Maurice Bastide, *Théâtre complet de Marivaux* (2 vols.; Paris: Les Editions nationales, 1946), I, 17.

entitle them to be placed in several categories at once. There is no need to attempt still another classification here. Suffice it to say that no other writer in the French theater has worked successfully in as many genres as Marivaux.

Originality of thought is another of Marivaux's traits. Mostly new on the stage, always sparkling, his ideas give added pungency to a dramatic output already remarkable for its novelty and style. Marivaux did not create a philosophical system; rather, he moralized on diverse subjects without plan. One might say that his predominant theme is the innate goodness of man and the necessity of being kindly disposed toward one's fellows. His whole theater exudes a buoyant optimism that springs from his faith in mankind. The expression "le bon cœur" appears repeatedly;[4] a good heart is what distinguishes one man from another, Marivaux implies. The epitome of the philosophy of goodness is in his famous line: "dans ce monde, il faut être un peu trop bon pour l'être assez." When the theme is not actually developed in a particular play, the spirit of it is usually present.

Man is born naturally good, and character is of more fundamental importance than birth. Throughout his writings (and some twenty-five years before Rousseau popularized the doctrine), Marivaux places greater value on character than on birth.[5] There is no instance in Marivaux's theater where birth triumphs over personal merit.

Making character the basis for evaluating merit implies social equality. Marivaux dwelt at length on this subject and made startling observations thereon. The central theme of *L'Ile des esclaves* is that equality springs from natural goodness and that social injustice is a malady that can be cured. A courageous plea for equality is made in *La Colonie,* in which the aristocratic Arthenice sweeps away social barriers between herself and the bourgeois women. Even if in the end Arthenice's ideas are shown not to work, their mere expression

---

[4] See *Le Prince travesti* (I, 4); *L'Ile des esclaves* (Sc. 9, 10); *La Double inconstance* (III, 5); and *L'Ile de la raison* (I, 4, III, 9).

[5] See in particular: *Le Prince travesti* (I, 1); *La Mère confidente* (II, 2, III, 12); *Le Jeu de l'amour et du hasard* (III, 8); and *Le Préjugé vaincu.*

on the stage was bold in the eighteenth century. In the same play Marivaux broached the still more venturesome topic of women's suffrage. The previous flurries of discussion on the education of girls and the rights of women by Montaigne, Molière, La Bruyère, and Fénelon had not yet touched on that point. Perhaps in Marivaux's day no one took him seriously, but he deserves credit for introducing the subject on the stage. Marivaux extends his thesis of social equality so far as to propose marriages that cut across the usual social lines,[6] a proposal that violates the accepted social code of the eighteenth century. This kind of attitude gives a distinctive touch to Marivaux's theater and places him generations ahead of his fellow dramatists. It is one of the factors that account for Marivaux's popularity in the twentieth century.

Marivaux had advanced ideas for his day on the duties of a monarch. At a time when the theory of the divine right of kings was still accepted in France and when the Regency displayed a callous disregard for the welfare of the people, Marivaux expressed stimulating views[7] on *le métier du roi,* which later in the century became part of the concept of the enlightened despot. His admonitions to monarchs to bestow equal justice on all, to follow the simple habits of their subjects, to show paternal concern for their people, to reject flattery, must have brought a smile to those who still remembered the obsequiousness practiced before Louis XIV.

Altogether, these diverse ideas create an ensemble of *philosophie,* of wholesome moralizing, that had not before been expressed on the stage in such straightforward terms. In the classical theater writers had tended to avoid expounding ideas directly; if they wanted to teach a lesson, they attempted to do so by irony, caricature, and other devices. For example, Molière believed that fathers should not force incompatible marriages on their children, but instead of presenting

---

[6] See *Le Jeu de l'amour et du hasard, Les Fausses confidences,* and *L'Epreuve.*

[7] See *La Double inconstance* (III, 5); *Le Prince travesti* (I, 4); and *L'Ile de la raison.*

liberal-minded fathers on the stage, he ridiculed obstinate ones such as M. Orgon in *Tartuffe,* Harpagon in *L'Avare,* and M. Jourdain in *Le Bourgeois gentilhomme.* Marivaux, on the other hand, presented his philosophy with disarming simplicity. If he had a point to make, he went straight to the heart of the matter and expressed his conviction as an integral part of the text without deviousness.

Marivaux did much to create the vogue for *philosophie* in the theater. Even while he was still writing, other dramatists were beginning to insert a bit of *philosophie* in their plays; and by the time he finished his professional career in the 1740's, other dramatists were weighting their plays heavily with *philosophie.* The *comédies larmoyantes* of La Chaussée and the *drames* of Diderot, not to mention the philosophical tragedies of Voltaire, were soon to fill the stage with sententious maxims. But one will look in vain for a writer who before Beaumarchais presents his ideas with such sparkling grace and clarity, and, as has already been shown, Beaumarchais borrowed some of his best ideas from Marivaux.

When one discusses the style of Marivaux, one enters an area of extremes: few techniques have been as thoroughly scrutinized as that of Marivaux, and criticism over the generations has ranged from the highest praise to heated scurrility and back to adulation. It is not that a particular epoch was hostile to Marivaux; rather, all degrees of praise and disfavor have been expressed concurrently.

Marivaux's style has brought into being the term *marivaudage,* commonly used in a derogatory sense to refer to an extreme affectation in phraseology and a fatuous analysis of sentiment. In reality, the question of *marivaudage* scarcely enters into an evaluation of Marivaux himself, for he is less guilty of it than his imitators. When Marivaux uses a precious figure of speech reminiscent of the seventeenth-century novel, when he pursues love into hitherto unexplored regions of the heart, when he dwells on subtle nuances of feeling, or when he enters the realm of elfin gaiety, he does so with complete mastery and without affectation. Yet when his successors during a good part of the eighteenth and nineteenth centuries imitate these same artifices, they drift into the silly verbiage and clumsy hyperbole known as *marivaudage*. Lacking the taste and artistry of Marivaux, these imitators have tended, knowingly or not, to associate their own faults with him and have thereby cast disrepute on his name. But on examining his style objectively, one realizes that his personages speak and act in a manner befitting the powdered elegance and beribboned grace of eighteenth-century drawing rooms. Marivaux fuses style and character into an indissoluble whole with an art that few writers have achieved. Fortunately, recent scholarship has led to a re-evaluation of Marivaux's qualities, and the general trend in the twentieth century is to absolve him from the taint of *marivaudage*.

The most frequent charge against Marivaux during the eighteenth century and since was that he had "trop d'esprit." Most of his comedies are full of scintillating badinage, and often even the servants speak with a polished wit that is indistinguishable from the elegance of their masters. But the overabundance of wit has led some critics to speak disparagingly against Marivaux: Voltaire made sarcastic remarks;[8] Geoffroy deplored Marivaux's influence on young writers;[9] Faguet[10] condemned his dramatic style as leading to *marivaudage;* Lièvre acrimoniously indicted Marivaux for concealing nefarious traits under his exquisite style.[11] But such remarks are in a distinct minority. Most often critics have yielded insensibly to the enchantment of his style and have been effusive in their praise of Marivaux. "Un magique ballet verbal," "la poésie de la première moitié du XVIIIe siècle," "une perfection soutenue," and the like recur ad infinitum in reviews of his plays.

Besides, now that revivals of Marivaux's plays are more and more popular, critics are finding new qualities in his writing. Of particular interest is the revelation of the rhythmic beauty inherent in the

[8] See p. 155.
[9] See p. 213.
[10] *Le Dix-huitième siècle* (Paris, 1890), pp. 117–38.
[11] See pp. 44n, 138–39, 217, 238.

words spoken on the stage. Modern actors have rediscovered, and spectators have learned to appreciate, the subtleties and purity of eighteenth-century language.[12] In addition, twentieth-century critics have noted a musical quality in Marivaux that previous generations seem to have missed. They perceive in his phraseology the melodic strain and orchestral variations found in musical compositions.[13]

All these elements of originality in subject matter, thought, and style give Marivaux a modernness that makes his plays as enjoyable today as they were when he wrote them. In the mid-nineteenth century Théophile Gautier,[14] comparing Marivaux's heroines with those of Shakespeare, found that "A travers l'œuvre ancienne, le caractère de l'époque où on la représente se fait jour malgré tout," and since then each generation of critics has drawn attention to the contemporaneous qualities in Marivaux's theater.

In reviewing *Le Jeu de l'amour et du hasard,* Brisson[15] says of Dorante: "Il avance sur son siècle comme la plupart des personnages de Marivaux; il est moderne"; and apropos of the same play, Antoine[16] declares: "on aperçoit qu'aucune comédie du XVIIIe siècle ne fut aussi contemporaine. . . . Silvia domine encore ses sœurs modernes." Truffier[17] feels that "*La Mère confidente* est très près de nous."

Far from being museum pieces like the plays of Destouches, Piron, and La Chaussée, the comedies of Marivaux have something that attracts each generation. His characters have enduring appeal, and his ideas are often more akin to the twentieth century than to the eighteenth. Like the plays of Molière and Racine, those of Marivaux transcend the moment of their conception and by reason of their

[12] See pp. 60–61, 105.
[13] See pp. 39, 60, 107, 217.
[14] *Histoire de l'art dramatique en France depuis vingt-cinq ans* (Paris: Magnin, Blanchard et Cie, 1858–59), V, 340.
[15] *Le Temps,* September 14, 1908.
[16] *Dossier sur Marivaux,* Rf 11782, Bibliothèque de l'Arsenal.
[17] *Les Annales politiques et littéraires,* December 1907, p. 525.

basic truth and inherent beauty are highly valued in the twentieth century.

The paucity of source material for Marivaux's plays only emphasizes his originality. Marivaux is at his best when he is not burdened with someone else's ideas. The most notable achievements in his theater—*La Double inconstance, La Surprise de l'amour, L'Ile des esclaves, Le Jeu de l'amour et du hasard,* and *La Mère confidente*—are those in which his inspiration stems entirely from within. For the most part, attempts to trace sources for Marivaux's comedies have yielded only wisps of information.

He draws but little from the usual sources. Of classical antiquity,[18] there is almost nothing. To be sure, in his only tragedy, *Annibal,* he uses a historical character, and there is a touch of Petronius in *La Seconde surprise de l'amour* and of Plautus in *La Méprise.* But there the classical influence ends.

The seventeenth-century novel influenced Marivaux to some degree.[19] The liberal father, depicted so often by Marivaux, appears in *L'Astrée,* and the *mère-amie,* in *La Princesse de Clèves.* The pedant Hortensus goes back to *Francion.* The heroics of *Le Triomphe de l'amour* are typical of *Le Grand Cyrus.* At times the detailed discussion of love by Marivaux is reminiscent of d'Urfé, Scudéry, and La Calprenède.

Much as Marivaux disliked Molière, he could not entirely escape his influence.[20] *L'Ecole des mères* is the most noteworthy case in point in that it shows similarities to *L'Ecole des femmes, Les Femmes savantes,* and *L'Avare.* The Lélio-Arlequin dialogue in *La Surprise de l'amour* (I, 2) recalls a similar conversation between Cléonte and Covielle in *Le Bourgeois gentilhomme.* The scene of the portraits in *Les Sincères* echoes Célimène's description of her friends in *Le Misanthrope.* Marivaux would probably have repudiated the charge of borrowing from Molière, but in these few instances the evidence is

[18] See pp. 26–29, 103, 174. [19] See pp. 102, 131, 146, 184, 188n, 263.
[20] See pp. 31, 41, 160–64, 176, 210, 226, 253, 259.

there. It can be said, however, that Marivaux did not imitate the more typical qualities of Molière's work, he did not use Molière as a standard, and he did not write a *comédie de caractère*.

Marivaux has often been likened to Racine, but their likeness is in natural talent. Both men possessed the gift of analyzing love; they portrayed the inner lives of their characters and reduced exterior events to a minimum. Racine excelled in depicting tragic passion; Marivaux, in revealing the awakening of love. Their works are entirely different, and Marivaux borrowed nothing from Racine.

Likewise, critics have found points of similarity between Shakespeare and Marivaux,[21] but as with Racine the similarity is one of talent. Marivaux did not know Shakespeare's theater; hence there is no precise relationship between the authors. However, in spite of their obvious dissimilarities, both writers possessed a certain elfin gaiety and a lyrical manner of projecting love scenes that are curiously akin.

To what extent Marivaux was influenced by his contemporaries is difficult to estimate. On occasion instances of borrowing can be identified with reasonable certainty,[22] but in each of these instances Marivaux has merely utilized a fragment and has so revitalized it that a charge of plagiarism is unjustified. Scholars have often strained a point in an effort to associate an item in Marivaux with some other work.[23] Borrowings by Marivaux are slight, to say the least.

Perhaps the greatest single source of Marivaux's plays is the most intangible one: the *canevas*—and, even more, the spirit—of the Théâtre Italien. As one reads his plays, one is conscious of a detail reminiscent of some other farce. But since Marivaux had to write for stock characters, he could scarcely avoid using some stock material. Whatever Spanish or Italian elements one notes in Marivaux can be traced to the *canevas* of the Riccoboni troupe.

Viewing Marivaux's complete theater in perspective, one realizes

[21] See pp. 24, 37–38, 40–41, 136, 148, 262.
[22] See pp. 55, 75, 132, 178–79, 198.   [23] See pp. 26, 132.

that he is less guilty of borrowing than most writers; the rather nebulous comparisons indicated above reflect only on a minor aspect of his theater.

If Marivaux borrowed sparingly from his predecessors and contemporaries, the same cannot be said of his successors. The names of dramatists who quarried in Marivaux's plays make a rather impressive list in the eighteenth-century theater. Destouches patterned Lisimon of *Le Glorieux* after Plutus of *Le Triomphe de Plutus*.[24] La Chaussée imitated Marivaux in *L'Ecole des mères*.[25] Gresset drew on *Le Petit-maître corrigé* for many of the characters and ideas in *Le Méchant*.[26] Voltaire adopted "Le Préjugé vaincu" as a subtitle for *Nanine,* and used the basic idea of Marivaux's comedy for the plot.[27] La Noue copied *L'Heureux stratagème* in *La Coquette corrigée*.[28] Borrowings of lesser importance were made by less well-known writers.

Marivaux is the outstanding precursor of the *drame*.[29] In *La Mère confidente,* especially, and in *La Femme fidèle* he created plays that illustrate the *drame* some twenty years before Diderot enunciated his theory. Although the eighteenth century did not give Marivaux credit for his innovation, the nineteenth and twentieth centuries have recognized his contribution to the evolution of the genre. Diderot himself did not borrow material from Marivaux for his two *drames*— the two men were too far apart in style and thought for that—yet one of Marivaux's claims to fame is that he anticipated Diderot in the writing of a *drame*.

One of the outstanding facts about Marivaux is his influence on Beaumarchais, particularly with respect to the creation of the character of Figaro.[30] Repeatedly in his theater Marivaux injects a strain of aggressiveness in the servants, the sum total of which constitutes the personality of Beaumarchais' famous valet. The Trivelin of *La Fausse suivante* and Cléanthis of *L'Ile des esclaves* contain the very

[24] See p. 112.
[25] See p. 164.
[26] See pp. 180–81.
[27] See pp. 246–47.
[28] See p. 171.
[29] See pp. 188–90, 222, 250.
[30] See pp. 46–47, 67–68, 81–82, 211, 246.

essence of Figaro, even down to certain phrasings; they lack only his revolutionary truculence. Beaumarchais borrowed so thoroughly and minutely from Marivaux that he could not have been unaware that he was indulging in overt plagiarism. It should also be noted that he copied some of the guileless innocence of Chérubin from the Arlequin of *Arlequin poli par l'amour.*[31]

Alfred de Musset is generally considered the lineal descendant of Marivaux, and rightly so, for he seems to have inherited Marivaux's penchant for portraying young love and for contriving witty dialogue.[32] In style and spirit Musset carries on the Marivaux tradition, albeit with the moodiness of the romantic period, which Marivaux himself never had. More specifically, Musset found the inspiration for *La Nuit vénitienne* in *Le Dénouement imprévu;* for *On ne badine pas avec l'amour* in *Les Serments indiscrets;* for *Il ne faut jurer de rien* in *Le Petit-maître corrigé;* and for *L'Ane et le ruisseau* in *Le Legs.* Less precise analogies can be drawn that further associate Musset with Marivaux. Since Musset's time no writer in the French theater has been designated as Marivaux's heir.

Aside from the positive influences just discussed, Marivaux has had intangible influences without number. Critics in the second half of the eighteenth century complained of the *marivaudage* in current dramas, and in 1810 Geoffroy laments Marivaux's dominion over young writers of the day. Even after Musset's time numerous nineteenth-century plays evoke some remembrance of Marivaux. Twentieth-century critics have caught glimpses of Marivaux in Curel, Porto-Riche, and Sartre.

Today Marivaux occupies a position of pre-eminence in the French theater, and not without justice. His contemporaries—Destouches, Piron, La Chaussée, Voltaire, Gresset, Diderot—are all but forgotten figures in the modern theater. The secret of Marivaux's popularity in the twentieth century, like that of Shakespeare and Molière, rests on the simple fact that he faithfully depicted the society

[31] See p. 21.   [32] See pp. 40, 73–77, 103, 151–55, 175–81, 195–201.

in which he lived and at the same time endowed his characters with the universal and enduring truths of human nature. If the area in which he wrote is somewhat narrower than that of Shakespeare and Molière, he is no less a master within his sphere. Perhaps Brisson,[33] in a review of *La Mère confidente* that applies with equal justice to most of Marivaux's plays, gives the best account of his position in the French theater: "L'ouvrage . . . dépasse le temps où il fut écrit; il est de tous les temps, il est du nôtre. Marivaux est l'auteur classique le plus près de nous; son œuvre exhale un extraordinaire parfum de 'modernité'!"

[33] *Le Théâtre* (1907–12), III, 277, 284.

INDEX

This list includes the titles of plays, periodicals, newspapers, and secondary sources cited in the book.

Acteurs de bonne foi, Les, 251–52, 254
Action française, L', 50n, 60, 201n, 242n
Age ingrat, L', 242
Aïeux de Figaro, Les, see Monnier
Alembert, d', vii, 190, 199n
Allainval, d', *L'Ecole des bourgeois,* 70–71, 89, 253
Allan, Mme., 215
Allard, Louis, *La Comédie de mœurs,* 200
Amans ignorans, Les, see Autreau
Amant malgré lui, L', see Carmontel
Amante frivole, L', 6, 251
Amasis, see La Grange-Chancel
Amour et la vérité, L', 14, 17–18, 141
Amoureuse, see Porto-Riche
Ane et le ruisseau, L', see Musset
Annales du théâtre et de la musique, Les, see Noël and Stoullig
Annales politiques et littéraires, Les, 23n, 129n, 136n, 148n, 192n, 238n, 262n
Année littéraire, L', 7
Annibal, 19, 26–29, 57, 74n, 149n, 256n, 263
Anouilh, Jean, *La Répétition,* 51, 252n
Antoine, 137, 262
Argens, Marquis d', *Réflexions historiques et critiques sur le goût,* 40
Aristophanes, *Lysistrata,* 117n
Arland, Marcel, vii, 89, 112n, 144, 164, 166, 175, 207, 241, 243, 254; *Théâtre complet de Marivaux,* 26n, 147n, 151n, 163n, 179n, 200n, 244n, 257n
Arlequin poli par l'amour, 19–25, 26n, 35, 37n, 40, 44, 56, 129, 131, 163, 202, 219, 231, 256–57, 266
Arlequin sauvage, see Drevetière de l'Isle
Arnould-Plessy, Mme., 134, 199, 215
As You Like It, see Shakespeare

Astrée, L', see d'Urfé
Athalie, see Racine
Atkinson, Brooks, 218
Augier, Emile, *Le Gendre de Monsieur Poirier,* 247
Autreau, 12; *Les Amans ignorans,* 21
Avare, L', see Molière
Aventures de***, Les, ou Les Effets surprenants de la sympathie, 5n, 17n, 55, 146

Baculard d'Arnaud, *Le Comte de Comminges,* 100n
Bajazet, see Racine
Balletti, Antoine Joseph, 11, 36
Banès, Antoine, 24
Banville, Théodore, 40
Bar, Mlle. de, 151, 179
Barbier de Séville, Le, see Beaumarchais
Baron, Michel, 10, 29; *L'Homme à bonne fortune,* 176; *Le Rendez-vous des Thuilleries,* 175n
Barrault, Jean Louis, xiii–xvii, 51, 105–6, 139, 194, 217–18
Bartet, Julia, 104, 134–35, 199
Beauchamp, *Le Portrait,* 132
Beaumarchais, 7, 21, 47, 49, 68–69, 82, 85, 211, 260, 265–66; *Le Barbier de Séville,* 67–68, 80; *Le Mariage de Figaro,* 21, 47, 67–68, 82
Beaunier, André, 60
Beckley, Paul V., 140
Bell, Maria, 139
Bellesort, André, 60
Benozzi, Zanetta-Rosa-Giovanna, see Silvia
Berr, Georges, 137
Berr de Turique, Julien, 249
Bertin, Pierre, 49–50
Bertrand, 165
Bertrand, Eliane, 218
Bibliothèque française, La, 200, 227
Bidou, Henri, 60, 148

Biographie universelle ancienne et moderne, 101n
Boissy, 12, 58; *Les Dehors trompeurs,* 121n
Boissy, Gabriel, 38, 48
Bordeaux, Henri, *La Vie au théâtre,* 192
Boudet, Micheline, 143
Boulanger, Marcel, 60
Bourgeois gentilhomme, Le, see Molière
Bourgeoises de qualité, Les, see Dancourt
Boursault, Edme, *Les Nicandres,* 174
Boutet de Monvel, *Les Victimes cloîtrées,* 100n
Bovy, Mlle., 192–93
Brisson, Adolphe, 24, 137, 192, 215, 217, 262; *Le Théâtre,* 267n
Brisson, Pierre, 49, 50
Brohan, Mlle., 104, 134, 199, 215
Brunetière, F., 40, 162–63

Cabinet du philosophe, Le, 5n
Calderón, 62
Campistron, *Le Jaloux désabusé,* 71, 74
Candeille, Mlle., 151
Candide (newspaper), 137n, 193n, 216n
Candide, see Voltaire
Caprice, Un, see Musset
Capus, 193
Caraguel, 165
Carmontelle, *L'Amant malgré lui,* 201n
Catulle-Mendès, Jane, 49
Causeries du lundi, see Sainte-Beuve
Cerny, Mme., 199
Cervantes, *Pérsiles y Sigismunda,* 22
Chaponnière, Paul, 254; *Piron: sa vie et ses œuvres,* 179n
Chauveau, Paul, 228
Chénier, M. J., *Henri VIII,* 236
Chevalier à la mode, Le, see Dancourt
Chez Silvia, see Clerc
Cid, Le, see Corneille
Clairon, Mlle., 84
Claretie, Jules, 23
Clède, M. de la, *Histoire du Portugal,* 142
Cléopâtre, see La Calprenède
Clerc, Charles, *Chez Silvia,* 36n
Clermont, Comte de, 189, 195, 240, 248, 253

Collé, Ch., 190
Colonie, La, 78, 89, 113–19, 161, 257–58
Combat, 62n, 97n, 228n, 239n
Comédie de mœurs, La, see Allard
Comédie en France au XVIIIᵉ siècle, La, see Lenient
Comedy of Errors, see Shakespeare
Comme il vous plaira, see Shakespeare
Commedia, 199n
Commère, La, 6
Compagnie de l'Equipe, 91n, 96–97, 194
Comte de Comminges, Le, see Baculard d'Arnaud
Condé, Le Grand, 175, 248
Conservateur, Le, 251, 254
Contat, Louise, 12, 134, 199, 213–14
Copeau, Jacques, 39, 49
Coquette corrigée, La, see La Noue
Coquette du village, La, see Dufresny
Corneille, Pierre, 7, 29; *Le Cid,* 143, 219; *Horace,* 143; *Polyeucte,* 29, 219
Corneille, Thomas, 26
Correspondant, Le, 148
Cours de littérature dramatique, see Geoffroy
Courville, Xavier de, vii, 21, 41, 48, 49, 60, 105, 148; *Le Théâtre de Marivaux,* 56, 58, 72–73, 98; *Luigi Riccoboni dit Lélio,* 21n
Cousin, Jules, 248
Crébillon, 29, 48, 144, 162; *Sémiramis,* 53n
Crébillon *fils,* 179
Curel, 236, 266
Curieux impertinent, Le, see Destouches

Dame aux camélias, La, see Dumas *fils*
Dames vengées, Les, see Donneau de Visé
Dancourt, 14, 39, 163; *Les Bourgeoises de qualité,* 253; *Le Chevalier à la mode,* 71, 176, 253; *La Femme d'intrigue,* 253; *Les Vendanges de Suren-nes,* 75
Dangeville, Mlle., 143, 152
Daudet, A., 40, 132
Dazincourt, 120n, 213
Debucourt, 62
Dehelly, 38, 192
Dehors trompeurs, Les, see Boissy
Deligne, *Le Fat dupé,* 175

Deloffre, Frédéric, ix, 5n, 146, 175n; *Marivaux et le marivaudage*, ixn, 14n; *Mélanges d'histoire littéraire offerts à M. Paul Dimoff*, 22n, 198n

Demay, M., 97

Démocrite, see Regnard

Dénouement imprévu, Le, 16n, 64, 73–77, 130, 133, 266

Desboulmiers, *Histoire anecdotique et raisonnée du Théâtre Italien* . . . , 22n, 35n, 59, 67n, 87, 96n, 133n, 147, 148n, 164, 166, 191, 203, 227, 236

Deschamps, Gaston, vii

Desmares, Mme., 29

Desmarets, 26

Destouches, 6, 39, 42, 140, 163, 262, 265–66; *Le Curieux impertinent*, 232n; *Le Glorieux*, 112, 132n, 265; *L'Obstacle imprévu*, 178

Deux Arlequins, Les, see Lenoble

Diderot, 7, 78, 182, 189–90, 250, 260, 265–66

Dispute, La, 78, 240–43, 248, 257

Dix-huitième siècle, Le, see Faguet

Donneau de Visé, *Les Dames vengées*, 178–79

Dossier sur Marivaux, 24n, 25n, 37n, 137n, 215n, 262n

Double inconstance, La, 39, 43–51, 56–57, 68, 81n, 130, 154, 163, 188, 219, 238, 244n, 256n, 258n, 259n, 263

Double veuvage, Le, see Dufresny

Drevetière de l'Isle, *Arlequin sauvage*, 79; *Timon le misanthrope*, 79

Dubech, Lucien, 24, 50, 60, 73, 137, 193, 201, 216, 219, 242; *Histoire générale illustrée du théâtre*, 73n

Dubisson, 200

Duchesne, La Veuve, vii

Dufresne, 29

Dufresny, 10; *La Coquette du village*, 89; *Le Double veuvage*, 91n

Du Gard, Roger Martin, 39

Dugazon, 120n

Dumas, André, 24

Dumas fils, *La Dame aux camélias*, 107

Duminil, Mlle., 192

Durry, Marie-Jeanne, 5n, 36; *Quelques nouveautés sur Marivaux*, 36n

Dussane, Béatrix, 52, 62–63, 135; *Reines de théâtre*, 135n

Duviquet, Pierre, vii, 135, 214; *Œuvres complètes de Marivaux*, 135n

Echo de Paris, L', 60

Ecole des bourgeois, L', see d'Allainval

Ecole des femmes, L', see Molière

Ecole des maris, L', see Molière

Ecole des mères, L' (Marivaux), 100n, 130, 134, 156–65, 188, 222, 234, 246, 263

Ecole des mères, L', see La Chaussée

Eliot, T. S., 242

Emigrés aux terres australes, Les, see Gamas

Ephésienne, L', see Mainfray

Epreuve, L', 23, 49, 61, 134, 136, 139, 188n, 192, 210, 231–39, 244n, 248, 256n, 259n

Epreuve réciproque, L', see Legrand

Epreuve villageoise, L', 237n

Esprit de Marivaux, L', see Lesbros de Versan

Etienne and Martainville, *Histoire du théâtre français*, 151, 213, 237

Faguet, Emile, *Le Dix-huitième siècle*, 261

Fanal, Le, 242

Fantasio, see Musset

Fat dupé, Le, see Deligne

Fatouville, 10; *La finta matrigna, ou La Fausse prude*, 10; *La Matrone d'Ephèse*, 103

Fausse suivante, La, 64–72, 87n, 102n, 144, 145n, 174, 246n, 265

Fausses confidences, Les, 23, 36n, 49, 68–69, 131, 132n, 134, 136, 139, 188n, 202–19, 223, 229, 231, 237, 239, 244n, 246n, 253, 256n, 257, 259n

Favart, Mme., 231n

Félicie, 251

Femme d'intrigue, La, see Dancourt

Femme fidèle, La, 89, 188n, 189, 248–50, 257, 265

Femmes, Des, see La Bruyère

Femmes savantes, Les, see Molière

Fénelon, 259; *Traité de l'éducation des filles*, 113

Feuillet, O., *Le Roman d'un jeune homme pauvre*, 210n

Figaro, viii, 46–47, 67–69, 80–82, 85, 211, 246, 265–66

Figaro, Le, 36n, 39n, 52n, 60, 61n, 85n, 97n, 105n, 149, 193n, 228n, 229n
Figaro et ses origines, see Toldo
Figaro littéraire, Le, 50n
Finta matrigna, La, ou La Fausse prude, see Fatouville
Flers, Robert de, 193
Fleury (actor), 120n, 213, 237
Fleury, Jean, vii, 144, 241; Marivaux et le marivaudage, 129, 171n, 253n, 257n
Folies amoureuses, Les, see Regnard
Fontanelle, 5n; Le Testament, 198n
Fourbe puni, Le, see La Fausse suivante
Fournier, Edouard, vii, 163, 165, 191, 244
Fournier and Bastide, Théâtre complet de Marivaux, vii, 36, 74n, 102n, 112, 134n, 144, 149n, 190n, 196, 240–41, 243, 249, 254, 257n
Francion, see Sorel
Frederich, Edna, 154–55
Fréjaville, Gustave, 216
French Tragedy in the Time of Louis XV and Voltaire, see Lancaster
Frères Parfaict, 67n, 74, 76n
Fresnay, Pierre, 137
Fuzelier, 12

Gaiffe, Félix, 85, 119
Galant coureur, Le, see Legrand
Galante, La, 36n
Gamas, Les Emigrés aux terres australes, 84
Gaulois, Le, 38n
Gaussin, Mlle., 143, 152, 171, 195, 246
Gautier, Jean-Jacques, 61, 97, 105
Gautier, Théophile, 40, 135–36, 191, 215, 219, 262; Histoire de l'art dramatique en France depuis vingt-cinq ans, 40n, 135n, 215n, 262n
Gendre de Monsieur Poirier, Le, see Augier
Geoffroy, 135, 164, 213–14, 219, 261, 266; Cours de littérature dramatique, 214n
Georges Dandin, see Molière
Gide, André, Journal, 51
Giraudoux, Jean, vii, 242
Glorieux, Le, see Destouches
Grand Cyrus, Le, see Scudéry

Grandval, 181
Grasset, Dr., Le Médecin de l'amour au temps de Marivaux, 19n
Gresset, 140, 265–66; Le Méchant, 180–81, 204n, 265
Greuze, 190
Grimm, 171, 190
Gueullette, J. E., Notes et souvenirs sur le Théâtre-Italien au XVIIIᵉ siècle, 18, 22, 35n, 48, 59, 83, 132, 202
Guillot de Saxe, 24, 216
Gulliver's Travels, see Swift

Hamburgische Dramaturgie, see Lessing
Hawkins, William, 218
Henri VIII, see Chénier
Henrik and Pernille, 132
Herbault, Jean, 61, 106
Héritier du village, L', 86–89, 161
Heureuse surprise, L', 6
Heureux stratagème, L', 166–72, 174–75, 257, 265
Hirsch, Robert, 61
Histoire anecdotique et raisonnée du Théâtre Italien . . . , see Desboulmiers
Histoire de l'art dramatique en France depuis vingt-cinq ans, see Gautier
Histoire du Portugal, see Clède
Histoire du Théâtre Français, see Etienne and Martainville
Histoire générale du théâtre en France, see Lintilhac
Histoire générale illustrée du théâtre, see Dubech
Homme à bonne fortune, L', see Baron
Horace, see Corneille
Houville, Gérard d', 85, 105, 228
Hus, Mlle., Plutus rival de l'amour, 112

Il ne faut jurer de rien, see Musset
Ile de la folie, L', 96
Ile de la raison, L', 78, 81n, 90–98, 163, 194, 257, 258n, 259n
Ile des esclaves, L', 68, 78–83, 94, 131, 202, 229, 257–58, 263, 265
Iliade travestie, L', 5n, 17n, 70
Illustre aventurier, L', see Le Prince travesti

Impromptu de Versailles, L', see Molière
Indigent philosophe, L', 5n, 226

Jaloux désabusé, Le, see Campistron
Janin, Jules, 214
Jean-Bernard, 199n
Jeener, J. B., 229
Jeu de l'amour et du hasard, Le, 16n, 23, 49, 58–59, 64, 71, 77, 81n, 120–40, 141, 152, 154, 156, 163, 188, 192, 195, 202, 206, 209, 214, 216, 218–19, 222, 232, 244n, 245n, 246, 256n, 257, 258n, 259n, 262–63
Joie imprévue, La, 6, 130, 167, 189, 203n, 220–23, 246n
Joly, Mlle., 213
Joubert, Louis, 148
Joueur, Le, see Regnard
Journal, see Gide
Journal de l'Empire, Le, 164n
Journal de Paris, Le, 213, 236–37
Journal des débats, Le, 59–60, 135n, 148, 165n, 213n, 214, 228
Journal littéraire, Le, 96, 147, 148n
Journal officiel, Le, 132n
Judith, Mlle., 135
Jugement dernier des rois, Le, see Maréchal

Kemp, Robert, 62, 143, 149, 218, 228, 242
Kerr, Walter, 25, 218
Korène, Véra, 49–50, 228–29

Labiche, *Le Misanthrope et l'Auvergnat*, 229–30
La Bruyère, 259; *Des femmes*, 114
Lacache, Bernard, 24
La Calprenède, 263; *Cléopâtre*, 142
La Chaussée, 6, 42, 70, 140, 163–64, 190, 242, 250, 260, 262, 265–66; *L'Ecole des mères*, 164, 265; *Le Préjugé à la mode*, 70
La Fayette, Mme. de, *La Princesse de Clèves*, 184n, 187n, 263
La Fontaine, *Tircis et Aramante*, 22
La Grange-Chancel, *Amasis*, 53n, 146
La Harpe, J. F., 21, 22, 171, 219; *Lycée, ou cours de littérature ancienne et moderne*, 21n; *Mélanie*, 100n

Lalique, Mme., 62
Lalou, René, 50, 210, 229
Lambert, Mme. de, 5, 19; *Œuvres de Mme la marquise de Lambert*, 238n; *Réflexions sur les femmes*, 119, 238
La Motte, Houdar de, 5n; *La Matrone d'Ephèse*, 103
Lancaster, H. C., *French Tragedy in the Time of Louis XV and Voltaire*, 26n
La Noue, 171; *La Coquette corrigée*, 171–72, 265
La Rochefoucauld, 41, 131
Larroumet, Gustave, vii, 23, 39, 40, 52, 87, 89, 103, 144, 189, 192, 210, 219, 230, 241, 249, 254; *Marivaux: sa vie et ses œuvres*, 3, 23n, 39n, 48n, 52n, 67n, 87n, 103n, 112n, 152n, 165n, 187n, 191n, 209n, 230n, 238n, 254n, 259n
Leconte, Mlle., 38
Lecouvreur, Adrienne, 99, 152n
Légataire universel, Le, see Regnard
Legouvé, Ernest, *Par droit de conquête*, 247
Legrand, 12; *L'Epreuve réciproque*, 132, 237n; *Le Galant coureur*, 132; *L'Usurier gentilhomme*, 87
Legs, Le, 23, 49, 69, 74, 134, 136, 170, 195–201, 202, 226, 232, 238, 266
Lemaître, Jules, 23, 60, 129, 136, 148, 227, 238
Lemarchand, Jacques, 62, 97, 239
Lemercier, Népomucène, *Pinto*, 53
Lenient, Ch., *La Comédie en France au XVIIIᵉ siècle*, 85, 171n
Lenoble, *Les Deux Arlequins*, 174
Lesage, Alain-René, 12; *Turcaret*, 111–12, 253
Lesbros de Versan, 14n, 36; *L'Esprit de Marivaux*, 36n
Lessing, 77, 164; *Hamburgische Dramaturgie*, 89
Lettre à d'Alembert, La, see Rousseau
Lettres persanes, Les, see Montesquieu
Lettres philosophiques, Les, see Voltaire
Lièvre, Pierre, 44n, 138–39, 212, 217, 238, 261
Lintilhac, Eugène, 59; *Histoire générale du théâtre en France*, 59n, 190n

Lope de Vega, 62; *El perro del hortelano*, 171n
Louis XIV, 8, 10, 248, 259
Louis XV, 142, 246
Louis XVI, 190
Love's Labor Lost, see Shakespeare
Lugné-Poë, 24
Luigi Riccoboni dit Lélio, see Courville
Lulli, 144
Lycée, ou cours de littérature ancienne et moderne, see La Harpe
Lysistrata, see Aristophanes

Mademoiselle de la Seiglière, see Sandeau
Mainfray, *L'Ephésienne*, 103
Marcel, Gabriel, 61, 96–97, 106, 139, 217, 219, 236, 239
Maréchal, *Le Jugement dernier des rois*, 84
Maria Theresa, 190
Mariage de Figaro, Le, see Beaumarchais
Mariage forcé, Le, see Molière
Maricourt, André de, 38
Marie Antoinette, 190
Marionnettes, Les, see Picard
Marivaux et le marivaudage, see Deloffre; Fleury
Marivaux: sa vie et ses œuvres, see Larroumet
Mars, Mlle., 104, 134–35, 164, 199, 214–15, 228n
Matrone d'Ephèse, La, see Fatouville; La Motte
Matthews, Herbert L., 25, 140
Maxon, Lois, 140
Méchant, Le, see Gresset
Médecin de l'amour au temps de Marivaux, Le, see Grasset
Médecin malgré lui, Le, see Molière
Meilhac and Halévy, *La Veuve*, 103
Mélanges d'histoire littéraire offerts à M. Paul Dimoff, see Deloffre
Mélanie, see La Harpe
Menaechmi, see Plautus
Ménechmes, Les, see Regnard; Rotrou
Méprise, La, 167, 173–74, 263
Mercure de France, Le, 5n, 11, 14, 17, 19, 22, 29, 35, 36n, 37n, 48, 58, 64n, 74n, 83, 87, 96, 104, 111n, 113–15, 117n, 132, 142, 147, 148n, 151–52, 163, 166n, 171, 175n, 191,

199–200, 202–3, 223, 227, 231n, 236, 242n, 246, 251, 253
Mercure de France, Le (Nouvelle Série), 44n, 52, 138n, 212n, 217n, 238n
Mercy-Argenteau, Comte de, 190
Mère confidente, La, 64, 69, 131, 134, 157, 162, 182–94, 195, 202, 222n, 229, 257, 258n, 262–63, 265, 267
Meyer, Eugène, vii
Misanthrope, Le, see Molière
Misanthrope et l'Auvergnat, Le, see Labiche
Mithridate, see Racine
Molé, 199
Molière, viii, 5, 7, 8, 10, 11, 13, 38, 41, 74, 104, 106, 160–64, 176, 182, 189, 210, 219–20, 253, 259, 262–64, 266–67; *L'Avare*, 161–63, 260, 263; *Le Bourgeois gentilhomme*, 25, 31n, 87, 260, 263; *L'Ecole des femmes*, 22, 161–63, 263; *L'Ecole des maris*, 161, 163; *Les Femmes savantes*, 113, 154, 263; *Georges Dandin*, 87; *L'Impromptu de Versailles*, 252; *Le Mariage forcé*, 162; *Le Médecin malgré lui*, 220; *Le Misanthrope*, 162, 219–20, 225–26, 228; *Monsieur de Pourceaugnac*, 15; *Les Précieuses ridicules*, 137; *La Princesse d'Elide*, 41; *Le Sicilien*, 162; *Tartuffe*, 15, 219, 260
Monde, Le, 62n, 143n, 149n, 218n, 228n
Moniteur universel, Le, 191, 213
Monnier, Marc, *Les Aïeux de Figaro*, 69n, 82n
Monsieur de Pourceaugnac, see Molière
Montaigne, 259; *De trois commerces*, 113
Montesquieu, 5n, 78, 114; *Les Lettres persanes*, 82, 93n, 114
Mouret, 111
Mozart, 39
Musset, Alfred de, 30, 40, 103–4, 179–81, 193, 201, 238; *L'Ane et le ruisseau*, 201, 266; *Un Caprice*, 139; *Fantasio*, 40; *Il ne faut jurer de rien*, 40, 103–4, 171, 201n, 266; *La Nuit vénitienne*, 77, 266; *On ne badine pas avec l'amour*, 154–55, 266

Nanine, see Voltaire
New York Herald Tribune, 25n, 140n, 218n
New York Times, The, 25n, 140n, 218n
New York World Telegram, 140n, 218n
Nicandres, Les, see Boursault
Noël and Stoullig, *Les Annales du théâtre et de la musique,* 23
Nota, Alberto, *La vedova in solitudine,* 103
Notes et souvenirs sur le Théâtre-Italien au XVIII⁰ siècle, see Gueullette
Notre temps, 49n
Nouvelles littéraires, Les (Amsterdam), 26
Nouvelles littéraires, artistiques et scientifiques, Les, 49n, 50n, 52n, 61n, 62n, 96n, 106n, 138n, 139n, 210n, 217n, 228n, 229n, 236n, 239n
Nuit vénitienne, La, see Musset

Obstacle imprévu, L', see Destouches
Occasions perdues, Les, see Rotrou
Œuvres complètes de Marivaux, see Duviquet
Œuvres de L. B. Picard, Les, see Picard
Œuvres de Mme la marquise de Lambert, see Lambert
On ne badine pas avec l'amour, see Musset
Opinion nationale, L', 191
Orléans, Duc d', 50

Panard, 111
Pandore, La, 200
Par droit de conquête, see Legouvé
Patrie, La, 165n, 191
Paysan parvenu, Le, 6n, 181, 202, 241
Peines d'amour perdues, see Shakespeare
Pensées sur divers sujets, 5n
Perdrière, Hélène, 139
Père prudent et équitable, Le, 14–16, 29
Perro del hortelano, El, see Lope de Vega
Pérsiles y Sigismunda, see Cervantes
Petit, Mlle., 237
Petit de Julleville, *Le Théâtre en France,* 84, 183

Petite Scène, La, 48, 49, 60, 105, 148, 227–28
Petit-maître corrigé, Le, 71, 130, 175–81, 222, 265–66
Petits hommes, Les, see *L'Ile de la raison*
Petronius, 103, 263
Pharsamon, 5n, 17n, 146
Phèdre, see Racine
Picard, L. B., *Les Marionnettes,* 89; *Œuvres de L. B. Picard,* 89n
Pinto, see Lemercier
Pirandello, 242
Piron, Alexis, 12, 42, 140, 262, 266
Piron: sa vie et ses œuvres, see Chaponnière
Plaisir de France, 52n, 61n, 106n
Plautus, 263, *Menaechmi,* 174
Plutus rival de l'amour, see Hus
Polyeucte, see Corneille
Porte, Abbé de la, 67
Porto-Riche, 236, 266; *Amoureuse,* 227
Portrait, Le, see Beauchamp
Précieuses ridicules, Les, see Molière
Préjugé à la mode, Le, see La Chaussée
Préjugé vaincu, Le, 131, 244–47, 248, 258n
Presse, La, 49, 191
Préville, 200
Prince travesti, Le, 52–63, 64, 80, 96, 105, 107, 130–31, 144, 172, 194, 256n, 257, 258n, 259n
Princesse de Clèves, La, see La Fayette
Princesse d'Elide, La, see Molière
Provinciale, La, 6, 253–54
Provost, Mlle., 38

Quarante ans de théâtre, see Sarcey
Quelques nouveautés sur Marivaux, see Durry
Quinault, Dlle., 152
Quinault, Philippe, 144
Quinault *aîné,* 99, 152

Racine, 7, 29, 30, 60, 62, 106, 138, 219, 238, 262, 264; *Athalie,* 218; *Bajazet,* 53n, 55; *Mithridate,* 143; *Phèdre,* 137, 143, 218
Réflexions sur les femmes, see Lambert
Regnard, 10, 14, 39, 163; *Démocrite,* 147; *Les Folies amoureuses,* 75; *Le*

Joueur, 103, 223; *Le Légataire universel,* 15; *Les Ménechmes,* 174
Reines de théâtre, see Dussane
Rémi, 149
Renaud, Madeleine, 49–51, 105–7, 217–18
Rendez-vous des Thuilleries, Le, see Baron
Répétition, La, see Anouilh
République française, La, 165n
Réunion des amours, La, 17n, 18, 78, 141–43, 156, 251
Revenants, Les, see *La Femme fidèle*
Revue de France, La, 212n
Revue de Genève, La, 253n
Revue de la semaine, La, 60
Revue des deux mondes, La, 163n
Revue hommes et monde, La, 106n
Riccoboni, 11, 17, 17n, 37, 73, 167, 209, 223, 226, 231, 264; *Les Sincères à contretemps,* 226
Rideau à neuf heures, see Verneuil
Rivain, Mme. Jean, 60
Romagnesi, 12, 36
Roman d'un jeune homme pauvre, Le, see Feuillet
Romanic Review, The, 154n
Rotrou, 62; *Les Ménechmes,* 174; *Les Occasions perdues,* 55
Rousseau, 23, 78, 82, 129, 136, 258; *La Lettre à d'Alembert,* 93
Roux, François de, 50n

Sabouret, Mlle. Marie, 61
Sainte-Beuve, *Causeries du lundi,* 84, 224–25
Saint-Jean, Mlle., 6n
Saint-Jory, Le Chevalier de, 14, 17, 17n
Saint-Victor, Paul de, 40, 191
Sandeau, Jules, *Mlle. de la Seiglière,* 247
Sarcey, Fr., 40, 136, 165, 183, 191, 215, 219, 238; *Quarante ans de théâtre,* 136n, 152n, 183n, 214n
Sarment, Jean, 39, 49, 85
Sartre, Jean-Paul, 239, 266
Saurel, Renée, 228
Schneider, Louis, 216
Scudéry, 26, 263; *Le Grand Cyrus,* 263
Seconde surprise de l'amour, La, see *Surprise de l'amour, La Seconde*
Sémiramis, see Crébillon
Serments indiscrets, Les, 16n, 40n, 130,

141, 144, 151–55, 156, 188, 222n, 245n, 246, 256n, 266
Shakespeare, 19, 24, 40–41, 62, 148, 262, 264, 266–67; *Comedy of Errors,* 174; *Comme il vous plaira* (*As You Like It*), 148; *A Midsummer Night's Dream,* 19, 24n, 37, 38, 136; *Les Peines d'amour perdues* (*Love's Labor Lost*), 38, 40; *The Tempest,* 37, 40
Sicilien, Le, see Molière
Silvia (Zanetta-Rosa-Giovanna Benozzi), 11, 35, 37, 57, 64, 71–73, 83, 130, 144, 240
Simiot, Bernard, 106–7
Sincères, Les, 170, 224–30, 231, 257, 263
Sincères à contretemps, Les, see Riccoboni
Socrate, see Villedieu
Sorel, *Francion,* 102, 263
Souday, Paul, 216
Spectateur français, Le, 5n, 70, 143, 157, 202
Surprise de l'amour, La, 30–42, 44, 48, 57, 71, 99n, 101, 119, 134, 153n, 154, 163, 172, 188, 219, 229, 256, 263
Surprise de l'amour, La Seconde, 37, 40n, 74, 91, 99–107, 130, 141, 152, 162n, 181, 194, 256n, 263
Swift, *Gulliver's Travels,* 90

Talma, 120n, 134, 151, 200, 213n, 236
Tartuffe, see Molière
Télémaque travesti, Le, 17n
Tempest, The, see Shakespeare
Temps, Le, 39, 49n, 50n, 137n, 192n, 215n, 238n, 242n, 262n
Tencin, Mme. de, 5n, 19
Testament, Le, see Fontanelle
Théâtre, Le, see Brisson
Théâtre complet de Marivaux, see Arland; Fournier and Bastide
Théâtre de Marivaux, see Courville
Théâtre en France, Le, see Petit de Julleville
Thibaudet, Albert, 138
Thierry, Edouard, 212
Thomassin, 12, 240
Thorillière, La, 99

Timon le misanthrope, see Drevetière de l'Isle

Tircis et Aramante, see La Fontaine

Toldo, Pierre, *Figaro et ses origines,* 68, 82n

Traité de l'éducation des filles, see Fénelon

Triomphe de l'amour, Le, 64, 144–50, 156, 263

Triomphe de Plutus, Le, 18, 78, 108–12, 141, 251, 265

Trois commerces, De, see Montaigne

Truffier, Jules, 23, 37, 38, 192, 262

Turcaret, see Lesage

Urfé, Honoré d', *L'Astrée,* 131, 146, 263

Usurier gentilhomme, L', see Legrand

Vaganay, Hugues, 131n

Vaudoyer, Jean-Louis, 104

Vedova in solitudine, La, see Nota

Vendanges de Surennes, Les, see Dancourt

Verneuil, Louis, *Rideau à neuf heures,* 137

Vestris, Mme., 120n

Veuve, La, see Meilhac and Halévy

Victimes cloîtrées, Les, see Boutet de Monvel

Vie au théâtre, La, see Bordeaux

Vie de Marianne, La, xvn, 45, 143, 156, 188–89, 202, 241

Villedieu, Mme. de, *Socrate,* 146

Voiture embourbée, La, 5n, 17n, 146, 155, 190

Voltaire, 34, 48n, 72, 78, 93n, 162, 176, 179, 199, 229, 240, 246, 256, 260–61, 265–66; *Candide,* 48; *Les Lettres philosophiques,* 41; *Nanine,* 246–47, 265

Watteau, 24

INDEX